THE
NATIONAL DEBT

'Slater has done a superb job, combining a fantastically clear explanation of what the National Debt actually is with an entertaining account of its history. This remarkably readable book will appeal to many a concerned citizen.'

—Evan Davis

'Short, clear and readable. Slater shows how the National Debt has been enveloped in a miasma of misunderstanding and misinformation, and valiantly sets out to clear up the mess.'

—Robert Skidelsky

'A tremendously satisfying book. Slater does not just recount and enliven history; he also explains the evolution of economic theories that influenced politicians, divided economists, and that continue to fire up public debate. A must-read for all those concerned by austerity.'

—Ann Pettifor, author of *The Production of Money*

'A comprehensive and comprehensible explanation of Britain's National Debt over the centuries. Slater provides much-needed perspective on why, and when, our government should borrow.'

—Alistair Darling, Chancellor of the Exchequer, 2007–2010

'A fascinating tour of British economic history.'

—Jonathan Portes, author of *50 Capitalism Ideas You Really Need to Know*

'Slater has written insightfully about one of the biggest economic issues of our times. Placing the National Debt in its historical context, this book is a must-read on whether our debt levels are too high.'

—Linda Yueh, author of *The Great Economists*

Martin Slater

THE NATIONAL DEBT

A *Short History*

HURST & COMPANY, LONDON

First published in the United Kingdom in 2018 by
C. Hurst & Co. (Publishers) Ltd.,
41 Great Russell Street, London, WC1B 3PL
© Martin Slater, 2018
All rights reserved.

A Cataloguing-in-Publication data record for this book
is available from the British Library.

ISBN: 9781849049412

This book is printed using paper from registered sustainable
and managed sources.

www.hurstpublishers.com

Endpapers: 'John Bull and the sinking-fund-a Pretty scheme for reducing
the taxes and paying off the National Debt!' © The Trustees of the British
Museum

Printed and bound in Great Britain by Bell & Bain Ltd, Glasgow

For Paul, Fiona, Emma,
Chloe and Luke
and children and grandchildren everywhere

CONTENTS

CONTENTS

LIST OF FIGURES, TABLES AND BOXES

FIGURES

TABLES

BOXES

LIST OF FIGURES, TABLES AND BOXES

ACKNOWLEDGEMENTS

I am indebted to many individuals for their help and support in the writing of this book. My daughter Fiona encouraged me in the concept and worked unceasingly to interest the publishing industry in it. Gerard Lally and Michael Kell valiantly read the whole manuscript at different stages and provided exceptionally valuable feedback. Thanks too to various editors and publishers' reviewers for valuable comments, and particularly to Jim Ferguson and to Michael Dwyer and Jon de Peyer of Hurst Publishers, who ultimately brought the project to fruition.

Stephen Broadberry and Nicholas Dimsdale guided me to the most up-to-date sources of economic historical data.

Other thanks are due to Linda Yueh, Adam Swallow, Sir Ian Byatt, Sir Jon Shortridge, Wes Williams, the Press Officers at DMO, John-Mark Considine and Gareth McKeever.

I would also like to thank the University of Oxford, my college St Edmund Hall, and my colleagues therein, for the supportive and wide-ranging academic environment throughout my career.

Above all I am grateful for the support and forbearance of my wife Lucy Newlyn.

PREFACE

In 2014, I was asked to contribute to a day of commemoration at my college—St Edmund Hall, University of Oxford—to mark the centenary of the outbreak of the First World War. As an economist, this was not really my subject at all, but eventually I offered to give a short talk on John Maynard Keynes and his role in the financing of the war. In the course of researching the talk I was struck first by the colossal economic cost of the war, second by the consequent explosion of National Debt, and third by the complicated web of international indebtedness which blighted the subsequent peace. All these continue to have an effect on our lives even to the present day. The story was shocking enough in its own right but it also had an uncomfortable resonance for the post-2008 economic climate in which the issue of national and international debts was becoming increasingly prominent, and indeed strident.

So after the talk I thought I should find out more about the evolution of Britain's National Debt beyond the narrow window of the First World War. But this was not as easy as I had imagined it would be. There were surprisingly few accessible books written by economists on the subject, and particularly no current overview of its complete history. The most recent such overview I could find was by Eric Hargreaves, *The National Debt*, published in 1930. It was a useful starting point. From there I discovered the *magna opera* of many distinguished historians, like Chandaman, Dickson, Brewer, Ferguson, Daunton, and Wormell, each targeting some sub-period of the debt's history. My debt to all these and other writers is immense. But again, none provided a complete overview, and their very large erudite tomes are not for the faint-hearted. Economists, too, have written extensively on national debt problems, but their approach is usually very technical and analytical, and usually more about general principles than specific instances, so again this produces little that is really accessible to the general reader.

Hence the genesis of this book. It is a combination of economics and history, and it is the fate of most such books not wholly to satisfy the professional experts of either constituency. My apologies in advance to them. But for the wider reading public I hope it will stimulate interest in an otherwise forbidding subject and make some contribution towards a better-informed general discussion of a crucial economic policy decision, one particularly fundamental to our democratic institutions.

A NOTE ON DATA AND THE VALUE
OF MONEY OVER TIME

We can be fairly precise about the data on the National Debt itself, even back to the very earliest days. For obvious reasons Parliament was always intensely concerned about the Debt and called for regular reports on its progress. There can be disagreements at the margin about what should go in and what should remain outside the definition of the National Debt (and some of these disagreements are encountered in the course of the book), but the core numbers provided from parliamentary reports and government statistical sources are well agreed.

However, Parliament always measures the Debt in the money of its own time, and the value of money has obviously changed enormously over the very long period of time covered by this book. The current Debt of £1.7 trillion is almost incomprehensible at an individual level; but how should this be compared to, say, the original loan of £1.2 million from the Bank of England in 1694 (see Chapter 3)? £1.2 million would hardly buy a small house in central London nowadays.

Normally economists face such problems by revaluing money variables to some constant price level, but price comparisons over such long time periods are notoriously difficult. Price indices attempt to weight the ups and downs in the prices of individual commodities according to their relative importance in consumers' budgets, but unfortunately the composition of consumers' budgets changes over time. Over short periods of comparison this may be only a minor annoyance, but over very long periods it can render the exercise almost meaningless: twenty-first century consumers' budgets mostly comprise products which were unknown to their eighteenth century predecessors. Nevertheless, economic historians have attempted to construct very long-run price index series. From these we can at least gain a general impression of the inflationary background to our history.

Generally speaking, although prices fluctuate from year to year and over short cycles of a few years' duration, there is no pronounced long-term inflationary trend until after 1945. The eighteenth century saw only a very slight rise in the price level, the nineteenth a slight fall. But there were short, sharp bursts of inflation in the Napoleonic Wars and in WWI and WWII.

For the reasons stated above, it is dangerous to rely too heavily on more specific conclusions, but for those who like this kind of comparison, £1 at various crucial dates might be worth (very roughly) the following sums in 2017 money:

1694	Foundation of Bank of England	£130
1793	Beginning of French Revolutionary and Napoleonic Wars	£100
1815	End of Napoleonic Wars	£60
1914	Beginning of WWI	£80
1918	End of WWI	£40
1939	Beginning of WWII	£45
1945	End of WWII	£30
1979	Margaret Thatcher elected Prime Minister	£4
2017		£1

According to this methodology, one pound in 1694 might have been worth about £130 in 2017 money, so the Bank of England's original loan of £1.2 million might be thought of as about £156 million in 2017 money. This is a significant magnification, but even this might not sound to us enormously large; such a figure would be well within the capabilities of many of today's super-rich individuals. But that would still be very misleading, because the British economy of 1694 was so much smaller than in 2017: the population was much smaller, and the economic activity was much, much smaller. Even the wealthiest merchant of 1694 could not have run to £1.2 million. Relative to the size of the economy at the time, £1.2 million was probably about 1.5 per cent of GDP. Uprating this to today's level of GDP, it is more equivalent to £30 billion in our own time. That sounds more like it—well beyond the capabilities of even the richest individuals.

This leads us to the view that a better standard of comparison, one which better captures the degree of comfort or discomfort with which contemporaries might have viewed their debt position, is the value of the debt relative to the size of the economy. We normally measure the size of an economy by its Gross Domestic Product (GDP). But again, since the very concept of GDP was only formalised in the 1940s, long-run historical series have had to be constructed retrospectively by economic historians, using whatever hard information they can find.

This also implies that contemporary observers would not themselves have thought explicitly in terms of a Debt/GDP ratio: they were more likely to think in terms of the ratio of the Debt and its servicing requirements to the government budget, on which they did have equally clear figures. A large debt pressing on the government budget was likely to lead to higher tax demands, which was most people's immediate individual concern. But that also led them to worry about whether the country as a whole could meet such tax demands, so there were often attempts to compare the Debt with some estimate of the taxable capacity of the economy.

Not surprisingly there are significant disagreements among the economic historians, and the margins of disagreement get larger the further back in time we go, but some very recent research work (*British Economic Growth, 1270–1870*, by S. Broadberry et al [Cambridge, 2015] and Bank of England, *A Millennium of Macroeconomic Data*) has greatly improved our understanding, and their estimates are used in this book.

In general, the movements of the Debt relative to GDP are so pronounced that even quite large margins of error on the GDP estimates would make little difference to the overall picture presented in these pages. One of the strange advantages of dealing with such large numbers is in fact the corollary of Senator Dirksen's aphorism (see the epigraph to Chapter 1): a billion or two here or there does not in fact make a great deal of difference to the conclusions in the very long run. So the reader is advised to treat most numbers in a fairly approximate fashion. Throughout this book I prefer to use mainly the original nominal values of debt, and debt/GDP ratios; and use constant-price comparisons sparingly.

1

INTRODUCTION

SHOULD WE WORRY?

'A billion here, a billion there, and pretty soon you're talking serious money.'

Attributed to US Senator Everett Dirksen, 1896–1969

I

After years of relative obscurity, the National Debt is newsworthy again. It is larger now than it has ever been, and since the financial crisis of 2007–8 it has been rising rapidly. In December 2007, the net National Debt of the government of the United Kingdom of Great Britain and Northern Ireland was £562.5 billion; in December 2017 it was £1,759.5 billion, so in ten years it has more than tripled.[1] It still is rising, although now at a slower rate. Since December 2016 it has increased by £62.3 billion, a growth rate of about 3.7 per cent per annum. That is £1,976 per second. On the web and elsewhere one can find 'National Debt clocks' which alarmingly illustrate the rapid ticking-up of the total.

There is no doubt these are massive sums of money, edging now (*pace* Dirksen), into trillions, not billions: £1,759.5 billion is £1.7595 trillion, or £1,759,500,000,000, or £1.7595 x 10^{12}, depending on your mathematical preferences. If measured out in a single pile of one pound coins, the pile would be 4.9 million km high—it would reach to the moon and back six and a half times.[2]

These may seem depressing, even overwhelming figures. But in dealing with the overall economics of a country of 65 million people, all numbers are likely to be beyond our own personal experience. Almost every aggregate financial variable in Economics is larger now than it ever has been. And flashy illustrations like the National Debt clocks and the pile of coins stretching past the moon may be arresting—they are intended to be—but are they really helpful? The pile of pound coins might get us well beyond the moon, but nothing like as far as Mars. And suppose, instead of piling all our pound coins up in a single pile, we spread them all out on the ground, in a massive carpet, one coin high. How many times would they cover the surface of the earth? The answer, possibly surprising, is nowhere near—they would struggle to cover even a third of a per cent of Britain's surface area.[3] Somehow—I don't know quite why—that seems much less impressive. This may be all good knockabout stuff, but it doesn't really tell us very much. Let us try to get some better perspective.

The government is ultimately only the representative of ourselves, the tax-paying citizens. Britain's population is about 65.6 million.[4] The debt is therefore about £27,000 per person. Or if you like, since there are 27.2 million households, the debt per household is about £65,000.[5] The debt increase between December 2016 and December 2017 was equivalent to £950 per person, or £2,290 per household, in a single year.

Let us also consider some more financial perspectives. At the end of 2017, Britain's Gross Domestic Product (GDP), a measure of the total national income, was running at about £1.963 trillion per annum,[6] so the National Debt is currently about 90 per cent of GDP. Is this a small or a large figure? We will use this ratio of debt to GDP a lot in this book, and we will see that there have been times when this ratio has been considerably higher.[7]

Since the Debt is explicitly the government's, rather than that of the nebulous economy as a whole, it might be more appropriate to consider its size also relative to the government's own income. In 2017, the central government's total revenue, mostly from taxation, was £731.9 billion (so the government takes about three-eighths of the national income).[8] The Debt is therefore 240 per cent of government revenue. That is a rather larger ratio, but not necessarily a dangerous one, since British government debt is mostly very long-term—actual demands for repayment are a very long way away in the future, and as we shall see may perhaps be deferred almost indefinitely. The current requirements for payment are therefore only for the interest, which amounts to £47.3 billion per annum: only 2.4 per cent of GDP and 6.5 per cent of government revenue.[9] These do not look to be dangerous levels, although of course they are not negligible either; without a national debt to service the government could afford to reduce taxes or increase expenditure on deserving causes by £47.3 billion per annum. That's £720 per person, £1,740 per household—or equivalent to the entire defence budget at the time of writing (though not as large as the education, health or welfare budgets). But again, as we shall see, that too is a little misleading: the net effect on persons and households would be very much less, since most of the interest payments are directly or indirectly received back by persons and households).

It might also be informative to consider these figures relative to some orders of magnitude in private-sector lending. Before the financial markets began to lose touch with reality in the run-up to the 2008 crisis, a reputable mortgage lender would usually be willing to lend long-term to a reputable applicant about 300 per cent of the applicant's income. The lender would be concerned if mortgage repayments came to more than 25 per cent of the applicant's income. As we shall see, there are important similarities but also important dissimilarities between individuals' debts and governments' debts, so such simple comparisons can be dangerous. But at least on the face of it this particular comparison, too, is not overly alarming (we will also see that at some times in the past the British government has gone well beyond both of those criteria).

Let us also compare our public indebtedness via the government with the debts we directly incur on our own behalf. Total Household Debt in Britain is estimated at £1.566 trillion (a very similar order of magnitude to the National Debt), of which £1.36 trillion is mortgages, and £206 billion is consumer credit lending.[10] Some 11.1 million households have mortgages, so therefore the average mortgage among those households is £122,554, with an average annual interest bill of £3,280.

So the debts the government has incurred on our behalf are not in fact astronomically out of our comprehension; they are about the same order of magnitude as the debts we choose to incur directly ourselves. That does not make them negligible and of course they are incurred on top of, and not instead of, our private indebtedness—we would seem to be about twice as indebted as we might superficially think we are.

But government debt is also in some ways very different from our private debts. We are not faced with explicit demands for interest and repayment. No large men with baseball bats knock on our doors to demand repayment. Most citizens have lived most of their lives in blissful ignorance of this invisible debt without baleful consequences, and will probably continue to do so. Mortgage or credit card debt is not the same. So why the doom and gloom? Is it really justified?

Since 2008, debt and deficits have been widely discussed, and indeed have come to be central to political debate. But the debate has been more pugilistic than enlightening. The National Debt has become something of a bogeyman. But there is little real understanding of what it is; where it came from; what might be done with it; how it really affects the economy; or whether it is good, bad, or dangerous.

Is the National Debt a monstrous millstone around the necks of our children and grandchildren, or is it actually something we have lived with quite comfortably for centuries, and quite normal that our children and grandchildren should too? Is a national debt the same sort of creature as an individual, personal debt? We are all familiar with the ground rules of the latter, but is a national debt something very different and arcane? Does a national debt actually have to be repaid? If so, the numbers are pretty daunting, but we seem to have avoided repayment for several centuries. How?

We read of the predicaments of countries like Greece, unable to pay their debts, effectively bankrupt (whatever that means), therefore somehow at the mercy of the diktats of foreign creditors, with the consequences mysteriously spreading far from the financial markets into the real economy of output and employment, and threatening the very nature of the political system. Could it happen to us?

In other circumstances it appears that a national debt can simply be rolled over painlessly, to mutual benefit, from generation to generation. Government bonds and national savings certificates are a very useful form of low-risk, moderate-return savings. In saving, say, for our retirement, we sensibly hold much of our savings in this form, either directly or more usually indirectly via pension funds and insurance companies. When we retire, we will wish our own particular bonds and certificates to be repaid so that we can live on the proceeds, but the next generation will at the same time be hoping to build up their savings, so the government should face little financial difficulty. Indeed if the population is increasing and getting wealthier the new savings should outweigh the withdrawals of the pensioners and the government could actually increase the National Debt at the same rate without danger to its credit. A nation, unlike an individual, does not have a finite life, and can therefore postpone repayment without limit. (The possible danger though is that the population might at some time in the future be expected to fall, or become less wealthy, or that the existence of the nation itself might be called into question.)

Is a national debt therefore a debt we owe largely only to ourselves, 'the right hand pays the left hand', as the eighteenth-century French economist Jean-François Melon first suggested? Are we getting into a frightful financial panic levying taxes on ourselves merely to make unnecessary and ultimately undesired repayments to ourselves? If we do want to do this, is there in fact a more or less painless way in which both sides of the balance sheet could be simply netted off against each other, so that we could start again with a clean slate?

Or is the Debt perhaps actually rather more sinister than this? Is it owed by domestic citizens mostly to foreign residents, companies and governments (as is usually the case with developing countries)? Even if it is mainly domestically held, is it largely held by the wealthy and paid by the poor? Is it a mechanism through which an idle rentier class can maintain their luxurious lifestyles at the expense of the industrious working classes? Is it in fact a backdoor mechanism of class oppression?

Could it be better for a government to tackle an economic slump with deficit financing, borrowing money to keep people in work and economic output higher—but at the cost of a higher national debt (the so-called 'Keynesian' approach); or should the government pursue 'austerity' measures, cutting expenditure and raising taxes in an attempt to prevent the Debt rising further, but at the cost of increased unemployment and lower economic output? Could—miracle of miracles—the deficit financing option even end up with a lower national debt, as increased tax revenues from the hoped-for higher output and employment eventually more than repay the initial outlays? Or, equally, could the austerity approach ultimately end up with higher employment because lower debt will mean lower interest rates and more business and consumer confidence in the future? Clearly this is the stuff of current political debate in Britain and throughout Europe. Perhaps less obviously to the general citizen, essentially the same debate dominated the 1920s and 1930s. Given the very real impact austerity policies have had on the availability and quality of public services in Britain, the stakes are high. Is this pain really justified?

III

Let us admit at the outset that there are no easy answers, or magic bullets, to these and other questions concerning national debts. The problems in practice are usually more complicated than the bare outlines drawn above, and any solutions are very, very long-term. Furthermore most 'solutions' cannot make the problems actually disappear; at best they can shift burdens between people and across time in a more helpful fashion. Almost always there will be gainers and losers from such rearrangements. In most periods this does not make for attractive political programmes, and, as we shall see, politicians have usually opted to duck the issues with a short-term fix, in the hope that if there is any ultimate crisis, it will be deferred to their successors.

In the short run, management of the National Debt is highly technical, even arcane. It is difficult for even the most intelligent outsider to grasp what is going on. This complexity and lack of transparency can be a great help to politicians and technocrats in constructing their short-term fixes, which usually depend on some sleight-of-hand to obscure where the real burdens have been transferred. It might also explain why there are few popular books on the subject of national debt.

In these pages we will have to confront some of these technicalities, but it is more the very long-term nature of the National Debt with which this book is concerned. We have got to where we are now through some very long processes, and any effective solutions will be similarly very long-term. It is impossible to put our current situation in perspective, and to be able to frame constructive proposals for the future, without some understanding of the history of the Debt. So the purpose of this book is to look also at the history of the evolution of the Debt; at the contexts in which it was contracted and the motivations behind it; at the different forms which borrowing has taken over the centuries; at the various attempts to manage the Debt and its consequences; and at the ebb and flow of contemporary controversies about and attitudes toward the Debt. In this way I hope the reader will gain a better understanding of the complex and subtle issues posed by a national debt—the political constraints, the distributional implications, the balancing of risk—and will thereby be better able to participate in what inevitably will be one of the important political issues of the next decades.

IV

Let us start by looking at Figures 1, 2 and 3 below. They illustrate, in different ways, the path of the National Debt from 1692 to the present day.

Figure 1 shows simply the value of the National Debt itself. This is, in fact, not very helpful.

While perhaps alarming at first sight, it is not necessarily so—almost all economic variables look like this over the very long run because of the combined effects of the growth of the economy and inflation after the Industrial Revolution.

Much more revealing is Figure 2, which shows the ratio of the debt to GDP.[11] Starting from near zero at the end of the seventeenth century it climbs dramatically, although irregularly, to reach over 200 per cent by the 1820s. Then follows a century of almost steady descent, to about 25 per cent in 1914. The first half of the twentieth century sees it suddenly ratchet up again, to even higher than its 1820s level. After 1945 we see another period of steady decline, and finally a tantalising glimpse of what could be the beginnings of another upswing in the years after 2008.

That tantalising glimpse is where we started this chapter; it is, of course, why this book has been written, and probably why you're reading it. But as you can see, it is only a tiny slice of the whole history, and not apparently a very significant one. The National Debt is rising, yes. But its level seems, as yet, nothing particularly special. It may indeed have tripled in the last ten years, but that was from historically a rather low point. Relative to GDP, there have been times in the past when the debt burden was well over twice what it is now.

Figure 3 shows another way of looking at the debt: the debt interest burden on the government, again relative to GDP. This follows much the same pattern as the second. Although there is a small upswing (but notably rather less in this graph than in the second) in very recent years, the relative interest burden is still close to its lowest level in a century. In the 1920s this, too, was almost three times as high.

So is there really nothing to worry about? Not necessarily. To anticipate some of the themes which will be developed in this book, let me suggest here four possible general areas of concern:

1. Although the current levels are not historically high, they are moving in the wrong direction, and at a time when they should normally not be.
2. The past historical context has perhaps been relatively kind to Britain and its public debt; we cannot guarantee that it will continue to be so.
3. The official figures for National Debt may exclude and conceal other public commitments for the future, which are themselves increasing rapidly.
4. The National Debt is only the debt of the government—the public sector. But the private sector has debts of its own—as we have seen these are of comparable magnitude and they have also increased rapidly in recent years. The overall situation of the country is the combined effect of private and public debts, and the 2008 crisis was more a crisis of private than of public indebtedness.

To gain more perspective on these issues, we must turn to the stories behind these figures.

Figure 1: British National Debt (£ billion)

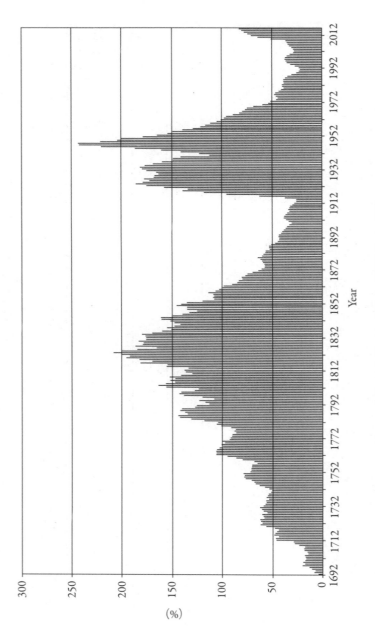

Figure 2: British National Debt/GDP Ratio (%)

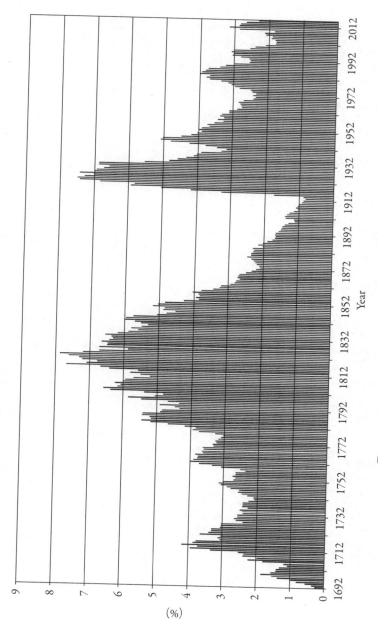

Figure 3: British National Debt Interest/GDP Ratio (%)

2

PRE-HISTORY

The origin of Britain's National Debt is normally dated to 1694, with the foundation of the Bank of England.[1] Certainly, this date signifies the beginning of a modern era of permanent indebtedness—permanent by design, not simply through fecklessness—but of course borrowing in some form has always been a feature of government, and it will help us understand subsequent developments better if we start our story somewhat earlier.

MEDIEVAL PUBLIC FINANCE

The monarch sat at the apex of the feudal system in the Medieval Period. Although the King had a distinct constitutional status, in economic terms he was simply the biggest of the country's barons. He had his own royal estates which furnished revenues and men, to provide a small amount of peacetime central administration and the nucleus of a royal army. But he could also call upon his subordinate barons' feudal obligations: they provided local administration in their own regions, and were bound to support their overlord with men and materials in times of war.

The medieval state had few social responsibilities: the only major expenditures were likely to be military, or occasionally the conspicuous consumption or prestige projects of the sovereign.

As described above, a feudal monarch should in theory not have had a great need to borrow. But in practice feudal tenants might prefer to buy out their personal participation with cash. They did not always make the best soldiers (consider the grossly out-of-condition Falstaff following his prince to the Battle of Shrewsbury in Shakespeare's *Henry IV, Part I*); and feudal levies would probably be poorly trained and poorly equipped, nor could they be relied on for long campaigns without disastrous effects on the agriculture of their home regions. It was therefore wise to augment them with professional mercenaries, who needed paying in cash. Increasingly sophisticated armaments also needed to be paid for. So the King's requirements from his underlings also became increasingly financial rather than in kind, leading to taxation and to borrowing.

Originally the distinction between a gift, a tax, and a loan was to some extent academic. The King's right to tax derived from his feudal right to expect support from his tenants. This idea of assistance, or feudal aid, entered the terminology of taxation: early French taxes were called *aides*, and English parliaments for many centuries have voted 'aids' to the government. In early years the King sometimes literally asked for voluntary offers of support rather than formulaic taxes, and those asked could refuse, at least in theory. Presumably they calculated their responses carefully. 'Loans' were probably unlikely to be repaid either promptly or in full, but even if there was no explicit *quid pro quo*, a generous offer might lead to a larger share of any booty from the campaign, or ensure the King's favour and possible gifts in return in the future. On the other hand, a niggardly offer might attract negative consequences for the future. In 1095 Anselm, Archbishop of Canterbury, made an insubstantial offer in response to such a request—he was probably making the point that churchmen enjoyed immunity from having to support martial purposes—which the King equally pointedly refused as being unworthy.[2] The Archbishop's fellow bishops, fearful of reprisals, tried to persuade him to be more accommodating.

But open-ended requests soon gave way to more formulaic demands, crystallising into different forms of tax: *scutage*, being the financial equivalent of a knight's wartime service obligation; *carucage*, being calculated on the number of ox-ploughing teams possessed (and therefore really a proxy for cultivable land), and taxes on revenues and the value of movable property, usually expressed as some customary fraction, e.g. a fifteenth or a thirtieth.

But did the King have a right to demand tax or merely a right to ask? In other words, did taxation require some kind of consent from the taxed? And if the King did have a right to demand, was it an absolute right, or only a right to make reasonable demands? If the latter, who was to decide what was reasonable?

In practice, the King rarely acted alone; major decisions were normally taken in conjunction with a Council, comprised of the major barons of the country. The Council members must thereby have given their consent, and as the major barons they were probably the major tax-payers too. In turn, they would collect most of their own liabilities from their own sub-tenants; but did those sub-tenants have any say? Also, a minority of Council members might have disagreed with the policy or been absent when the decision was taken; did majority consent also bind the minority and the absent? Many other barons were not members of the Council at all; and some citizens, particularly town-dwellers, were not in a direct feudal relationship with the Crown anyway. Did the consent of the Council bind them too, or did their consent have to be sought separately?

These issues were not simple. Much of the Plantagenet kings' military campaigning was in France, protecting their substantial family possessions there. But was such campaigning a legitimate demand on barons and citizens of the Kingdom of England? Some barons, like the King, had estates on both sides of the Channel, and would have had no problem with this; others were wholly England-based and would therefore be more likely to resent the financing of what would have been to them a foreign adventure. The Church, which was one of the wealthiest potential tax-payers, claimed to have a moral aversion to warfare and therefore no obligation to finance it. Some merchants might resent the disruption to trade caused by warfare; others might benefit from military purchasing. Opposition to royal plans was frequently voiced in the Council and outright refusals of taxation, on grounds of unreasonableness or some claim to exemption, were not uncommon. Sometimes such refusals were overridden with violence, but if opposition was widespread, a king might tactically withdraw.

Thus began the whole dispute over the control of taxation that played out over many subsequent centuries. The Magna Carta in 1215 and Simon de Montfort's Parliament in 1265 were milestones in a long struggle for security of private property rights and consultation on matters of taxation. Unsurprisingly, the greatest incentive at first lay with the major barons, but as the basis of taxation widened other sectional groups, such as the lesser nobility, the commons, the Church, merchants, and towns also required their say. Parliament therefore evolved as a much broader assemblage of separate sectional interests than the Council. In 1362 a parliamentary statute explicitly claimed the right to approve all taxes, and in 1407 King Henry IV recognised this right as being specifically vested in the House of Commons (rather than the House of Lords). But Henry was in a weak position, having usurped his predecessor Richard II, and probably needed to curry favour wherever he could. In practice the struggle for control continued—a struggle that would eventually lead to the English Civil War (1642–1651).

Another source of money for the King was borrowing. Borrowing at least avoided these political difficulties, but did of course require repayment. A successful military campaign might provide enough in booty, in territorial gains or in indemnity from a defeated opponent, but this was a risky strategy: few campaigns were really successful in this way. The King's own revenues from the royal estates were unlikely to be sufficient to repay a loan for a significant campaign. So ultimately, repayment would usually force the King back to taxation.

These days economics students are taught to think of taxation and borrowing as alternative means of financing government expenditure: ideally expenditure should be defrayed by taxation, and only if this is not possible should resort be made to borrowing. But in these early days of public finance the two methods were more complementary than alternative: borrowing presupposed some command of taxation in the future for there to be any realistic expectation of repayment; and, perhaps less obviously, taxation almost always involved some element of borrowing as well. To some extent this complementarity continues, in subtler forms, throughout later history.

The problem was that taxation was cumbersome to administer and slow to materialise, while the demands of warfare were immediate and peremptory. At the beginning of a war taxation might be agreed by the King and/or Parliament, but the revenues might take months or years to come in; meanwhile, the troops had to be paid now, in hard cash. Hence the government had to borrow in the short term to pay the troops and then use the tax revenues to pay off borrowing over the next few years. Modern analysts of public accounts diagnose serious problems if they observe interest and debt repayments absorbing a large proportion of the government budget. But early public accounts, if reconstructed, would not necessarily bear that implication: as the government had few expensive peacetime responsibilities, the main purpose of peacetime taxation was to pay off the debts of the last war.

Where was such borrowing to come from? Possibly from the King's own subjects, particularly wealthy landed nobles, wealthy Church institutions, and the growing merchant class in towns; and also from European banking families. Medieval English kings particularly favoured Italian bankers. Loans were usually short-term and for the financiers it was a risky business: monarchs often defaulted, and there was little financiers could do to enforce repayment. Kings Edward I, II, III and IV all defaulted in various ways on their Italian bankers, bringing down in succession the Ricciardi, the Frescobaldi, the Bardi, the Peruzzi, and the London branch of the Medici.

Perhaps the best security against default was a country's crown jewels: a monarch was unlikely to survive the revulsion of public opinion at the loss of such valuable symbols of the country's prestige and heritage, so a financier who could get his hands on such assets as collateral was unlikely to be bilked. Famously, King John did lose the country's crown jewels, apparently in a freak accident of the tides in the Wash, while campaigning against rebels. But he was seriously in debt. At the very least it is notable that he should take such valuable assets with him into a very vulnerable situation.

Alternatively, security could be sought through linking repayment to the proceeds of specific taxes, or by taking direct control of tax collection itself. This latter course was not necessarily unwelcome to the government. With only very rudimentary administrative resources at its disposal, the actual business of tax collection was difficult. In some way or other the task had to be delegated to local officials, or local magnates, or even to representatives of the local tax-payers themselves. Monitoring was difficult and efficiency of collection low. It could be more convenient to the Crown to delegate the business to an individual who would contract to pay the agreed total revenue up-front, immediately, and then use his own resources to extract the underlying tax payments for himself over a period of time. Such 'tax-farming' arrangements could be structured in various ways; they were used intermittently in England and very extensively in France. In this model a tax-collector was therefore necessarily also a banker and a money-lender, thereby gaining himself a multiple unpopularity which could be exploited by populist rabble-rousers or by a cynical monarch wanting to avoid repayment or distance himself from the unpopularity of taxation.

From the government side a decision to tax was therefore also usually simultaneously a decision to borrow, either explicitly from outsiders on the security of the future tax revenue, or implicitly from its own tax collectors and suppliers. Ideally this kind of borrowing was merely 'anticipation of revenue'—in a well-regulated system government would continually pay off its short-term debts and no permanent indebtedness was envisaged. The trouble, of course, was that the system was in practice difficult to regulate, and the indebtedness was likely to spiral out of control. More insidiously, the system tended to obscure the fact and the degree of indebtedness. Many monarchs and their advisors considered they were living within their means because they were simply spending their tax revenues as provided obligingly by their tax-farmers; but if revenues had already been anticipated for several years to come, this could be far from the truth, and the Crown might have little flexibility to deal with any new emergency.

Crucially, the debts of this time were usually thought of as the King's debts, certainly not Parliament's, and only indirectly the country's. The repayment of royal debts was considered to be a legitimate use of taxation, but Parliament might refuse to recognise debts which it thought had been irresponsibly or improperly contracted. Furthermore, a succeeding monarch could easily repudiate his predecessor's debts. In such circumstances, although medieval kings were almost always desperately short of money, and always tempted to borrow, the caution of potential lenders usually set fairly low limits on the level of indebtedness. Financial fortunes fluctuated, but there was little possibility of any significant level of national debt becoming permanently embedded.

TALLIES

The traditional medieval instrument of public credit was the Tally. This was a wooden strip, of varying lengths, given as a receipt for a tax payment, or for a loan, or as a kind of IOU for goods supplied on credit. It was notched crosswise in a code denoting the sum of money and other terms involved, then split lengthwise, one half being given to the creditor and the other retained by the Crown. On eventual repayment, or to settle any dispute, the two halves would be matched to prove the validity of the claim. For loans or IOUs it was understood that they would eventually be paid out of tax revenues, and creditors were instructed to apply for payment either to the central exchequer or direct to local tax collectors—but no guarantees were given as to the time at which sufficient revenues would be available. The payers would only release payment on receipt of a written order to repay from a responsible official, presentation of the tally only serving to validate the payee. Thus, the ultimate timing of repayment was entirely at the future discretion of the government. But a considerable backlog of payment would result in tallies becoming less acceptable to creditors, except at a discount, raising the cost of government purchases.

Tallies had the advantage of being very difficult to forge, but they were cumbersome, and we will see that they were eventually superseded by paper instruments, from the seventeenth century onwards. Tallies nevertheless continued to be cut right up until the nineteenth century. When they were finally abolished in 1834, government officials decided to dispose of this considerable stock of wood in the furnaces of the heating system of the Houses of Parliament. It would be comforting to think that this decision was at least made on the grounds of sensible economy, but apparently not; it was just a convenient rapid way of getting rid of material whose storage space was urgently needed for other purposes. Parliament was not sitting at the time and the Chambers had no need for the additional heating. But something went wrong with the furnaces, and both Houses of Parliament were burnt to the ground—perhaps the most tangible example ever of government being brought down by overheated finance.[3]

TOWARDS THE CIVIL WAR

At the end of the Middle Ages, Tudor kings and queens created a more powerful centralised state, with a steadily increasing need for financial resources. In turn, this required a new kind of public servant, skilled in finance and in the raising of revenue through taxation, borrowing and other means: people like Henry VII's Morton, Dudley and Empson; and Henry VIII's Wolsey and Thomas Cromwell. Such positions offered the opportunity for significant personal enrichment, but necessarily also attracted powerful enemies, so their holders could experience rapid ascent to dizzy heights and equally rapid—and often fatal—decline when they lost the favour and protection of the monarch. (Although Thomas Gresham managed to serve such diverse monarchs as Henry VIII, Edward VI, Mary Tudor and Elizabeth I, and die a natural death—he was obviously a natural survivor.)

The financial health of the state varied with the monarchs and their proclivities and policies. Henry VII was cautious in matters of finance and carefully rebuilt the fortunes of the Crown after the disasters of the late Middle Ages. Henry VIII was more profligate, given to conspicuous consumption and adventurous for-

eign policy, but the suppression of the monasteries and the seizure of the very large land holdings of the English Church gave
him enormous extraordinary revenues and disguised the weakening financial position.

Elizabeth I was another monarch more cautious with expenditure—famously she refused her captains' requests for more
ammunition even during the most crucial days of the Spanish
Armada naval battles—and was able to announce in 1574 that
she had cleared the debts of her predecessors.[4] This was in fact a
political side-swipe at the alleged profligacy of her predecessor
Mary and her husband Philip II of Spain, now hate-figures in
Elizabethan England (the political compulsion to denigrate the
financial competence of one's predecessors is nothing new).
However, she failed to reform an increasingly ineffectual tax sys-
tem and was in debt again by the end of her reign. She had her
own source of unorthodox revenue: the piratical expeditions of
Francis Drake and others were surprisingly profitable, and the
Crown was a large shareholder in them.

The Stuart monarchs faced both a weakening financial position,
but now also a suspicious and increasingly hostile Parliament. Both
James I and Charles I were seen as personally extravagant, lavishing
money on favourites, conspicuous consumption and unpopular
foreign projects. With an inadequate tax system and little enthusiasm in Parliament to reform this to provide more adequate
resources to a profligate and suspect Crown, both monarchs
resorted to non-parliamentary sources of revenue: the 'farming' of
tax revenues, the sale of Crown lands, monopolies, offices and
titles, the levying of fines for trivial or imaginary offences, even the
direct seizure of bullion. Both attempted at times to rule without
calling Parliament (Charles for eleven years from 1629 to 1640) but
were forced back through lack of funds.

Charles also vigorously attempted to bend (rather than overtly
break) the rules of parliamentary approval of taxation. He con-

tinued to collect the traditional Tunnage and Poundage duties, although Parliament had pointedly voted these only for the first year of his reign rather than, as was customary, for its entirety. His famous and controversial attempt to extend Ship Money from its traditional base of coastal towns to the whole country could perhaps be represented as not a new tax, but a reinterpretation of the rules of an existing, parliamentary-approved tax. Finally, he attempted to impose forced loans instead of taxation. He was able to get at least some of the judiciary to support the legality of these manoeuvres, but eventually when Parliament had to be recalled (because Charles had no money to resist a Scottish invasion in 1640), it reasserted their absolute illegality.

He was, though, unable to use borrowing in any significant degree to escape this financial straitjacket. Many of his high-handed actions had offended the City of London merchants, who refused him a loan outright, and cautious foreign bankers would be unwilling to lend much to a monarch who so obviously could not command the tax revenues necessary for repayment.

THE COMMONWEALTH AND RESTORATION

Charles' disputes with Parliament culminated in the English Civil War, which commenced in 1642 and ended with his defeat in 1645 and execution in 1649. But surprisingly the King's defeat was not a simple victory for Parliament. A Commonwealth on republican lines was declared, and Parliament was nominally its supreme governing body, but real effective power now lay with the parliamentary army rather than Parliament itself, and army views had become more radical than those of the Members of Parliament. A period of fractious relations ensued, with Members inimical to the army being removed ('Pride's Purge'), and eventually General Oliver Cromwell (a descendant of Henry VIII's Thomas) dissolved even the remainder of Parliament (the 'Rump') in 1653, instituting what was effectively a military dictatorship.

A paradoxical side-effect of all this was that, with Parliament sidelined, there was again no legal or consensual basis for taxation. Cromwell simply imposed taxes (including discriminatory taxes against royalists) and forced loans. While Cromwell lived, the force of his personality and his arms was able to hold things together, but on his death in 1658, neither his son nor any other leader seemed able to command conclusive support. A dangerous and potentially anarchic situation threatened, resolved by the most powerful military commander, General Monck, negotiating the return of the monarchy in the person of Charles' son, as Charles II.

The deal securing Charles' return in 1660 had to involve a resolution of financial responsibilities, although in retrospect parliamentarians would regret that they had not been strict enough. Parliament reasserted its sole right to approve all taxation other than customary feudal dues. However, as a gesture of goodwill it voted sufficient tax revenues to Charles for the duration of his reign to enable 'the King to live of his own', i.e. to cover all normal peacetime state expenditures (it estimated this need at about £1.2 million p.a.). Additional expenditure to cover emergencies such as wars would require explicit parliamentary approval of additional taxation on each occasion. Unfortunately, Parliament had been over-optimistic in estimating the yields of the taxes providing Charles' permanent income, and Charles had inherited his family's extravagant tastes, so the financial settlement soon came under strain.

'Extravagance' was of course a perennial parliamentary criticism of monarchs—just as it is today of contemporary recipients of public money—but it was not always justified. Kings were expected to maintain the dignity and international reputation of the state, and to demonstrate its wealth and power through architecture, the arts, sumptuous entertainments, and generosity in rewarding service. Louis XIV of France was, of course, an extreme case, but any monarch who failed to do at least some of this would be conversely accused of miserliness or incompetence. Charles II also attempted to compensate out of his own resources many impoverished former supporters of his father. But there was indeed corrupt extravagance as well: permanent grants exceeding £45,000 p.a. were paid to the royal mistresses the Duchesses of Cleveland and Portsmouth, and £70,000 of 'Secret Service' expenditure was diverted to Portsmouth and to Nell Gwyn, a third mistress.[5] As we have seen, the total annual budget was about £1.2 million, so these were significant sums. And Charles had other mistresses too.

The Restoration settlement definitely envisaged a monarchical, not a parliamentary government. The King had the right to choose his own ministers and policies, irrespective of parliamentary wishes. Parliament's power lay solely in the right to authorise taxation, and refusal could of course restrain major policies which it disliked. But Parliament did not collect that taxation, which was in the hands of royal officials; nor, at least so far as the substantial permanently-voted general income of the King was concerned, did it control or even have reliable information on what it was actually spent on. Nor did it control the King's borrowing. These major loopholes gave the King considerable discretion to spend on policies that Parliament would not approve, with the added concern in the case of borrowing, that Parliament might ultimately be faced with the unpalatable choice of repaying the King's unauthorised borrowing or allowing an embarrassing royal bankruptcy.

Sceptical parliamentarians were unwilling to grant an extravagant and suspect monarch more resources, being concerned about the opacity of his finances and the true destination of the funds already voted. This limited Charles' policy options, but also led him further into borrowing, ultimately with disastrous consequences (see Chapter 3), and into non-parliamentary sources of income, most notably accepting a subsidy from the King of France in exchange for secret policy obligations which would have been unacceptable to Parliament. But despite all the difficulties, neither Charles nor Parliament wished to provoke a return to civil war, and each side was flexible and pragmatic enough to walk the necessary tightropes of the age.

Charles was succeeded by his brother James II, who was considerably less flexible in matters of both politics and religion. And unfortunately James' accession coincided with an economic boom which produced a remarkable improvement in tax revenues and freed him from the financial constraints that had dogged his brother. Financially able to pursue more confrontational and absolutist policies, he soon provoked the so-called 'Glorious Revolution' of 1688, in which Parliament effectively deposed him and offered the Crown instead jointly to the protestant Dutch prince William of Orange and his wife Mary (Mary had the better hereditary claim, being James' daughter, but it was William who really combined all the desired religious, political and military qualifications).[6]

This time Parliament resolved to avoid the mistakes of 1660, and to spell out definitively the limitations of monarchical powers, particularly with regard to finance. The arrangements put forward then are now widely thought of as the origins of Britain's current system of constitutional monarchy and parliamentary government, and it is at this point that our story of public finances and public debt really begins to take off.

3

THE BEGINNINGS OF THE NATIONAL DEBT

The Glorious Revolution of 1688 brought the prospect of significant change: a constitutional monarchy in which the financial control of Parliament would restrain the Crown's tendencies to extravagance and absolutism. Parliament hoped it could look forward to a new era of financial stability.

However, the immediate prospect was of greater financial demands: the new regime would need to defend itself militarily against the domestic and foreign supporters of the deposed Stuart monarchy, and one of William's principal purposes had been to detach England from her Stuart pro-French policy and bring her into alliance with the Netherlands against the French. War against France broke out almost immediately and lasted until 1697. Government expenditure, and unregulated short-term indebtedness, grew alarmingly, even more alarmingly than under the Stuarts. The purchasing agents of the Navy and the Army placed orders for materials and employed sailors and soldiers. But when the bills came in the agents simply did not have the money to pay them.

In principle, of course, this was not a new problem, and was handled by the use of the Tally. As before, in the first instance the government would have to use tallies to purchase military supplies and pay its troops, and then hope to pay off these debts in the reasonably near future when tax revenues began to come in. But warfare was becoming more expensive, and it was difficult to control the purchasing agents, who were increasingly now stationed all over the globe. Furthermore, a new and fragile government was not in an ideal position to levy large increases in taxes. As a result, the number of tallies outstanding was increasing rapidly and in uncontrolled fashion, and it was by no means obvious that the taxes voted would be sufficient to pay them all off. Suppliers' willingness to accept tallies was coming into question, with possible disruption of war supplies looming.

To avert a crisis, the government looked for ways of reducing its reliance on hand-to-mouth methods.

THE ORDER OF REPAYMENT
AND THE STOP OF THE EXCHEQUER

Under similar financial pressure during Charles II's reign, in 1664, Sir George Downing (after whom Downing Street is named) had attempted to improve on the tally by introducing the Order of Repayment.[1] This was a paper instrument, secured on a specific tax revenue, originally produced in addition to the tally for a loan or IOU. It would be repaid with interest (6 per cent p.a.) as an inducement to suppliers to bear their waiting patiently until the eventual repayment; it would be transferable from one holder to another, so that if suppliers could not be patient they could sell their claim to another citizen who would hold it until the eventual repayment; and it would be registered and numbered and would be paid off in strict numerical order as the tax revenues became available. This last feature was particularly important: as we have seen, the tally was a clear acknowledgement of a debt, but it provided no guarantee of any timescale for repayment. The Order of Repayment similarly had no commitment to a firm date, but since the estimated yield of its securing tax could be known from parliamentary papers, and the Register of Orders was also open to public inspection, an intelligent holder could form a good estimate of the ultimate date of repayment (like one of those telephone answering systems where at least the disembodied voice tells you what position you are in the queue). In return for this greater certainty, bankers would be more willing to lend, and suppliers more willing to extend credit, than under a simple tally system.

On the face of it these Orders were an admirable innovation, and they might have developed smoothly into an organised system of short-run lending, such as our modern Treasury Bills, or even into a state-backed paper currency system.[2] But the smooth working of such a system did require one important commitment from the government, and one whose dangers it perhaps did not sufficiently appreciate: no other uses for the securing taxes could be allowed to jump the queue. Indeed, to avoid breaking faith with the existing creditors, even urgent requirements for new expenditure must take their turn behind the repayment of existing debt. If a large volume of debt repayments pre-empted the incoming revenue streams for the year, all new expenditure would itself in turn have to be borrowed, perhaps on increasingly unfavourable terms as the potential lenders could easily see the mounting difficulties of the government.

In its early stages, when the system was applied only to some of the time-limited additional taxation streams explicitly voted, where there was an obvious limit to the amount of credit that could be safely created, and urgent current expenditure could be met from other unrestricted revenue streams, these dangers were not so apparent. But the early success of the system—and the government's increasing problems with Parliament—encouraged the government to extend it to the whole of the open-ended permanent revenue, and the volume of credit grew alarmingly. When a war threatened in 1672, the government had little choice but to spend its current revenues on war preparations instead of on the promised repayments for the year. This so-called 'Stop of the Exchequer' was not complete: those Orders secured on the explicitly-voted additional taxes continued to be honoured; similar Orders were issued on a small scale subsequently; and the government eventually guaranteed the interest on the Orders that were stopped. But the stopped Orders themselves remained in limbo, with now no plan for eventual repayment.

The Orders concerned, being transferable, had indeed largely been transferred. The original creditors, wanting early repayment, had mostly sold their claims to private banking firms, many of whom were ruined by the Stop. This so-called 'Bankers' Debt' remained an unresolved issue for some years; eventually in 1699 an Act of Parliament effectively wrote down the principal by a half, but agreed to pay the interest of 6 per cent on the remainder until an unspecified repayment date, thereby bringing this originally short-term debt into the newly-established category of Permanent Debt.[3] Repayment was actually achieved in 1720 as part of the South Sea Bubble scheme (of which more later).

But the reputational damage had been done. The Stop was clearly a default. An unaccountable monarchical government, left to its own devices, had shown itself again to be too powerful, and too capricious, to be a reliable financial partner. Few would trust any further financial innovations coming from such a state alone.

FIRST LONG-TERM LOANS

The debt on tallies and Orders was a short-run debt, with the government continually being embarrassed by pressure for repayment. This pressure might be relieved by raising money explicitly on a longer-term basis. In 1692 the first attempt to raise serious long-term money from the public was a tontine (see Appendix I) loan at 10 per cent p.a., for £1 million. This was not a success: only just over £100,000 was raised on the tontine terms, although nearly £800,000 was raised from the second-string offer of a life annuity (see Appendix I) at 14 per cent p.a.

In 1693 the government followed up, raising the remainder of the million also by life annuities at 14 per cent. But more importantly for the future, the 1693 Act guaranteed holders of these annuities exemption from any taxation upon them. In the circumstances of the time this was perhaps not an unreasonable thing to clarify: there was no general income taxation, and any subsequent government attempt to tax the returns on government loans would really have been a unilateral change of the terms—effectively a partial default. However, it sowed the seeds for much political dissension in the future in which those elements of society which did pay taxes of various sorts—particularly the 'landed interest'—railed against the 'moneyed interest', which did not.

In 1694 the government tried again with another 'Million Loan'. This time the added attraction was a lottery. Losers in the lottery received interest of 10 per cent for sixteen years, winners (2,500 of them) considerably more. Again, the average cost of the loan to the government was 14 per cent.

Additionally, £300,000 was raised by the sale of more life annuities, although these could be on one (14 per cent), two (12 per cent), or three (10 per cent) lives. These could be very long-term commitments indeed. (And subsequently the single-life annuities were offered the chance to convert to very long fixed-term annuities of ninety-six years.)

These loans suggest the actions of a financially desperate government. Despite increasingly frantic marketing appealing to the gambling instinct, future revenues were being mortgaged very expensively for long periods. It is not clear how long this could have been continued. But the next move set the tone for an altogether more stable set of arrangements.

THE BANK OF ENGLAND

In this period there were many proposals for the setting up of banks of various descriptions. Some were quite frankly bizarre, others were more sensible. Banks did already exist, of course. They had grown up spontaneously from various roots: from straightforward money-lenders; from international trading merchant houses who necessarily dealt in large sums of money; or from goldsmiths and silversmiths who accepted deposits of coin and precious metals for safe-keeping and issued receipts. But there were limitations. In the absence of any well-developed company law, such enterprises were usually family-based or partnerships, limiting their size and reach. The acceptability of their paper was similarly limited by the limits of their personal reputations.

Joseph Paterson, an enterprising Scot, was a prolific producer of potential financial innovations. Few innovations of the time did not have his fingerprints somewhere on them, although many of his ideas were unrealised, and others were disastrous (see the Darien expedition, Chapter 11). The age produced many such financial promoters. On this occasion, Paterson joined with a group of City of London merchants to promote the formation of a Bank of England. The Bank would offer to make a permanent loan to the government of £1 million at 6 per cent p.a., in exchange for the granting of certain privileges: a Royal Charter of incorporation as a joint-stock company with limited liability, and the ability to issue paper bank notes as legal tender—indeed, a monopoly on issuing such bank notes. The government baulked at legal tender and monopoly (although both of these eventually came in the fullness of time) but liked the general idea. After negotiations, in 1694 a loan of £1.2 million at 8 per cent was agreed in exchange for the Charter and non-monopoly issue of bank notes.

The advantages to the Bank were substantial: the grant of joint-stock limited-liability status (not generally available in the laws of the time) allowed expansion to a size otherwise unthinkable; the steady interest income from the government of £100,000 p.a. (£96,000 interest and £4,000 for administrative costs) gave the Bank stability and credibility. Even without formal monopoly and legal tender status the Bank's notes soon dominated the London financial markets.

The government had reason to be pleased too; it had borrowed a very large sum of money (as we have seen, Parliament had estimated the same sum as a reasonable year's expenditure for Charles II's government) at a much lower rate of interest than before, without any fixed date of repayment. If the arrangement proved successful to both parties, further loans could be negotiated similarly.

The first important innovation here was in the permanence of the loan: there was no requirement on the government to pay it back at a specific date, or even at all—except in the case of the government terminating the Bank's privileges, which it could do after 1705 with a year's notice. In practice this simply meant that terminating the Bank's privileges would be too expensive, although at periodic renegotiations of the Charter the government could and did extract further loans or better conditions. Both parties had locked themselves into an indissoluble relationship.

Of course, the short-run loans on tallies and Orders similarly had no precise date of redemption, but the public presumption was that they would be paid, and relatively swiftly. When this did not happen the government's credit and the acceptability of tallies and Orders for the future suffered. In this case there was no such presumption, therefore the government's credit was safe.

But another, perhaps even more significant, innovation was that the Bank bound itself by its charter only to lend to the government with the express authorisation of Parliament, and with the explicit allocation by Parliament of sufficient tax revenues ('funding') to service the debt fully. As the Bank (and models based on the Bank) would quickly establish itself as the almost exclusive route of government borrowing, this effectively closed off the danger of unauthorised royal borrowing.[4] The government's debt was now firmly based on the credit of Parliament, not of the King personally—a true 'national' debt—and the credit of Parliament depended in turn on its un-assailed control of taxation. From about this time writers begin to use the terminology of 'the publick credit'.

The government followed up this success with another, pre-existing chartered company—in fact the largest of all, the East India Company. Founded in 1600 for the purpose of trading with India, it had been very successful and profitable. However internal dissensions of policy had broken out between two factions, one of which decided to cut out and set up a rival company of its own. In granting a charter to the New East India Company in 1698, the Crown extracted a permanent loan of £2 million on similar terms to the Bank of England. The New East India Company operated in competition with the Old East India Company for only a few years. Both factions soon realised there was more profit in cooperation, recombining to form the United East India Company in 1708–9, and making a further loan of £1.2 million for the privilege.

But not all of the government's ventures were successful. A large lottery loan of £1.4 million in 1697, secured on the excise duty on malt, was a disastrous failure, selling only £17,630.

More worryingly the 'floating debt', the unsecured short-term debt, still mainly in tallies arising from uncoordinated military purchasing, was still much larger than that which had been stabilised into longer-term forms. This problem was tackled in three ways: first Parliament passed the first of a series of 'General Mortgages' indefinitely prolonging taxes which were due to expire, until their associated loans, and other loans which had no tax associations, were truly paid off. As the terminology suggests, this acknowledged that earlier profligacy had effectively mortgaged future tax revenues for some years to come. But as a measure on its own it would only work if future revenue requirements were reduced, and that was unlikely.

A second measure was the introduction of Exchequer Bills, which were similar to the earlier Orders of Repayment, interest-bearing and transferable, but with two crucial improvements: they were acceptable in the payment of taxes, and trustees were appointed who would guarantee, for a fee, to cash such bills if the holders found it necessary. This greatly improved their acceptability and liquidity, and increased the incentives for holders to refrain from demands for early repayment. These Exchequer Bills are the forerunners of today's Treasury Bills.

Thirdly, the short-term debts might be converted into longer-term. An extension of the Bank of England's charter allowed it to expand its capital by a further £1 million, of which 80 per cent might be subscribed in tallies. The extra capital would be remunerated by the government at 8 per cent, as with the Bank's original capital. Thus tally-holders would be converted into holders of permanent debt as Bank shareholders. The success of this 'Ingraftment of Tallies' led on to an even more ambitious scheme.

THE SOUTH SEA COMPANY

Direct marketing of debt to the public had had some successes, but the failure of the malt lottery suggested it had reached its limits for the moment. On the other hand, borrowing from chartered companies had been a resounding success. The incorporated company effectively acted as a wholesaling agent for the government, but it also served to reassure investors, still suspicious of the arbitrary powers of the Crown in financial matters. The Directors of the Bank of England and the East India Company performed a credible monitoring function, and possessed significant bargaining power. But with its ability to control the terms of the charters, the government had some bargaining power too.

There were few such incorporated companies in existence—incorporation at this time was not a right, it could only be obtained by the specific grant of a charter from the Crown—so the government's next move was a bold attempt to expand the market. A proposal was brought forward to establish a third chartered company, to be called the South Sea Company. Like the East India Company, its ostensible purpose would be to exploit trade, in this case with the South Seas, i.e. what we would now call Latin America. But, like the Bank of England, its secondary purpose would be to make permanent loans to the government in exchange for a fixed-interest income stream, which in turn would give assurance and permanent credibility to its operations. In contrast, however, its initial loans would not be new money: the holders of the floating debt would be invited to exchange their claims for shares in the new company, thereby converting the embarrassing short-term debts to a more stable long-term footing. The company was chartered in 1711, and the financial conversion was an immediate success: £9 million of floating debt was incorporated, solving that particular problem almost overnight.

Several important things should be noted about the South Sea Company. With a capital of £9 million, it dwarfed the Bank of England, and its contribution to the public finances was considerably larger than the East India Company. Together, the three companies now accounted for nearly half the entire National Debt, with the brash newcomer clearly in the lead.

On the other hand, the South Sea Company's ostensible principal purpose was more tenuous than either of its rivals. Most of Latin America belonged to Spain, which was notoriously unwilling to grant trading rights to foreigners and was frequently (and indeed currently) at war with Britain. The American trading prospects were therefore at best a very speculative gamble on success in the current war leading to a peace treaty which might open up the continent to British trade. In the event, this did not happen. Furthermore, despite its impressive balance sheet, the South Sea Company in fact had very little money to exploit any trade potential that might arise, as all its shares had been simply transfers of debts and not in-payments of cash.

A third feature was its party-politics. From its inception the Bank of England was seen as a very Whig institution. Moneyed city interests were predominantly Whig, and they had combined with like-minded members of the government to found the Bank in 1694. Tory politicians distrusted this financial–political nexus, and Tory landowners resented the merchant classes' ability to make more money out of their money assets. Tory landowning interests had therefore already proposed the foundation of a competing Land Bank, but this had been a resounding failure. However, Tories had become more influential in the government (despite an ill-judged and much-resented attempt by the Bank of England to warn the Queen away from this), and saw in the South Sea Company a useful potential Tory competitor to the Bank.

The implications of these features would only become apparent in the future.

THE SOUTH SEA BUBBLE

Most people know the general story of the South Sea Bubble, the earliest British example of stock market hype, hysteria, hucksterism and hubris. The South Sea Company was formed to exploit trade with South America in much the same way as the East India Company had been formed to exploit trade with India; for a short time it was the ultimate stock market darling, but when it was discovered that its trade prospects were limited at best, the bubble burst, amid a welter of bankruptcies and much exposure of fraud and sharp dealing. It has an honoured place alongside Tulip mania and other quaint episodes of speculative frenzy and bizarre human gullibility—well, they would be quaint had we not the example of the 2008 crash before us.

Up to a point all this is true, but the South American trade story was really only a diversion—as we have just noted, the real purpose of the South Sea Company was to do with the National Debt. It had been founded in 1711 to mop up the floating debt, with great success. The trade prospects with South America were still only a speculative future prospect, but they could wait. Half the National Debt was now safely very long-term at reasonable rates of interest with the three chartered companies.

The government now turned its mind to the conversion of the rest of the National Debt to lower rates of interest. Here there was an assortment of different forms of longer-term debt: annuities, lottery loans, tontines. Some were permanent, some (eventually) self-liquidating; some had options of redemption, others not. They had been contracted at very high rates of interest, but with the coming of peace, market rates of interest fell well below those rates. Where these debts were redeemable, this gave the government the possibility of borrowing at the current rates of interest to redeem them, with a considerable saving on the interest bill. More conveniently, the government could simply use the threat of doing so to coerce the existing debt-holders into accepting a lower rate of interest (a technique known as 'Conversion', of which we will hear much more, see Appendix I). In 1717 the chief minister Stanhope successfully completed the conversion of most of the potentially redeemable debts to 5 per cent (including the South Sea Company's £9 million). But this left the unre-deemable ones, for which the government had no credible inducements. How could the holders be persuaded to give up their secure and very long-term income streams, for something less expensive to the government?

Here, the public's awakening interest in the potentials of com-mercial speculation could be of service. The South Sea Company had already successfully taken over some parts of the National Debt. The Company had shown it could provide its investors with a steady interest stream, just like the government. But it might provide more. If its South American trading prospects paid off, it might provide considerably more. The government's intransigent irredeemable debtors might be tempted to relinquish their certain government claims for the prospect of getting in on the ground floor of an eighteenth-century Google. Essentially it was the idea of 'equitizing' the debt, and it captured the spirit of the age (much the same idea was being simultaneously pursued in France by the maverick Scottish financier John Law, and his Mississippi Company was even more ambitious, initially more successful and ultimately more disastrous than the South Sea Company—but his initial successes had been noted in England, and English events were partly driven by a desire not to be left behind by the French).

In 1719 the Company took over some of the Lottery loans, and plans were made to offer similar terms to the holders of the remainder of the irredeemable debt. The problem was on the way to being solved. But at this point enthusiasm and over-ambition really took over. If equitisation was such a good idea, why stop at the irredeemables? Why not take over the whole of the National Debt? Essentially this was the proposal the Company made in 1720: to take over the whole of the long-term National Debt, apart from that held by the Bank of England and the East India Company, and to take over the Bank of England's

41

functions of administering the shorter-term floating debt. This seriously alarmed the Bank of England, which made counter-proposals of its own to protect its position. A short bidding war ensued, which was won by the Company. If it worked, the scheme would be a great benefit to the government. But in its efforts to undercut the Bank of England, the Company had recklessly cut its margins to an unsustainable level: it offered to accept an interest rate of 5 per cent from the government, whereas many of its proposed new investors had been receiving up to 14 per cent. The fees it would accept (or prices it would offer) for other aspects of the administration of the public finances were equally unrealistic. The only way it could deliver its investors' expectations was if the South American trading prospects did indeed prove to be a gold mine, and the value of the shares would rise accordingly. In reality this was highly unlikely, but for some time at least the prospects could be talked up— talked up and fraudulently manipulated.

A highly-charged speculative boom ensued, and ultimately collapsed, ruining many investors. This is not the place to recount the ins and outs of the whole story.[5] Like Gordon Brown in 2008, Prime Minister Robert Walpole earned considerable credit for eventually resolving the crisis, but equally some criticism about his possible role in instigating it in the first place. Some members of the government were clearly fraudulently involved. Unlike the bankers of 2008, many of the principal participants were pursued relentlessly at law by a vengeful Parliament, and some had their fortunes confiscated (although the involvement of other senior members of the government and even royalty was carefully hushed up).

However, despite the financial mayhem, from the narrow viewpoint of national debt management, the episode was a great success. Debt-holders had been persuaded to give up their expensive claims on the government for other claims which ultimately proved worthless.

Walpole hoped to resolve the situation by having the Bank of England and the East India Company each take over half the South Sea Company. Unsurprisingly, the two stronger companies declined the poisoned chalice, and eventually the Bank took over only a part of the South Sea Company's assets. The South Sea Company itself survived, although with a considerable write-down of its assets, and soon the abandonment of any pretension to South American trading. It reverted to what it had always really been: an organisation which simply managed its members' investments in the National Debt—rather like a modern-day pension fund manager. These functions became increasingly routine, and even unnecessary as the instruments of national debt were progressively simplified. Nevertheless, very large sums of money continued to flow through its hands. For more than a century to come many middle-class families would continue to hold their savings in and draw their incomes from South Sea Annuities—Jane Austen's parents held South Sea Annuities and handed them down to their children. You can find on the internet many references to South Sea Annuities in contemporary wills and benefactions.

The Company was finally wound up only in 1853. Its grand headquarters building, South Sea House (the second building of that name), was completed, interestingly, after the Bubble.[6]

Economists' Views on the National Debt: 1. David Hume

In general, the views of well-known economists on the National Debt were almost universally hostile, pessimistic and even doom-laden.

One of the earliest, David Hume (1711–1776) was particularly apocalyptic. He identified both economic and political consequences. The taxes required to service the Debt either oppressed the poor or raised the price of labour. Incomes derived from the Debt encouraged the wealthier classes into idleness and luxury. But more dangerous were the political consequences: as the Debt inexorably mounted, ultimately the state would be at the mercy of the stockholders. In the end the nation would have to destroy the Debt before it was destroyed by it. By Hume's time, the ability actually to repay the Debt was seriously in doubt, so Hume predicted a catastrophic repudiation in the near future.

4

WAR AND PEACE IN THE EIGHTEENTH CENTURY

For Britain the eighteenth century was a period of almost incessant warfare, broken only by small interludes of peace.

Table 4.1 shows the major wars in which Britain was involved between 1688 and 1815. These wars accounted for 68 out of 127 years. There were many minor wars as well, and the major wars were often untidy patchworks of conflicts among participants with very diverse objectives, spawning further subsidiary conflicts sometimes with unlikely enemies. From the British point of view they were mostly a long struggle for dominance with France (and to a lesser extent Spain), involving also all of the other European powers from time to time in a continually shifting web of alliances and counter-alliances. They were fought all over the world: on the oceans, on the European mainland, in the Mediterranean, in North America, the West Indies, India, Africa, even Latin America. Even the American Revolutionary War (or American War of Independence, 1775–1783) could be seen as a proxy war with France, who supported the colonists, and it drew in the Spanish and Dutch as well. It was the least successful of Britain's

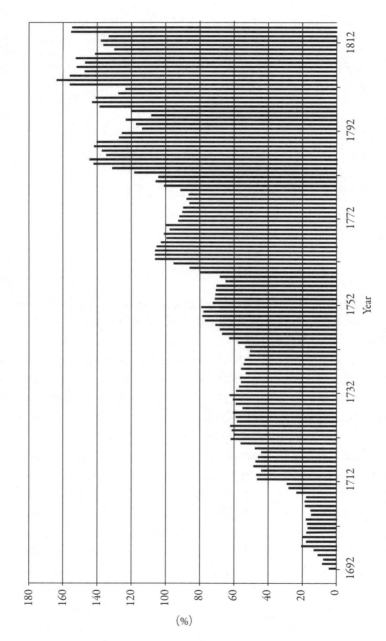

Figure 4: British National Debt/GDP Ratio (%), 1692–1815

wars, partly because it was the only one in which the government found itself completely bereft of allies. By the end of the period Britain had lost its first colonial empire in the United States, but had successfully excluded the French from large parts of the globe and thereby established a second, larger colonial empire with India at its heart.

Table 4.1: Wars and Terminal National Debt, 1688–1815

Years	Conflict	Concluding Treaty	National Debt at End
1688–97	Nine Years' War	Concluded by Treaty of Ryswick 1697	£14.5 million
1701–14	War of the Spanish Succession	Concluded by Treaty of Utrecht 1713	£36.2 million
1740–48	War of the Austrian Succession	Concluded by Treaty of Aix la Chapelle 1748	£75.4 million
1756–63	Seven Years' War	Concluded by Treaty of Paris	£128.6 million
1775–83	American Revolutionary War (American War of Independence)	Concluded by Treaty of Paris	£227.2 million
1793–1802	French Revolutionary Wars	Concluded by Peace of Amiens	£537.7 million
1803–1815	Napoleonic Wars	Finally concluded by Battle of Waterloo and Congress of Vienna 1815	£839.3 million

As shown in the table, each successive war ratcheted up the Debt (as a strange rule of thumb, each major war seemed roughly to double it) until financial exhaustion compelled a halt. The ensuing interlude of peace was then a desperate race to mend the finances before the next bout of hostilities began. The government fully appreciated that its military success depended on its financial strength. France was a much larger country than Britain; its land area and population were more than double. On the face of it France should have won a war of resources easily, but Britain's ability to borrow previously unheard-of sums enabled it to match the spending of its rival. Smaller traditional rivals like the Dutch simply could not keep up.

Some contemporary commentators, indeed, saw the National Debt as Britain's most potent strategic weapon. Others, less sanguine, saw the ease of borrowing as the cause of militarism and foreign adventures. Modern historians have coined the term 'fiscal-military state' to describe the nature of British governance in this period.

The government was haunted by two nightmares: one was that the French might actually get their public finances in order and be able to rearm quicker than the British could. The other was how long this increasing debt-cycle could continue.

THE STRUCTURE OF INDEBTEDNESS: REPAYMENT, CONVERSION, CONSOLIDATION

The structure of indebtedness, and its perceived problems, changed with each war. In 1688 the Debt, although chaotic and uncertain, probably amounted to only a few million pounds.

By 1697, at the close of the Nine Years' War, the Debt amounted to £14.5 million. Despite the founding of the Bank of England with its permanent loan the great majority of the Debt was still the floating debt: short-term, unsecured, volatile, posing a threat to the public credit.

By 1714, at the close of the War of the Spanish Succession, the Debt had risen to £36.2 million, but of this only £8.4 million was floating; the three chartered companies now accounted for £15.8 million, and the remainder was annuities, either for short-or long-fixed terms or for one, two or three lives. The government had not been able to prevent the Debt from more than doubling but it had been successful in converting most of the Debt to a longer-term, more stable basis.

There then ensued an unusually long period of peace, mostly under the political leadership of Robert Walpole, until the next major war in 1740, during which the government gave its attention to alleviating the debt burden in various ways. The most pressing problem now was the high rates of interest at which debts had been incurred, whereas market rates had since fallen with peacetime conditions.

We have seen that in 1717 Stanhope was able to convert the loans from chartered companies and redeemable annuities to 5 per cent; we have also seen how the attempt to use the South Sea Company to do the same with the unredeemable annuities led to the Bubble. Although in the wider scheme of things this was a complete disaster, when the dust had settled the government had indeed achieved its narrower, national debt objective: the unredeemable holders had been induced to swap their expensive claims for much more modest South Sea Annuities at 5 per cent (due to reduce further to 4 per cent in 1727).

But the overall context of the National Debt had undergone a qualitatively significant change. Thirty years earlier it had been possible to view national indebtedness still as an essentially temporary phenomenon, which in the natural course of events should and would be paid off. All the debts had been contracted under that assumption, however piously expressed, and all were associated with mechanisms that should in theory repay them. Either they were essentially trade debts, which obviously had to be cleared and taxation had been voted to do so, or they were annuities for lives or fixed terms, which would eventually lapse.

This was clearly no longer the case. Debt had been contracted explicitly on a permanent basis, and the taxation voted to service this debt explicitly covered only the interest payments, with no provision for automatic repayment of principal. Quantitatively, too, the scales had swung towards permanence: £5–10 million might conceivably have been paid off over a few years with a concerted effort, but £36 million was a different order of magnitude—repayment was no longer really practical politics.

WALPOLE'S SINKING FUND

There was considerable debate as to whether this situation was sustainable, and views were expressed which were to be traced and retraced at intervals over the next two hundred years.

At one, optimistic, extreme, it could be argued that this was no real problem; if the government had no legal requirement to repay, this was not a real debt at all. The only real burden was the annual interest payment and so long as this was adequately covered by taxation, public creditworthiness was perfectly safe. But this in turn did suggest the real problem: taxation to cover the interest was a burden on the economy; it was larger than it had been in the past; and it was now permanent. Furthermore, with no automatic mechanisms to enforce repayment, and no incentive to do so voluntarily, the Debt could only grow. With each successive war the Debt would get bigger and bigger until the interest burden alone was unsupportable. Therefore some determined extraordinary effort should be made to pay the Debt off. If not, the ability to fight future wars would be compromised, and even a national bankruptcy threatened.

One proposal was for a general levy on land for a few years; another proposed monetising the Debt into a non-interest-bearing paper currency; a third re-converting it all into floating debt, exchequer bills at 3 per cent, and using the consequent savings on interest to redeem them all over a period of thirty years; a fourth to tax the earnings of fund-holders (despite the promise given not to) and use the revenues to redeem.

All these proved too extreme and Walpole proposed the more modest idea of a 'sinking fund': the interest savings arising from the recent downward conversions would be paid into a fund which would apply them to redeem national debt, without the need for additional taxation, gradually over a period of years. In practice, though, the sinking fund moneys were largely diverted to other purposes. There will be more to say about the sinking fund concept later.

PELHAM'S CONSOLIDATION: THE BIRTH OF THE CONSOL

'"Heigho! I wish I could exchange my position in society and all my relations for a snug sum in the Three Per Cent. Consols"; for so it was that Becky felt the Vanity of human affairs, and it was in those securities that she would have liked to cast anchor.'

W. M. Thackeray, *Vanity Fair*

By 1739 little repayment had been achieved, but market interest rates had reduced further, and Sir John Barnard, a constant critic of government financial policy, proposed a further conversion operation to 3 per cent. Walpole was at first supportive of this, but in the face of determined opposition from the vested fund-holding interests, eventually backed down. The following year, war broke out again (the War of the Austrian Succession), and the government was forced into significant new borrowing, mostly at 4 per cent in the form of perpetual but redeemable annuities marketed directly to the public rather than to the chartered companies. By the peace of 1748 the Debt had doubled again, to £75.4 million.

But with peace, interest rates dropped sharply again and the new Prime Minister Henry Pelham was able to carry out a very successful conversion of almost all the Debt to 3.5 per cent, and subsequently to 3 per cent.

This conversion exercise was also accompanied by a considerable administrative simplification: all the various vintages of annuities were 'Consolidated' into two 3 per cent perpetual but redeemable stocks, the '3 per cent Reduced' (originally £17.5 million) and 'Consols' (originally £9.1 million). Subsequent government borrowing concentrated mainly on these two issues alone, and Consols, although originally the smaller, eventually became the classic British government stock of the nineteenth century, beloved of the British middle classes. Families held their savings in Consols and passed them down to their children. They were a particularly good way of ensuring a guaranteed income to daughters and younger sons who would not inherit the family's real property—which is why female characters in nineteenth-century novels always seem to have a suspiciously exact income of 'so many pounds per year'.

Although no new Consols were issued after 1927, they survived until 2015: the Cameron government took advantage of the current extraordinarily low interest rates to redeem and convert all the outstanding perpetuities—an eventuality which few would have thought likely before 2008.

Crucially, whereas each annuity issue had typically been secured on some particular tax, the new consolidated stocks were to be secured on government revenue in general. Previous streams of taxation had flowed into various funds, only the surpluses of which had been transferred into the Sinking Fund. Now all streams would flow directly into the Sinking Fund itself, from which all expenditure and all interest servicing would be carried out, and the surplus applied to debt redemption. Although this seemed to prioritise the role of the Sinking Fund, in fact it had the effect of turning its major function into that of an administrative channel through which all transactions relating to government finances must flow, rather than a device explicitly aimed at debt redemption alone. While this was itself a useful increase in transparency, the debt redemption objective became secondary. Soon the fund adopted a new name, the Consolidated Fund, which it retains to this day.[1]

And what of the Chartered Companies? The South Sea Company, although financially still very large, was now reduced to a simple administrative conduit: all its annuities and its permanent loan to the government were to be remunerated at 3 per cent, just like the consolidated stocks. In the 1750s its directors formally gave up any pretensions to the South Sea trade; the company made no further loans to government but continued to function for many years rather like a modern-day pension fund. Despite their lurid history, South Sea Annuities were now as safe as Consols. But in reality, the company had no useful function—its annuities might just as well have been Consols—and it was finally wound up by William Gladstone, the Chancellor of the Exchequer, in 1853.

The East India Company's loans were similarly reduced to 3 per cent, and the Company played no further active role in the National Debt. In 1793 its loans were in fact consolidated into the 3 per cent Reduced. It too was ultimately wound up by the government after the Indian Rebellion of 1857.

The Bank of England came out on top. In the preceding years it had not actually been a great supplier of long-term finance to the government. What it had supplied was reduced like all others to 3 per cent (although not its original foundation loan of £1.2 million). It had instead concentrated its recent efforts on supplying the government's short-term needs, and on helping the government issue and manage its public offerings, originally at the short end and more lately the long-term issues as well. In this it had faced competition from the two rival chartered companies, but as they were eclipsed its position as the manager of all government debt business was now unassailable.

Pelham's reforms marked the end of the first turbulent, exploratory phase of permanent public borrowing. He had reached a structure easily recognisable to modern eyes: a stable transparent structure based on simple perpetual but redeemable annuities at low rates of interest, well suited to secondary markets; consolidation of tax revenues into a single pot, with a sinking fund offering some hope of redemptions; a reputable Bank of England managing the Debt; and floating debt via Exchequer Bills well under control, with easy conversion into longer-term form if necessary. The Debt was still unfavourably large, but interest rates were as low as could reasonably be hoped.

The damage of past wars to the public finances had been contained, and if future wars could be avoided the debt problem should recede. But if the circumstances required it, the machinery that Walpole and Pelham had created would be only too capable of a further vast expansion of war finance.

THE SEVEN YEARS' WAR AND THE AMERICAN WAR OF INDEPENDENCE

Of course there were more wars. The Seven Years' War broke out in 1756 and borrowing soared again. Interest rates rose, and the government was obliged to offer rates of 4 per cent or more, or to attach additional inducements to its loans in the form of extra lotteries or annuities. However, when hostilities ceased, and interest rates fell again, the government was able to use its conversion tactics to pull the costs back to 3 per cent once more (in some cases this was written into the original loan contracts).

Next along was the American War of Independence (or American Revolutionary War). This conflict was particularly expensive, involving the support of large armies over very long lines of supply, and the financial system began to show some strain. Interest rates rose to 5 or 6 per cent, and lenders had become wise to the possibilities of conversion. Taking up a government loan at 6 per cent was obviously attractive, but less so if that rate could be reduced to 3 per cent on the return of peace. To protect themselves against this, lenders insisted on provisions restricting redemption until a minimum period of time had passed. Alternatively, they might protect themselves by taking up loans at low interest rates but under par (see Appendix I). In this way, during the American War, the National Debt rose by £115 million, although the government actually only received £92 million in borrowing. The French Revolutionary Wars that followed continued the trend. In such ways, the admirable simplicity of the Consol gave way again to greater complexity and lack of transparency.

LOAN CONTRACTORS

Another disturbing feature for the government was the emergence of the 'loan contractor'. Although government bonds were in theory marketed direct to the individual investor, with such large sums of money required the government found it more convenient in practice to use the services of middlemen: loan contractors would agree to take large chunks of a government issue, or even the whole issue, and distribute them to their own client lists, making a profit on the difference between buying and selling prices. The process was obviously open to abuse; explicit or implicit collusion among the small group of loan contractors suppressed competition in the market to the detriment of the government (Prime Minister Lord North complained that he was 'at the mercy of the money men'). The power and reputation of the contractors was significant: investors struggled to gain admission to what were thought of as the most privileged lists, and such admission could be used to curry favour and bribe influential people. The observation of such capricious and murky fortune-making did little to endear public opinion towards financiers and the financial markets.

Although strictly they belong to a slightly later period, and the few glimpses we get of their business activities suggest more the railway and international speculations of that period, the machinations of Mr Merdle in Dickens' *Little Dorrit* and Augustus Melmotte in Trollope's *The Way We Live Now* are typical of loan contractors, and the authors' treatment in both cases is savage. In real life, the famous economist David Ricardo made much of his fortune as a loan contractor, and his experience derived from those markets lent great authority to his economic pronouncements. Famous banks such as Baring Brothers and N. M. Rothschild also laid their foundations through operations in these markets.

By the end of the American War, the Debt had risen to £227 million, and Lord North's reputation had suffered as much from the general impression of financial ineptitude as from the conduct of the war itself. A further round of national soul-searching ensued, with the usual predictions of national bankruptcy and the inability to finance national defence in future. The new Prime Minister William Pitt the Younger decided that a serious effort was needed to restore public confidence and break the apparently inexorable rise of debt.[2]

FRENCH PUBLIC FINANCE IN THE EIGHTEENTH CENTURY

If British public finance and public borrowing were driven in the eighteenth century by the military rivalry with France, how did the rival fare? The simple answer is, not well.[3]

Economists' Views on the National Debt: 2. Adam Smith

Adam Smith (1723–1790) had a more measured approach than David Hume, but fundamentally he was no more optimistic. In the very last chapter of *The Wealth of Nations* (first published in 1776), he provided a survey of the development of public borrowing across Europe from primitive times and a detailed history of the growth of the English debts from 1688 onwards.

He had no truck with the argument that a national debt is a source of wealth in itself, nor with the lesser argument that the servicing of a domestically held debt is simply an internal transfer, 'the right hand paying the left', without serious economic implications. Even if the debt were genuinely entirely domestically held, which he doubted, the consequences could still be severe. The only true sources of wealth-generation were land and capital, and the taxation necessitated by the debt reduced the landowner's incentive to maintain and improve his land, and the capitalist's incentive not to consume his capital or to remove it to another, less taxed country. For Smith, landowners and capitalists had inbuilt incentives to look after and maintain their particular pieces of land and capital, but debt-holders had only a general and very dispersed interest in the overall health of the economy, and therefore no incentive to apply effort to any particular part of it. The result would inevitably be degradation of the wealth-producing resources.

He conceded that the British had in fact managed their debt fairly well up to that point, and that the performance of the British tax system compared favourably with its continental rivals. But that was only cause for false optimism.

He wrote: 'The practice of funding has gradually enfeebled every state which has adopted it [citing the Italian republics, Genoa, Venice, Spain, France, the United Provinces] ... Is it likely that in Great Britain alone a practice which has brought either weakness or desolation into every other country should prove altogether innocent? ... When national debts have once been accumulated to a certain degree, there is scarce, I believe, a single instance of their having been fairly and compleatly paid. The liberation of the publick revenue, if it has ever been brought about at all, has always been brought about by a bankruptcy; sometimes by an avowed one, but always by a real one, though frequently by a pretended payment.'

He concluded: 'Great Britain seems to support with ease a burden which half a century ago nobody believed her capable of supporting. Let us not however upon this account rashly conclude that she is capable of supporting any burden.'

Unlike most other commentators, Smith spent little time on ingenious schemes to pay off the debt. For him it was a hopeless task (unless a fraudulent one). Doubtless improvements to the tax system could increase revenue somewhat, but the required surpluses, and the time-scale over which they must be continued, were just too much. He really offered no solution.

To Smith there was only one possible glimmer of hope, and he devoted a surprisingly large proportion of this chapter to it: the ethical case for apportioning taxation among the different countries of the United Kingdom and extending taxation to the colonies in order to repay the debts. Since in Smith's view most of the borrowing had been on account of imperialist military adventures to found and protect colonies, it was only fair that the colonists should share the burdens of the resulting taxation. (This was part of Smith's general negative view of colonies—he thought that they were vanity projects, a drain on rather than a benefit to the parent economy.) But this, he noted, would have big political implications: if the colonies were to be taxed on the same basis as the home country, they must by rights have the same parliamentary representation at Westminster (and by implication not in their own territories). Neither colonists nor the British would be likely to find this satisfactory.

Smith was particularly insistent that the American colonists should pay their share or be cast adrift. He was well aware of what he called the 'present disturbances', but colonies 'which contribute neither revenue nor military force towards the support of the empire cannot be considered as provinces. They may perhaps be considered as appendages, as a sort of splendid and showy equipage of the empire. But if the empire can no longer support the expence of keeping up this equipage, it should certainly lay it down. ...' This was the very last paragraph of *The Wealth of Nations*. The American colonists had perhaps already taken note of Smith's earlier point, that high levels of taxation would encourage wealth-holders to remove their wealth from the jurisdiction—or the jurisdiction from their wealth.

Almost at the same time as the English were making their big statement against absolute monarchy and in favour of a constitutional monarchy with parliamentary control of finance, Louis XIV in France was making an equally emphatic statement in the opposite direction. He dismissed his ministers and parliament and reaffirmed a monarch's absolute right to rule in person. No parliament was called in France during the entire eighteenth century, until the fateful recall of the Estates General in 1789. Since there was no innovation in political control, the system of public finance also remained pretty much in its medieval form.

Firstly, the taxation system was quite cumbersome. Partly this was due to the historical development of France. While England had been a single coherent country since well before the Norman conquest, the French state had developed later, and in a piecemeal fashion. In the thirteenth century France was still a patchwork of independent Duchies and Counties (many claimed and fought over by English kings), and the French King only controlled a very small part of the whole. Gradually, the French Crown managed to eject the English and absorb the various Duchies and Counties. But for political reasons the absorption left many of the original statelets' local customs and privileges intact, including often their taxation systems. So the tax system was by no means homogeneous across the territory of France.

Secondly, again for internal political reasons, various important interest groups had bargained for themselves exemptions from taxation. As these included the Church and the nobility, large parts of the most lucrative tax bases were lost to the state and as a consequence taxation bore particularly heavily on lower-income groups.

Thirdly, the administration of the tax system remained largely in its medieval form. Whereas in England the older systems of tax farming gave way to professional tax-collectors in the public service, tax collection in France continued to be contracted out to a bewildering array of tax-farmers, collectors-general, or 'venal accountants'. (While to modern ears this last phrase sounds like a volley of abuse, it is in fact a neutral technical term. Venality is the system of purchasing offices, which most French opinion of the time thought was perfectly ethical and indeed efficient. An accountant was simply someone who 'ran an account' for the government.)

These were private-sector businessmen, combining the functions of tax-collector, lender and bank. They paid large sums of money for their offices (which were essentially advances on the taxes they had contracted to collect), and had to stand ready to provide further loans if requested. Most were also active in private-sector business, banking and investing, and there was little requirement to segregate the public- and private-sector funds in their care—so long as they delivered to the state the funds they had contracted for, the state had no great concern over their methods. It was a recipe for corruption and oppression which would reap its whirlwind only at the revolution. It is well known that the great scientist Lavoisier was guillotined during the revolution, with pleas for clemency on the grounds of his great usefulness to mankind being callously turned down: 'The revolution has no need for geniuses'. The real reason was not simply that he was an aristocrat, but that he had invested in a tax farm, albeit apparently to fund scientific research. There was no forgiveness for tax farmers.

Their offices were frequently hereditary and passed down from generation to generation. Although the original incumbents were not usually of noble stock, the offices were a vehicle for social advancement: second and third generation incumbents would be granted titles and would have amassed enough wealth to buy country estates and all the trappings of nobility. In the highly-stratified French society this was an important incentive for proud and ambitious parents. The nobility proper, although outwardly spurning these offices, also secretly benefited from them: the accountants were usually themselves operating on borrowed money, much coming from the wealthy aristocracy.

The relationship was very symbiotic: the accountant gained in his private-sector businesses by apparently having the weight of the state behind him, and through the liquidity of having large sums of tax revenues flowing through his books. On the other hand, the state benefited from the private-sector credibility of the accountant in that many of the state's bills could be settled by the accountant's paper credit notes instead of in gold. The upshot of all this was that the state's finances were very, very opaque, even to the state itself. At the outbreak of the Revolution in 1789, the problem was not simply that the state was massively in debt, but that nobody knew how big the debt was.

As to borrowing, the vulnerabilities of individuals lending to an absolute monarch precluded the expansion of publicly-available state securities, as in England. Instead the state tended to borrow through intermediaries. The Rentes de l'Hôtel de Ville de Paris were popular: individuals would lend to the City of Paris, who would then lend on in bulk to the government. The Church was another such conduit. In both cases the institutions were seen to have enough bargaining power with the state. It should be noticed that these arrangements are not so different in principle from the English government's dealings with the Bank of England and the Chartered Companies. But the eventual dominance of the Bank of England, the Consol and the Parliamentary guarantee was a much simpler, more efficient and more transparent system than the French networks. In particular, the English system enabled a much clearer line to be drawn between the operation of the tax system and the operation of the borrowing system.

No French equivalent to the Bank of England emerged until after the Revolution. Adam Smith cannily noted that Paris was not a big mercantile centre like London, where large amounts of cash had to be continually available for settling transactions. The Bank of England was able to provide a lucrative government use for such cash while still offering merchants almost comparable liquidity; but operations on such a scale would not be possible in Paris, where banking continued to be the province of small, private bankers. All attempts to set up a Bank of France attracted the enmity of the existing network of financiers, a large group of very influential people with much to lose.

There were several attempts during the eighteenth century to reform the French public finance system, but all foundered against the opposition of the various vested interests embedded within it. The most ambitious attempt was by the Scottish financier John Law, whose Banque Royale and Mississippi Company paralleled the English South Sea Bubble. Later attempts by the Controllers-General Turgot and Necker had some initial success in replacing parts of the venal system with professional civil servants but were both ultimately beaten back by vested interests. Only after the Revolution did a more coherent and professional system of public finance come into being.

5

PITT'S SINKING FUND AND THE FRENCH REVOLUTIONARY AND NAPOLEONIC WARS

REPAYMENT AND THE SINKING FUND

Broadly speaking there are two approaches to lessening the burden of debt on tax payers. One is to attempt to reduce the rate of interest payable on the debt, and we have seen how this can be achieved through Conversion. The other is to attempt to repay the capital. Although on the face of it these two approaches seem obviously complementary to each other, in practice the mechanisms required are sometimes contradictory, and policy over the centuries has veered between periods when repayment was the preferred option, and periods when repayment was seen as pointless and interest-rate reduction the only course worth pursuing.

We have looked at conversion; let us now consider repayment. Here the difficulties are immediate and obvious, and they are both financial and political. Once the debt has accumulated beyond the modest level from which the existing voted taxes will take care of it automatically, a serious attempt to repay will require either additional taxation or reduced current expenditure.

The significant expenditure of the time was military and therefore subject to the vagaries of international politics (although it was well realised that a determined 'peace policy' and eschewal of foreign adventures would probably have the most favourable effect on the public finances). But whatever the level of expenditure, debt repayment logically means that more taxes have to be collected than would otherwise be the case.

Taxation is never popular and only a bold politician will risk the opprobrium—and for what gain? £1 million of extra taxation will pay off £1 million of debt, and the immediate gain to the taxpayer will only be the avoidance of the interest payment on that debt—at, say, 5 per cent, £50,000 in the current year. Of course, in the long view, all the saved interest payments of the future may make this economically a good proposition, but taxpayers and politicians have notoriously short time horizons—£1 million to save £50,000 is a difficult story to carry through in PR terms.

At this point both taxpayers and politicians will remember that, although interest payments are a terrible burden on the economy, so too are taxes: taxes distort economic incentives, penalise the most industrious classes and reduce economic growth—who is to say that the taxation burden is not worse than the interest burden? Politicians realise that if they are to receive the opprobrium of having levied extra taxation, there are many more useful things they could do with it than merely repay debt—build some more ships for the navy, or roads or hospitals, or increase welfare payments for instance. Furthermore, were a current surplus to arise by chance, would it also not be better to seize the opportunity to cut taxes, and thereby reduce tax distortions and gain popularity, rather than to use it to pay off really a very insignificant proportion of the National Debt? If a new war comes along requiring an expenditure of £20 million, will it be more popular, and less distortionary, to cover this by levying £20 million extra taxes in the current year, or by borrowing £20 million in a perpetual loan at

5 per cent and voting only £1 million of extra taxation (but also in perpetuity) to cover the interest payments?

Looked at from the distributional angle, one encounters a similar double-bind. Lower-income tax-payers resent (possibly quite justly) having to pay taxes to hand over interest payments to higher-income bond-holders. But the immediate effect of trying to reduce this subservience will be higher, not lower, such payments. If handing over £50,000 p.a. to the rich is unpalatable, how much more unpalatable is handing over £1 million?

All these considerations mean we cannot be optimistic that the political process will automatically be able to discipline itself to ensure the orderly repayments of its debts. The reality is that repayment cannot make the burden of the National Debt disappear—all it can do is crystallise a particular time-profile of that burden. The only real solution to the distortion of the economy and the taxpayer's resentment is not repayment, but default—and if that is ruled out, all the incentives point in the direction of kicking the can down the road, for one's successors to sort out.

But far-sighted thinkers could see that at some point this must become unsustainable, culminating even in national bankruptcy. Hence there was interest in devising some formal scheme which might tie a government's hands and ensure that the public debt would eventually be paid off. The difficulty remained that any such scheme would be painful.

The idea of a 'Sinking Fund' held out the prospect of miraculously removing that pain. We have seen that Robert Walpole instituted a sinking fund in the 1730s, but his motivations were pragmatic, his commitment half-hearted and the results disappointing. Later in the century, though, the idea was taken up by several propagandists with vigour and even messianic zeal. It was held that the marvellous powers of compound interest could be harnessed to pay off any debt, however large, and from however small a starting-point, given enough time. In its most messianic form, the initial contribution towards repayment could itself even be borrowed, and during the repayment process the government could continue to borrow; nevertheless, the inexorable power of compound interest would still ensure the ultimate repayment of the debt.

The most important and persistent of these propagandists was the clergyman the Reverend Richard R. Price: 'One penny, put out at our Saviour's birth to 5 per cent compound interest, would, before this time, have increased to a greater sum than would be contained in a hundred and fifty millions of earths, all solid gold. But if put out to simple interest it would in the same time have amounted to no more than seven shillings and fourpence half-penny.' (Compound interest seems to have exercised a fascinating influence on the late eighteenth century clerical mind—Thomas Malthus' famous principle of population is similarly based on a naïve comparison of simple and compound interest.)

Although he was rather too given to purple prose, and his reputation ultimately suffered very badly from his sinking fund proposals, Richard Price (1723–1791) was no ignorant single-issue 'debt crank'. He was a well-known and important figure in political debate of the time, a dissenting clergyman who used his pulpit and a prodigious pamphlet output to propound radical views on many subjects. He corresponded with most of the big names in intellectual and political discourse in Britain, America and France. He was a supporter of American independence and the French Revolution, and his open letter of congratulation to the French revolutionary government provoked the counter-blast of Edmund Burke's famous *Reflections on the Recent Revolution in France*, and subsequently the counter-counter-blasts of Thomas Paine's *Rights of Man* and Harriet Wollstonecraft's *A Vindication of the Rights of Woman*. He was also a serious student of mathematics and probability theory, being a Fellow of the Royal Society, and having edited the works of Thomas Bayes and popularising the latter's famous theorem on conditional probabilities. This work also had very practical objects: he advised the Equitable Assurance Company and wrote in depth on actuarial issues, and he attempted to extend the benefits of insurance to low-income families—effectively a forerunner of the welfare-state social insurance of 150 years later. Clearly, his actuarial experience underlies his proposals regarding the National Debt. It speaks much for his technical reputation that Prime Minister William Pitt the Younger, the antithesis of radicalism, should seek out the advice of such an extreme political opponent. And the subsequent tarnishing of that reputation was as much due to others' inept implementation of his theories as to his own rash statements.

The idea is actually quite simple. Suppose one starts with a total debt of £1,000 million, paying interest at 10 per cent. There is a total interest bill of £100 million p.a., which is covered by existing tax revenues. Now suppose we make a commitment to raise an extra £1 million in taxes every year and devote this to our sinking fund. On the face of it this looks to be a very inadequate commitment and a very slow process: at £1 million per year this might take a thousand years to eradicate the debt. Not so, as Figure 5 demonstrates. In the first year the administrators of the sinking fund use this money to buy back £1 million of government bonds from the existing holders. Next year they receive a further £1 million of taxation, but also a payment of £100,000 interest on the bonds they bought last year; they devote this to buying more bonds, so now they own £2.1 million of bonds. In the third year they will receive another £1 million in taxation and £210,000 interest, so they will end that year with £3.31 million bonds. And so on. As the table shows, the fund grows faster than its contributions, initially modestly so—after ten years the fund has bought back nearly £16 million bonds, after twenty nearly £60 million—but its acceleration is dramatic, and it reaches its target of £1,000 million in only forty-nine years.

Table 5.1: Sinking Fund

Year	Contribution from Taxes	Sinking Fund at 10%			Sinking Fund at 5%		
		Opening Balance	Interest at 10%	Closing Balance	Opening Balance	Interest at 5%	Closing Balance
1	1.00	0.00	0.00	1.00	0.00	0.00	1.00
2	1.00	1.00	0.10	2.10	1.00	0.05	2.05
3	1.00	2.10	0.21	3.31	2.05	0.10	3.15
4	1.00	3.31	0.33	4.64	3.15	0.16	4.31
5	1.00	4.64	0.46	6.11	4.31	0.22	5.53
6	1.00	6.11	0.61	7.72	5.53	0.28	6.80
7	1.00	7.72	0.77	9.49	6.80	0.34	8.14
8	1.00	9.49	0.95	11.44	8.14	0.41	9.55
9	1.00	11.44	1.14	13.58	9.55	0.48	11.03
10	1.00	13.58	1.36	15.94	11.03	0.55	12.58
11	1.00	15.94	1.59	18.53	12.58	0.63	14.21
12	1.00	18.53	1.85	21.38	14.21	0.71	15.92
13	1.00	21.38	2.14	24.52	15.92	0.80	17.71
14	1.00	24.52	2.45	27.97	17.71	0.89	19.60
15	1.00	27.97	2.80	31.77	19.60	0.98	21.58
16	1.00	31.77	3.18	35.95	21.58	1.08	23.66
17	1.00	35.95	3.59	40.54	23.66	1.18	25.84
18	1.00	40.54	4.05	45.60	25.84	1.29	28.13
19	1.00	45.60	4.56	51.16	28.13	1.41	30.54
20	1.00	51.16	5.12	57.27	30.54	1.53	33.07
21	1.00	57.27	5.73	64.00	33.07	1.65	35.72
22	1.00	64.00	6.40	71.40	35.72	1.79	38.51
23	1.00	71.40	7.14	79.54	38.51	1.93	41.43

24	1.00	79.54	7.95	88.50	41.43	2.07	44.50
25	1.00	88.50	8.85	98.35	44.50	2.23	47.73
26	1.00	98.35	9.83	109.18	47.73	2.39	51.11
27	1.00	109.18	10.92	121.10	51.11	2.56	54.67
28	1.00	121.10	12.11	134.21	54.67	2.73	58.40
29	1.00	134.21	13.42	148.63	58.40	2.92	62.32
30	1.00	148.63	14.86	164.49	62.32	3.12	66.44
31	1.00	164.49	16.45	181.94	66.44	3.32	70.76
32	1.00	181.94	18.19	201.14	70.76	3.54	75.30
33	1.00	201.14	20.11	222.25	75.30	3.76	80.06
34	1.00	222.25	22.23	245.48	80.06	4.00	85.07
35	1.00	245.48	24.55	271.02	85.07	4.25	90.32
36	1.00	271.02	27.10	299.13	90.32	4.52	95.84
37	1.00	299.13	29.91	330.04	95.84	4.79	101.63
38	1.00	330.04	33.00	364.04	101.63	5.08	107.71
39	1.00	364.04	36.40	401.45	107.71	5.39	114.10
40	1.00	401.45	40.14	442.59	114.10	5.70	120.80
41	1.00	442.59	44.26	487.85	120.80	6.04	127.84
42	1.00	487.85	48.79	537.64	127.84	6.39	135.23
43	1.00	537.64	53.76	592.40	135.23	6.76	142.99
44	1.00	592.40	59.24	652.64	142.99	7.15	151.14
45	1.00	652.64	65.26	718.90	151.14	7.56	159.70
46	1.00	718.90	71.89	791.80	159.70	7.99	168.69
47	1.00	791.80	79.18	871.97	168.69	8.43	178.12
48	1.00	871.97	87.20	960.17	178.12	8.91	188.03
49	1.00	960.17	96.02	1057.19	188.03	9.40	198.43
50	1.00	1057.19	105.72	1163.91	198.43	9.92	209.35

At this point all the country's bonds are in the hands of the administrators, and they can simply be cancelled and the country will be debt-free. And all this is apparently achieved merely by forty-nine additional annual payments of £1 million.

Mathematically there is nothing at all controversial about this—it is a process very similar to the way in which we all pay off our mortgages on our house purchases. As with the mortgages, whether we end up in practice at the desired outcome will depend on whether we have stuck carefully to the rules through the entire duration of the process. But if the principle is hardly new, seeing the numbers is undeniably impressive. It is not surprising that the idea attracted adherents otherwise despairing of an apparently insuperable task.

You can see from Table 5.1 that by the end of its term the sinking fund has acquired a tremendous momentum. Extending it for just one further year would enable another £100 million purchases (if there were any bonds left to purchase). Price concluded that it would not therefore matter very much if, during the existence of the sinking fund, the government were to continue to make some further borrowings; these would easily be mopped up in just a few more years.

Extending this argument a little, it was suggested by some that additional taxation might not be required at all—if it were true that the government could borrow some more during the course of the process then even the initial contribution of £1 million p.a. might itself be borrowed. From our figure it would seem that a total sum of £49 million would only take an extra six months to pay off. This sounded too good to be true, and it was—a kind of financial perpetual motion machine. But the times were sympathetic to such notions, and it gained surprisingly wide support.

Price also correctly noted the crucial role of the rate of interest in this. Our table also shows the same process with an interest rate of only 5 per cent. The general principles are the same but the results are less impressive: after fifty years the fund has only amassed just over £200 million. From this Price deduced the paradoxical conclusion that repayment was easier and faster with higher interest rates. The government's attempts to convert debt to lower interest rates were therefore counter-productive; if anything, they should be doing the reverse. Taking this even further, Price argued that wars, which tended to raise interest rates, were therefore actually helpful to the cause of debt repayment—so long as the sinking fund mechanism was strictly adhered to.

The new Prime Minister Pitt had decided that a serious effort was needed to tame the roller-coaster rise of debt and restore public confidence. No mean financier himself, he was impressed by the more extreme arguments and took advice from Price, although the scheme he finally adopted was not quite to Price's liking. In 1786 he instituted a new Sinking Fund system, to be fed by regular additional taxation of £1 million p.a. This money would be entrusted not to the government or to Parliament, but to a body of Commissioners for the Reduction of the National Debt, who would use the money to purchase back government debt in the market-place, and then use the interest payments on this debt in turn to repurchase more debt. Pitt hoped the independence of the Commissioners would prevent the kind of governmental raiding that had nullified Walpole's earlier fund.[1] He followed up with provisions requiring similar sinking funds to be attached to any new loans, with a view to always ensuring repayment within forty-five years. With these public commitments Pitt aimed to repair the public credit before the next, even greater conflict.

THE FRENCH REVOLUTIONARY AND NAPOLEONIC WARS, 1793–1815

The French Revolutionary and Napoleonic Wars would prove the severest test yet of the financial system. Lasting eighteen years, with only one very short interval after the Peace of Amiens, and fought at an intensity not seen hitherto, they affected the whole nation in something akin to the total wars of the twentieth century. The government's strategy involved not only large expenditures on the navy and army, but also large subsidies to continental allies. Pitt and his ministers constructed a highly efficient military-industrial state, eradicating many of the inefficiencies and corruptions of the eighteenth century. But the ability to sustain this high level of activity depended in turn on the adequate supply of finance. Borrowing increased dramatically again, interest rates rose, and like Lord North, Pitt was faced by a financial market well able to extract the best deal from the weak bargaining position of its captive client. Between 1793 and 1802 the National Debt more than doubled, and it increased by a further 60 per cent by 1815.

But Pitt knew that ultimate success must rely on maintaining the public creditworthiness intact in the long run. He and his successors maintained the Sinking Fund in operation throughout the war in line with Price's doctrines, despite the massive increase in borrowing that the war entailed. At the time public opinion on the subject was not unfavourable, and it may even have helped to maintain the government's reputation for fiscal responsibility under the greatest of pressures. But in fact its effect was harmful: taxes were levied to redeem debt, which then had to be re-borrowed (and more) at a higher interest rate. Commissions and profits were paid to the loan contractors on an unnecessary churning of debt. Taxation or borrowing, or both, were therefore maintained at a higher level than was absolutely necessary at a time when both were being strained to their limits.

When at the end of the war the public learnt that their debts had massively increased despite their being constantly reassured that their high taxes were paying them off, they rightly felt cheated. The National Debt Commissioners announced proudly that they had paid off an enormous proportion of the pre-war Debt—but the public was shocked to discover that the National Debt was somehow now much bigger. The revulsion was the greater because public acquiescence to the high taxation of the war years had been partly due to the promise held out of paying down the Debt. The result was that the very notion of a sinking fund was regarded as fraudulent for over half a century.

The theoretical flaw of the most extreme sinking fund proponents lay in overlooking some apparently minor but in fact very important ways in which compound interest would also work *against* the aim of debt redemption. If the original £1 million were borrowed, there would be interest (£100,000) payable on that. If that were not itself covered by additional taxation, it too would have to be borrowed, and that would lead to further interest payments, and so on. This interest would accumulate in an equal and opposite way to the Sinking Fund itself, totally negating its purpose. Worse, if larger sums of money were being borrowed additionally to fight new wars, the same would apply, in much larger measure. The more perceptive proponents (including Price himself) had not, in fact, overlooked this flaw, and emphasised that the interest payments on any additional borrowing must be covered by additionally-voted taxation. But they did not seem to grasp the extent to which this might undermine the whole thrust of their argument, and they carelessly helped to create a climate in which mere adherence to the formal rules of a sinking fund came to be seen as a magic bullet, irrespective of fiscal common sense.

Worse, this caveat ultimately exposed the hollowness of the whole venture. For if Parliament was in fact willing to levy such additional taxation (which would certainly start off low, but would soon grow to considerably more than £1 million p.a.), these tax revenues on their own would directly pay off the Debt in the same time. If in theory Parliament might do this, in practice it was obviously not likely to do so, not even in the pre-revolutionary period of peace, and certainly not once war broke out and the war needs pre-empted all available tax revenues. The sinking fund concept was always respected on the surface: almost all new borrowings had sinking fund contributions attached to them; but only on the surface, because the money for these was in effect being borrowed as well.

Nor was there really any need for an elaborate fund structure holding large quantities of bonds: the government could simply cancel debt as it went along—so long as the government resisted the temptation to reduce the overall starting level of taxation of £100 million as its debt progressively fell throughout the forty-nine years. The only purpose of a Fund was in fact a psychological, or constitutional one, making it just a little more difficult for the politicians to deviate from the path of righteousness. But practice showed this too to be a broken reed. It is a parliamentary maxim that parliaments cannot bind their successors. In emergencies contributions to the Sinking Fund could be suspended and used for other purposes. Worse, the Sinking Fund itself could be raided for other purposes: the administrators could be instructed to purchase new government bonds rather than old ones, or feed their vast stock of bonds back into the market, thereby enabling the government to run a larger deficit.

Parliamentarians therefore began to view the Sinking Fund as a dangerous temptation: a vast piggy bank which a government could use to fund expenditure without parliamentary approval (politicians did indeed talk of it as their 'great war-chest' ready to be unleashed in any new hostilities). Financiers feared that as the Sinking Fund grew, the size of its potential bond purchases might seriously destabilise the markets. The public found it difficult to grasp why they were being taxed heavily to enable the government to make interest payments to itself, a point increasingly harped upon for instance by William Cobbett the radical political commentator: what is the point, he argued, of paying high taxes to pay off the National Debt, if the National Debt interest bill does not come down? (In our theoretical table, in the forty-ninth year of our scheme, £100 million is still being collected to finance interest payments, almost all of which are paid to the administrators.)

This last little point, not often noticed, actually shows that the magic of the Sinking Fund is really no more than a sophisticated version of kicking the can down the road. In the first year of their forty-nine year plan, the taxpayers are only contributing £1 million more than they are legally required to; but their plan assumes that the taxpayers of the forty-ninth year will be paying something like £91 million more than they are legally required to. Is this actually likely to occur? To the taxpayers of the forty-ninth year, reality will seem very different. They will start off that year with a national debt reduced to about £91 million, with the knowledge that their predecessors survived the past half-century with debts considerably larger. Why, then, should they bust a gut to pay this debt off all in one year? Surely no harm in slackening off now? Actually, this realisation will kick in well before this stage. Late-Victorian Chancellors of the Exchequer did in fact argue in exactly these terms to water down their own sinking funds. So although a sinking fund looks like a very praiseworthy commitment on the part of current tax-payers, the current tax-payers are really trying to commit their successors to doing most of the work.

The argument about higher interest rates was similarly flawed. Certainly, the scheme would accelerate faster at 10 per cent than at 5 per cent. But if interest rates could be cut from 10 per cent to 5 per cent, the government would have an extra £50 million p.a. from the very first year to devote to debt repayment if it so chose. If it did choose, the 5 per cent scheme would outperform the 10 per cent scheme for many, many years.[2]

The fiasco gave the sinking fund concept a bad reputation from which it has never completely recovered. In the end there is no escape from the simple financial reality that debt repayment depends on the resolve of the government to run a surplus over many years (as was argued conclusively and influentially in an 1812 pamphlet by Robert Hamilton, Professor of Mathematics at Aberdeen). If the government does not have the ability or the resolve to do this, nothing else will work. Any formal scheme can only be a cosmetic device to boost the level of commitment. At times this may indeed be beneficial, but at other times it might be counter-productive, as in Pitt's time, and subsequently in the 1920s and 1930s, where the quest for balanced budgets—which included a very large sinking fund component aimed at reducing the monstrous First World War debts—meant that every budget was in fact extremely deflationary when the macro-economic situation required the opposite.

LORD HENRY PETTY'S SCHEME

Pitt died in 1806, but his successors continued to prosecute the war against France and as we have seen they continued to adhere strongly to the principles of the Sinking Fund, which by now had become almost an article of faith. Minor adjustments were continually made but the general principle was inviolable. But it was something of a straitjacket for policy: with continuing large demands for war expenditure and to maintain the Sinking Fund payments on existing debt, Chancellors were continually obliged to increase already heavy rates of taxation or make further borrowings. Sleight-of-hand was used to appear to respect the principle while deferring the real reckoning further into the future. One particular episode is worthy of note.

In 1806 Lord Henry Petty became Chancellor of the Exchequer at the age of twenty-six. He reviewed the difficult financial situation he had inherited and wondered how he could maintain the required levels of war expenditure for the foreseeable future—for the war showed no sign of ending—without politically unacceptable rises in taxation.

His scheme was complex, but roughly speaking his calculation was as follows. He estimated the required war expenditure at £32 million p.a. To defray this he had £21 million p.a. in war taxes already voted by Parliament. To cover the shortfall he would have to raise a further £11 million p.a. in taxation, which was politically inconceivable. Alternatively, he could borrow to eliminate the shortfall, but he would still have to raise over £700,000 taxes to cover the interest and the sinking fund contribution required. Even that would be politically challenging. However, if he redeployed the existing war taxes away from the direct purchase of war material and used them instead to cover the interest and sinking fund contributions of new loans, he could plug the gap without the need for any additional taxation. The gap would now be bigger because the new loans would now also have to cover the purchases that the pre-existing taxes had been destined for; but that was acceptable, for the taxes would of course underwrite loans much bigger than the taxes. In fact, he could go on like this for a number of years. In the steady state he calculated that he could take out a series of loans, year by year, for which the existing taxes would cover the interest payments and sinking fund contributions necessary to pay each loan off in fourteen years. As each loan was paid off a new one could take its place under the same terms. In this way a war expenditure of £32 million could be prolonged indefinitely without any further addition to taxation. And as all loans would be duly repaid through sinking fund contributions in fourteen years, it would apparently be a very fiscally responsible policy too.

Perhaps fortunately for the country, the government fell the next year and Petty's budget was never implemented. It is an object lesson in both the power and the pitfalls of debt financing. For Petty's taxless war is of course only an illusion: the taxes are simply deferred until the end of the war. Under Petty's scheme the already high level of war taxation must be carried fourteen years into the peace to pay off the massive debt which would have accumulated. The plans of his predecessors had implicitly assumed that they would cease at the end of the war.

Worse, the scheme would really have been a fraud on the taxpayers. Parliament had originally voted the war taxes on the assumption that they would directly purchase war material, and that having so purchased, there would be no further claim on the taxpayer. By diverting them to underwriting new borrowing, Petty would have been committing taxpayers unwittingly to significant further expenditure. In fact, the borrowing policies of wartime governments do this to some extent all the time, but Petty's scheme would have taken it to its logical conclusion.

The scheme is also a lesson in how rigid adherence to the letter, but not the spirit, of a sinking fund scheme is no guarantee that debt will not increase to intolerable levels. Each individual loan may be on course for repayment within fourteen years but the overall total of such loans can be pushed to the limit of taxpayers' capacities. It is rather like believing credit card debt can never be a problem because the minimum monthly contribution will always ensure repayment within a finite time. Well, it will unless the consumer keeps increasing their debt until the minimum monthly contribution itself is intolerable. If at that point the consumer is still unable to rein in his excessive spending, he takes out another credit card and juggles the two. Both credit cards may seem on course for ultimate repayment, but the consumer's debt continues to go up, until a third card is necessary, and so on; until even the possibilities of juggling are exhausted and default occurs.

THE FLOATING DEBT

If the government's sinking fund policy was a terrible mess, other measures promoted by Pitt to contain the National Debt and maintain the public credit were more successful.

Firstly, the government was very successful in controlling the floating debt. As we have seen in previous wars uncoordinated military purchases brought about an explosion of short-term debt and unpaid IOUs, which undermined the future confidence of suppliers. The usual policy was to let this problem fester until the end of the war, when it could be gradually mopped up in peacetime. But with a very long war in prospect, Pitt resolved on a steady programme of conversion of these debts into properly funded, long-term debt. Although long-term rates of interest were temporarily high, long-term debt was more acceptable, and the government's purchasing ability was improved. At the end of the wars the proportion of floating debt was unusually low.

INCOME TAX

Secondly, Pitt took steps to improve tax revenues. In the first half of the wars, to 1802, tax revenues accounted for only about a third of government expenditure, but in the second half this rose to over 50 per cent. Partly this was due to much higher rates and new forms of customs and excise duties and other indirect taxation (thereby creating the great age of smuggling), but most significantly it was due to the introduction of Income Tax. This is worth considering in some detail.

Traditional tax was a mixture of indirect and direct taxation. Indirect taxation was largely customs and excise duties, particularly on alcohol (wines, spirits and malts), occasionally sugar, tea, and some specific taxes such as on carriages, domestic servants or windows. Direct taxation was cruder, being largely the land tax, dating from a period when land was really the only source of wealth.

Indirect taxation, in so far as it was on basic commodities, was thought of as being paid by the poorer classes, or ultimately by the employers of labour, as subsistence wages would have to rise to meet the increased prices. The wealthier classes on the other hand could be targeted directly through the land tax or through indirect taxes on luxuries (hence the taxes on carriages and domestic servants). But land was becoming an increasingly poor correlator with ability to pay. The profits of the new industrial capitalists were not taxed, nor were the salaries of the growing professional classes and government employees. Nor, particularly, were the interest payments of national debt-holders or other dividends arising from the financial markets. This was a great bone of contention between the 'landed interest' and the 'moneyed interest'. Pitt proposed to replace the land tax with a more comprehensive tax on all the sources of income equally.

This was hugely controversial and unpopular, despite the resentments towards the old system. It was seen as a terrible invasion of privacy. But it was accepted reluctantly, as an emergency measure, for wartime only. It was introduced in 1799, but it had hardly got into full operation when on the signing of the Peace of Amiens its opponents pounced and insisted on its immediate abolition. The vituperative tone of parliamentary debates of the time show the remarkable strength of feeling against the tax—all the tax records were to be destroyed by immersion and pestling in water-tubs in an extraordinary act of symbolic public humiliation.

But unfortunately for its opponents, the Peace of Amiens did not last, and the tax was quickly reintroduced. In fact, the little hiatus turned out to be an advantage because the re-introduced form was able to incorporate several changes that went some way to meeting public objections. One that is still with us is the separation of income assessment into various Schedules: A, B, C,

D, E—income from land; income from commercial occupation of land; income from public securities; income from trading, professions and vocations; and income from employment. Each schedule was to be assessed separately and no attempt was to be made to add them up into one total income figure. Public opinion would accept compartmentalised assessment but not a declaration of total income.

This system worked surprisingly well and generated significant revenue. But in 1815 public opinion again forced its immediate abolition with unfortunate fiscal effects (see Chapter 6). It was reintroduced by Prime Minister Robert Peel in the 1840s, again avowedly on a temporary basis—but this time it stuck. Ironically, by the end of the nineteenth century it was thought of as one of Britain's uniquely wonderful institutions, spreading the burden of taxation widely and fairly, with a respected and incorrupt administration, and capable of producing large additional revenues in emergencies with a high degree of public compliance. (It should be noted that still only a minority of the population were affected by it: average working families were well below the threshold, and their incomes fluctuated inconveniently with the fortunes of trade, which would have made them difficult to assess. The tax was mainly targeted at the steady rental and professional incomes of upper- and upper-middle-class families.)

INFLATION

Another issue was rather different, but no less momentous. Until now, money had been clearly understood to be the precious metals, gold and silver. The unit of account, the pound, was defined as being a certain weight of either, although by this time gold had become the dominant metal for large payments. In practice, private bank notes and paper credit notes were used for convenience, but the notes were understood to be ultimately only claims on the underlying precious metal. Banks always had to stand ready to supply gold for their notes (and the government gold for its debt obligations) if required. This meant that the gold price of commodities could never deviate far from their nominal pound prices. However, in the difficult circumstances of the war, gold reserves became dangerously low (partly because of the government's need to export gold as subsidies to its foreign allies) and the government suspended gold convertibility in 1797. For the rest of the war the country was on a purely paper-money standard. This was uncharted territory, and much debate in the newly-emerging field of economics concerned itself with the consequences. There was clearly inflation: the price of corn was high. Or was it really? How much of the price increase was due to real disruptions of corn supply and demand because of the war, and how much just due to depreciation of the paper money? The market price of gold bullion had increased well beyond its normal Bank of England bench-mark, but even this was difficult to establish with accuracy because the markets were highly imperfect and official statistics largely non-existent.

Economists like Ricardo, Malthus, Thornton, Torrens and McCulloch debated the issue in pamphlets at some length. Ricardo concluded that the problem was due to an excessive circulation of bank notes, resulting from the removal of any discipline on the supplying banks. He did not, however, favour any statutory control of the supply of paper, arguing that the problem would resolve itself with the re-establishment of convertibility, leading the banks voluntarily to curtail their circulations again to avoid bankruptcy. But after the war the debate would continue, leading to the Bank Charter Act of 1844 which did restrict the supply of paper money to the Bank of England and laid down a rule for the maximum supply of Bank of England notes.

However, the importance for the National Debt problem after the war was that debt had been incurred at inflated prices, by borrowing in a depreciated paper currency during the war. When convertibility was re-established, that debt would be repayable in a more valuable currency, thus giving a further twist to the debt burden, and to the resentment towards the windfall profits of the rentiers. Therefore, it might be both fairer and cheaper to take extraordinary steps to repay quickly, before prices fell; or afterwards to mark down the debt by a proportion equivalent to the currency movement. In the event neither happened, and the real burden on the taxpayer did increase.

Despite Pitt's and his successors' efforts, they had not managed to break the inexorable increase of debt with every war. By 1815, the National Debt was approaching £800 million, or 200 per cent of GDP, surely exceeding by far even the worst fears of the most anxious debt critics of the early eighteenth century.

6

THE NINETEENTH CENTURY
A CENTURY OF PEACE

The nineteenth century (or more precisely the period 1815–1914) was for our purposes in many respects the complete opposite of the eighteenth. Whereas the previous century was a period of almost continuous warfare the nineteenth was—for Britain at least—one of almost unbroken peace, apart from minor, mostly colonial, wars. Whereas the eighteenth century began with practically no debt and ended, post-Waterloo, with an almost intolerable level, the nineteenth saw an equivalent reduction from that peak to the lowest debt ratio since the very earliest days. These two features are of course not unrelated.

But perhaps the most significant point to note is that the improvement in the debt position was not achieved by large-scale repayment of debt. A debt of some £800 million in 1815 was reduced only to about £650 million in 1914. Nor did inflation reduce its real value: the price level in 1914 was if anything lower than in 1815. The really important factor was the growth of the economy itself. The industrial revolution and the onset of peace had ushered in a more modern-looking period of steady long-

87

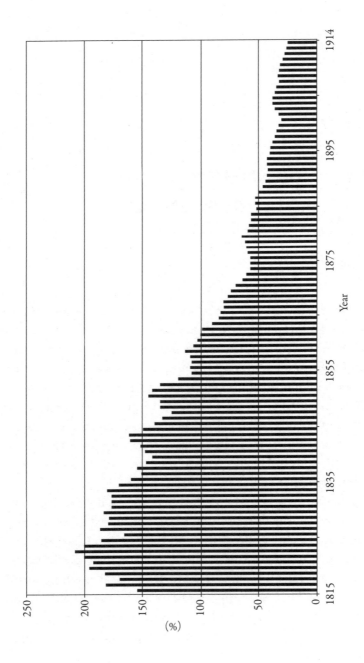

Figure 5: British National Debt/GDP Ratio (%), 1815–1914

run economic growth—not without its ups and downs, and at a relatively modest rate (about 2 per cent p.a.) by more recent standards—but the effect over a large number of years was very significant (the power of compound interest again). GDP increased almost sixfold between 1815 and 1914.

The population grew too, tripling from 15 million in 1815 to 45 million in 1914, so that the debt *per capita* also showed a marked improvement.

The long period of peace allowed politicians to turn their attention to schemes for debt alleviation, which in the earlier years seemed particularly urgent. The gradually improving economic and political situation freed resources for this purpose, but at the same time also gradually undermined the incentive to do so. Interest rates remained low, and as the interest burden became increasingly supportable and stable, politicians naturally reverted to their preferences for low taxation, punctuated only by occasional bursts of debt concern.

EARLY YEARS

The Napoleonic Wars had left the country with a massive debt legacy, but also some advantages. While there were some serious winners and losers (newer technological industries had benefited from wartime orders, and agriculture had gained from higher prices; industries whose export markets or raw materials had been cut off by the trade blockades, and workers put out of work by technological change were the main losers), overall the economy had actually prospered through the war. The tax system, while oppressive, was yielding large revenues. Pitt's income tax was a powerful and efficient new source of revenue, and with its aid a much greater than usual proportion of wartime expenditure had already been funded out of taxation rather than out of borrowing. Without it, the debt problem would have been worse still. Its continuation could help with the repayment. But the public was weary of the high taxation of wartime, and it had only accepted income tax as an explicitly wartime measure. Nicholas Vansittart, the Chancellor of the Exchequer, was unable to resist the pressures for the abolition of all explicitly wartime duties.

As we have seen, income tax had already been abolished once, immediately on the Peace of Amiens in 1802, only to be re-introduced quickly when that peace proved short-lived. The vituperative tone of the 1802 parliamentary debates was revived in 1815, showing the remarkable strength of feeling against the tax—whereas in 1802 all records were destroyed by immersion and pestling in water-tubs, in 1815 they were committed to be burnt by the public hangman in another act of symbolic public humiliation. But, ironically, the abolitionists had overlooked an obscure public official called the Public Remembrancer, whose department's job was to take copies of all government financial paperwork. Indeed, he was so obscure that he seems to have been overlooked by everybody; only many years later was it discovered, to historians' delight, that a copy of all the original income tax paperwork did in fact still exist, in a dusty archive.

But this 'bonfire of taxation' was an overreaction, plunging the country into deficit again when it should have been comfortably in surplus. The floating debt, which had been fairly well contained in wartime, paradoxically ballooned again in the first years of the peace. In the longer term it signalled a distinct lack of enthusiasm for tackling the debt problem head on. Perhaps unsurprisingly, more effort in the next few decades was addressed to reducing the burden and the inefficient structures of taxation that were left over from the war years. From the combined effect of the continuing deficits and a serious depression, the debt ratio carried on its rise until the early 1820s, peaking at over 200 per cent.

Pitt's sinking fund system struggled on for some years but was seen increasingly as a sham. In 1829 it was finally abolished: all

Economists' Views on the National Debt: 3. Lauderdale

James Maitland, 8th Earl of Lauderdale (1759–1839), is hardly remembered these days as an economist. But perhaps he should be, and I include him in this list because some of his unorthodox positions have an uncanny resonance with present-day controversies.

Although one of Scotland's top aristocrats, he espoused very radical views. He was a strong supporter of the French Revolution and was present in Paris during the 1792 massacres; but unlike many British intellectual radicals, these did not dim his enthusiasm. At times he styled himself Citizen Maitland and wore Jacobin costume, and he continued to oppose in Parliament anti-French policies abroad and repressive measures at home. The British government suspected him of having far too close connections with the revolutionary French authorities but were also happy to bring him in as a principal negotiator in abortive peace talks with Napoleon in 1806. In later life he became very much more conservative—he was a keen participant in the royal faction-fighting of the time, he was a very reluctant convert to the abolition of slavery, and he opposed the Reform Bill of 1832—and by the time of his death was probably generally regarded as an unreliable and cranky eccentric.

In 1804 he published his *Inquiry into the Nature and Origin of Public Wealth, and into the Means and Causes of Its Increase.* He was by no means over-awed by Adam Smith's reputation, and took issue with several of Smith's most important propositions, which had by then become accepted wisdom. For instance, he thought Smith had vastly over-rated the importance of his famous Division of Labour; Lauderdale argued that while the division of labour was probably very helpful in improving the quality of work in very skilled trades, the vast improvement of quantity in mass production was more due to the application of machinery to replace labour than to division of labour itself.

More importantly for our purposes, he maintained against Smith's Labour Theory of Value that value was determined by a combination of scarcity and desirability, hence injecting a demand-side element that foreshadows modern orthodoxy. From this it followed that private individuals could increase their wealth from an increased scarcity of the commodities they dealt in, whereas the public wealth could hardly be said to benefit from such a cause. Hence public wealth was not simply the sum of individual private wealth, and could suffer from policies aimed at increasing private wealth. From this it further followed that saving was not necessarily, as Smith had maintained, the only route and the infallible route to economic development—'every frugal man a public benefactor, every prodigal a public enemy'.

Lauderdale argued that this generally accepted doctrine—which he described as 'Parsimony', a term not far removed from our modern 'Austerity'—was a dangerous delusion. Parsimony might be the correct prescription for increasing an individual's private wealth, but for economic growth in the country as a whole, saving had to be accompanied by positive acts of production, and production could not be automatically relied upon to follow from acts of saving. Production was a matter of perceived profitability and therefore influenced by demand, which would be reduced by saving. Lauderdale campaigned vociferously against Parsimony. In all this one can see glimpses of a proto-Keynesianism.

The Sinking Fund was a particularly egregious example of Parsimony. The taxation required to fuel a sinking fund was a form of forced saving which would not necessarily find an outlet in profitable investment opportunities and would therefore be counterproductive. (True, but on the other hand, Lauderdale did not seem to take much note of the obvious corollary that the original incurring of the debt was a form of forced dissaving which was probably equally inappropriate. Thus there could be no presumption that the currently existing level of the National Debt was the right one.) Lauderdale became as assiduous a pamphleteer against the Sinking Fund as Price had been for it.

Although Lauderdale lived to see the demise of the Pitt/Price Sinking Fund, his economic views more generally were heavily criticised, even ridiculed, and were soon submerged by the success of Ricardo, who refined the Smithian position into the Classical Political Economy which held sway through most of the nineteenth century. Lauderdale's name largely disappeared from the economics literature, although Joseph Schumpeter made some favourable mention of him in his monumental *History of Economic Analysis*.

Economists' Views on the National Debt: 4. David Ricardo

David Ricardo (1772–1823) offers probably the clearest analysis of the effects of a permanent national debt. He was well placed to do so, since he had made his fortune in the debt markets. Despite this, his stance is as hostile as any of the other economists. This is perhaps not so surprising: by the time he started writing on economics he had retired from business and set himself up as a country gentleman, so he was able to bite the hand that had fed him.

The real problem with the funding system is that it makes us 'blind to our real situation', he wrote. If a war cost £20 million, then that would be £20 million capital withdrawn from productive enterprise and spent on a non-productive purpose. If the £20 million were taken away immediately by taxation from the citizenry they would appreciate how they had been impoverished and start saving to restore their positions. However, if the war were funded by a loan the capitalists would feel no worse off: they would have withdrawn from £20 million worth of productive business, but now have £20 million worth of government bonds instead. Non-capitalists would have taken no note of these transactions and also have no reason to believe they are any worse off than before. Nobody would feel any need to rebuild capital. But £20 million of capital would have been destroyed and everyone would in fact be poorer. Whether or not the interest should be duly paid in the future is irrelevant. The real cost to the nation is the £20 million, not the interest payments—the £20 million would never come back, and the interest payments, and the taxes necessary to fund them, would simply be devices to try to pin that loss on one or other segment of society.

'A country which has accumulated a large debt is placed in a most artificial situation. ... It becomes the interest of every contributor to withdraw his shoulder from the burthen, and to shift this payment from himself to another; and the temptation to remove himself and his capital to another country ... becomes at last irresistible ....' 'A country which has involved itself in the difficulties attending this artificial system would act wisely by ransoming itself from them, at the sacrifice of any portion of its property which might be necessary to redeem its debt.'

'A man who has £10,000, paying him an income of £500, out of which he has to pay £100 per annum towards the interest of the debt, is really worth only £8,000, and would be equally rich, whether he continued to pay £100 per annum, or at once, and for only once, sacrificed £2,000.'

'But where, it might be asked, would be the purchaser of the property which he must sell to obtain this £2,000? The answer is plain: the national creditor, who is to receive this £2,000, will want an investment for his money, and will be disposed either to lend it to the landholder or manufacturer, or to purchase from them a part of the property of which they have to dispose. To such a payment the stockholders themselves would largely contribute.'

Ricardo was writing at the end of the Napoleonic Wars, when the Debt was at its highest, so the apocalyptic tone and the espousal of dramatic remedies is understandable. He was not against a sinking fund in principle but emphasised that no sinking fund could be effective if not underpinned by a genuine surplus of revenue over expenditure; he regretted that the current Sinking Fund was only a sham.

Like Smith, Ricardo saw the harmful effects of the funding system in the distortion of important wealth-generating incentives. Unlike Smith he saw several feasible economic solutions, but he feared that the nation had neither the political wisdom nor the political will, to adopt them. But were they not adopted, he feared that another major war would bring the country to a 'national bankruptcy'. But even here he pointed out that such a bankruptcy would ensue not because the country was physically unable to sustain a larger debt, but because it was politically unwilling to do so: 'assuredly there are limits to the price which ... individuals will pay for the privilege merely of living in their own country.'

stock in the hands of the National Debt Commissioners was cancelled and any set payments into the fund were discontinued. All that remained was a return to Walpole's original structure: the public accounts were to be made up quarterly and at each quarter any surplus was to be applied immediately to debt redemption. Redeemed stock would be immediately cancelled, and would not therefore accumulate in the hands of the Commissioners. The Commissioners themselves survived, because they had by now gained other functions with regard to the management of the National Debt, but their ability to reduce the National Debt as implied by their official title was now severely limited. Debt redemption was again left to the mercy of accidents of budgeting. A budget surplus was as much a sign of sloppy budgeting as a deficit and therefore in principle to be avoided; and quick-witted ministers seeing a surplus beginning to emerge might increase their expenditure accordingly through supplementary estimates to absorb it. So the likelihood of any great debt redemption through this route was negligible.

In the ensuing decades, with explicit debt redemption off the agenda, efforts were confined to reducing the interest burden through a series of conversions, with reasonable success as market rates of interest returned to lower levels. As time progressed, this policy of benign neglect began to seem justified. Despite some serious domestic social turbulence, the country avoided foreign wars and therefore any further large-scale borrowing requirements. There were nevertheless some extra demands: in the 1830s £20 million had to be raised to fund compensation for slave-owners on the abolition of slavery, and in the 1840s £10 million to relieve distress in Ireland and the West Indies.

THE ABOLITION OF SLAVERY

The role of the National Debt in the abolition of slavery is worth some comment. In 1807 Parliament outlawed the slave trade and authorised the Royal Navy to enforce this, first against British slave traders, and later more generally. While this considerably hindered the creation of new slaves, it did not affect the position of existing slaves or their descendants, which was vociferously defended by slave-owning interests. However, the campaign for total abolition of slavery in the British Empire continued, eventually to meet with legislative success in 1833. An important element which ultimately eased the passage of the Act through Parliament was the award of compensation to the slave-owners. Unsurprisingly this was a highly controversial issue at the time, and indeed continues to be so to the present day.

To purist abolitionists the very idea of compensating slave-owners for crimes against humanity was outrageous. But the slave-owners of course argued that their past transactions in slaves had been perfectly legal in the laws of the land of the time, and that their plantations, long organised on the accepted basis of slavery, would suffer large economic losses on abolition. Many of the current owners of plantations had not themselves personally been active in the slave trade, but had inherited their estates, or had bought them at prices which reflected the current conventional way of operating plantations with slaves. Many owners were in fact absentees, living in Britain (in Jane Austen's *Mansfield Park*, the wholly upright and otherwise generally admirable country gentleman Sir Thomas Bertram has to absent himself from the story for some time to attend to affairs which have been mismanaged in his estate in Antigua), often with little first-hand knowledge of conditions on their own estates. Some, bizarrely, claimed to be theoretically opposed to slavery but in practice opposed to its abolition on account of their financial interests. More pragmatic abolitionists recognised that without compensation this opposition to abolition would continue, that the opposition was well represented in Parliament, and would continue to defeat the parliamentary process.

Thus, despite much acrimonious debate, the eventual Bill did provide for compensation. A total sum of £20 million was agreed and was distributed by what turned out to be a remarkably efficient administrative process. Slave-owners were invited to make claims to an office, detailing numbers, genders, ages, qualifications and locations of slaves. These claims were meticulously recorded, investigated, and paid out over several years by formulaic rules ascribing different values to different types of slave. The records still exist and have recently been the subject of an extensive research project.[1]

But £20 million was a very large sum of money—about 40 per cent of annual government expenditure in 1833, so far too large to be paid out of existing current tax revenues. Furthermore, levying significant additional taxation for the specific purpose of slavery compensation would surely have been controversial and unpopular on many fronts. So the money was raised, without difficulty, by an issue of Consols—the total National Debt of the time was around £800 million, so the addition was not a severe strain on the market.

One of the interesting results of the recent research project was to show that although the majority of slave-owners might fit our usual stereotype of the wealthy West Indian plantation owner, a significant minority were very different. Many people, some of relatively modest means, living in Britain and who had never been to the Caribbean, turned out to own slaves there. Many were widows who had been left slaves by their husbands as a form of pension. They had, of course, never seen their slaves, who were presumably physically managed by agents in the Caribbean, who leased them out to plantation owners and remitted the proceeds to their ultimate owners in England. In modern financial terminology, we might say that the slaves had been 'securitised'—converted into a safe homogeneous investment that could be traded anonymously at arms' length by people concerned only with the investment properties of the asset, and not its physical reality. But clearly the widows and orphans who relied in this way on the slave trade for pension security would be better served by assets such as the new Consols, and the compensation provisions of the Act effectively brought about such a transition. A repellent form of 'property' had been replaced by a more neutral form.[2]

GLADSTONE

By 1845 the economist John Ramsay McCulloch could write 'the stupendous inventions and discoveries of Watt, Arkwright, Crompton, Wedgwood and others have hitherto falsified all the predictions of those who anticipated national ruin and bankruptcy from the rapid increase of the public debt.' It was argued by others that since 1815 policy had managed to reduce the National Debt only by a few percentage points, but national wealth had increased several-fold. Was it not better to leave capital in industry earning a return of 6 or 8 per cent, than to tax it away to repay debt at 3 or 4 per cent?[3]

But this complacency was soon to be undermined by two events: one was the outbreak of the Crimean War in 1854.

Although only a short, minor war by eighteenth century standards, it turned out considerably more expensive both in lives and in money than anticipated—a sign of things to come—and underlined the crucial, but fortuitous, role of the absence of war in this rosy scenario.

The other was far less predictable, but in its way more fundamentally disturbing. In 1865 the economist William Stanley Jevons published *The Coal Question*. This remarkable and innovative book, the precursor of all the ecological resource pessimism literature of more recent times, argued that the coal resources of the country were finite and in danger of running out in the near future. Like many of its successors, it turned out to be a little premature, but its impact was significant. If it was now accepted that the taming of the National Debt was only achievable through economic growth, its message was alarming indeed. As McCulloch had pointed out, the country's economic strength was based on its energy-using technological innovations. If these failed, the future of the Debt might not be one of fading into insignificance.

These two issues coincided with the rise to prominence of a politician who was to dominate the scene for half a century and to personify for ever the Victorian attitude to public finance— William Ewart Gladstone (1809–1898).

Robert Peel, a liberal Tory, had reorganised the Tories from their reactionary, landowning roots into a more broadly-based Conservative Party wedded to 'moderate' reform. He was a moderniser, and more sympathetic to the newer industrial interests of the country, and he saw tax reform as a more urgent priority than debt policy. He was a free trader and aimed to revitalise industry by dismantling the chaotic network of indirect taxes and customs duties that had grown up during the wars. As Prime Minister in 1842 he swept away many of these, replacing their revenue by reintroducing the income tax at seven old pence in the pound (3 per cent), but only on a temporary basis. A few years later he carried his free trade agenda further by abolishing the Corn Laws, the protective duties on the importation of corn; but this was a step too far for his party, and he lost their backing and his office. Nevertheless his ministry had two significant effects: it set the country firmly on a free trade route for the rest of the century, and it caused a permanent realignment of the two-party system. Peel's supporters from the Conservatives now combined with similarly minded Whigs and Radicals to form what became the left-of-centre Liberal Party, leaving Benjamin Disraeli to take the Conservative party forward, firmly to the right of centre. William Gladstone had started his political life as a Tory and had served as a junior minister under Peel. He followed the Peelites to the Liberals, and in due course he would become the greatest Liberal politician of the century, and Disraeli's formidable sparring partner.

Gladstone was a man of steely determination, high intellect, firm principle and strong religious views, and he had one of the longest periods at the centre of power (as Chancellor of Exchequer and then as Prime Minister) of any Victorian politician. He had particularly pronounced views on public finance and stamped them indelibly on the British system—we still use the term 'Gladstonian public finance' to describe the ethos of that system.

Gladstone was the quintessential Victorian economic liberal. He believed in laissez-faire, free trade, balanced budgets, low taxation and minimal government. These days we would consider such a platform as being on the right of the political spectrum, but in Gladstone's time it was a radical left-wing agenda. His main target was the inefficiency, excess and corruption of the old elites, and he looked to create a new meritocratic and moral society, in which the poor would benefit from the technological and industrial developments currently being obstructed by 'old corruption'.

That minimal government should of course be as efficient, as economical and as accountable as possible. Not only should

Parliament authorise all taxation and all expenditure, but it should follow up with audit to ensure that all money was spent only for the purpose for which it had been voted. The Treasury's role in this process would make it dominant over all other government departments. Any money unspent for a particular purpose must be returned to the central Treasury and not redeployed by the ministry concerned to other projects under its control and in need of further funds. Any budgets unspent at the end of the financial year must similarly be returned to the Treasury; they could not be carried over to the next year. No taxes should be hypothecated to particular purposes: all taxation should go into a single pot (managed by the Treasury) and all expenditure allocations must be made on their own merits (supervised by the Treasury) irrespective of the source of revenue. The overall government budget should be balanced, and borrowing should be eschewed except in case of absolute emergency. Only the absolute minimum of taxation should be collected, in the fairest and most efficient way, so estimates must be as accurate as possible.

When Gladstone first became Chancellor of the Exchequer in 1852 he intended to let Peel's temporary income tax lapse as it was due to do. But first he wanted to complete Peel's project of getting rid of indirect taxes, so he extended the life of income tax a little further. Then the advent of the Crimean War confronted him with a serious clash of principles: if he disliked taxation, he disliked borrowing more.[4]

'In time of peace nothing but dire necessity should induce us to borrow.' But even in time of war borrowing was a moral evil. 'The system of raising funds necessary for war by loans practises wholesale systematic continued deception upon the people.' 'The expenses of war are the moral check which it has pleased the Almighty to impose upon the ambition and the lust for conquest that are inherent in so many nations.' (The Reverend Price sounds positively prosaic by comparison.) He therefore proposed—unlike almost any politician before or since—to fund the war entirely through taxation, doubling the rate of income tax. Unfortunately the government of which he was a part fell the following year because of public dissatisfaction with the conduct of the war, and his successor George Cornewall Lewis was made of less stern stuff—and was confronted by considerably higher estimates of the cost of the war. Lewis reverted to the traditional borrowing policy and at the end of two years' inconclusive warfare the Debt had increased by £30 million—but at least he intended to pay it off after the war with a dedicated sinking fund.[5] Disraeli succeeded Lewis and he objected to debt even less—he cancelled Lewis' Sinking Fund and let the war debts simply add to the permanent funded debt. By the time Gladstone returned to the Exchequer in 1860 this was all water under the bridge, so he turned his attention to a more fundamental attack on the total Debt. However, he again encountered the usual dilemma: debt reduction vs tax reduction.

Gladstone saw that after his desirable reduction of indirect taxes, income tax would have to be retained if there was to be any serious possibility of reducing the Debt. He probably also realised that income tax was efficient, not very distortionary in the circumstances of the time, and capable of delivering significant tax revenues. Therefore paradoxically it could be quite congenial to his minimal-interference aims; an ideal tax system might be one which combined income tax with only a small number of key indirect taxes. Ideally the income tax should be held at a fairly low level in times of peace but it would offer a rapid flexibility of revenue in emergencies.

But what actual means could he employ to reduce the Debt? The only extant mechanism was the chance occurrence of budget surpluses from time to time, and this was clearly too weak to achieve very much. The sinking fund concept was so discredited that politically speaking it was a non-starter. He therefore turned back to the old idea of Terminable (i.e. finite) Annuities.

The old annuities for life or for a fixed term of years had the great advantage for the government that at the end of their terms they simply lapsed, without the need for any final capital repayment. Of course, the annual payments during their lives were greater than those of perpetual annuities, but for long annuities not enormously so (the workings of compound interest again). If the public could be induced to switch their perpetual annuities into new, long-term but finite annuities, the Debt would be put on an automatic path to extinction with only a moderate current sacrifice.

Unfortunately, by now the public very much preferred their perpetual annuities. A terminable annuity in which the capital is effectively being repaid continually with each year is very inconvenient for long-term savers whose principal aim is to keep their capital intact (now one of the cardinal Victorian virtues); indeed, for trustees holding investments on behalf of others it was positively illegal. Also it was much easier to operate secondary markets in perpetual annuities where each bond was identical, than in terminable annuities where each bond was idiosyncratic, so that perpetual annuities were much more liquid. Lastly the new income tax would penalise the larger terminable annuity payments unless the capital repayment element were somehow exempted.

The National Debt Commissioners were empowered to offer schemes of voluntary conversion, but there were few takers. Compulsory conversions seemed possible only on exorbitant terms. But Gladstone noted an interesting fact: significant numbers of government bonds were actually held by the government itself, or by government agencies;[6] for instance, the Post Office Savings Bank and the Trustee Savings Bank both held most of their reserves in government bonds.[7] So did other government departments. These bodies at least could be instructed to convert to terminable annuities.

It was better than nothing, but it did only affect a minority of the Debt. For all his rhetoric Gladstone's practical impact on the

Debt was initially small. Nevertheless, as with the Reverend Price's Sinking Fund, even starting off in a small way might still eventually mop up the whole Debt. For as the Savings Banks' annuities were progressively paid off in cash, they could be instructed to reinvest the proceeds by buying ordinary interest-bearing bonds in the market, which could in turn be converted to terminable annuities, and so on. Eventually, assuming the government issued no further ordinary bonds (always the important assumption), the existing supply of ordinary bonds would be run through.

In fact, this was another little sinking fund in all but name, but Gladstone hoped that its peculiar constitution would at least protect it from the usual past raids on sinking funds. Alas that hope, like all others of its type, proved misplaced. A cash-strapped government in 1885 simply suspended the capital part of the yearly payments. If Gladstone could set up such a scheme with ease because he was both payer and payee, his successors could equally easily dismantle it. But for a while terminable annuities were the policy *du jour*. Nobody seemed to notice that making new borrowings while operating terminable annuities would be just as illogical as Pitt's borrowing while operating his Sinking Fund.

'PRODUCTIVE' INVESTMENT

One other minor aspect of borrowing at this time might be noted. As we have seen, government borrowing had almost always been for the purposes of warfare. It was almost a technical term of the time that the National Debt was 'powder and shot'; i.e. irrevocably gone, to no future benefit. Most politicians in fact shared Gladstone's view that there was something wrong in borrowing in times of peace, and as the government's responsibilities in peacetime were still few, this was not usually too difficult to avoid. But towards the end of the century government began to borrow, in peacetime, for the purposes of long-term civilian productive investment.

Economists' Views on the National Debt: 5. John Stuart Mill

John Stuart Mill (1806–1873) was also generally hostile to the Debt itself: debt withdraws capital surreptitiously from productive purposes, he thought, and its servicing arrangements distort incentives. A nation with a debt should make strenuous efforts to pay it off. But, writing in the middle of the century when the air of crisis had somewhat abated, he was a little more cautious about the more drastic remedies. Ricardo's immediate general levy on property had much to recommend it, except that Mill felt this would be discriminatory against property-owners, who had not been the only beneficiaries from the debt-financed expenditures. A wider levy, including non-property-owners, would be more ethically defensible, but this would presumably involve the non-property-owners having to borrow their contributions. While, again following Ricardo, this would be feasible in a perfect market and indeed desirable—simply crystallising citizens' shares of public indebtedness into private debts—in practice there would be serious complications: the non-property-owners' credit being so much worse than the government's would mean that the interest they would have to pay would be much higher than that which the government had been paying on their behalf. They would therefore unfairly lose out. In the face of these difficulties Mill reluctantly ruled out a general levy.

There remains the alternative of slower repayment via continuing budget surpluses, the case for which Mill takes as incontrovertible. He has little time for the counter-argument of leaving money 'to fructify in the pockets of the people'—in fact he argues it is more likely to fructify if removed from the pockets of the people and given to the holders of the National Debt. For the people in general will either consume or save their incomes if left untaxed, but the holders of the National Debt have already made their choice to hold their bonds as savings. If the bonds are redeemed with cash the bond-holders will therefore almost certainly want to reinvest in some other asset. So total savings are likely to be higher if bonds are redeemed out of general taxation.

Mill acknowledges the argument that the Debt is useful as a home for small savers looking for a low-risk asset. But he notes that the development of commerce has now produced alternative similar assets in the private sector. Furthermore, the attractiveness of government debt lies simply in its government guarantee: a government-guaranteed savings bank would more suitably meet this need.

So the Debt should definitely be paid off, but a balance must still be struck. The purpose of redeeming the Debt is to relieve the population from oppressive taxation in the future. However, redemption requires the taxes to be higher in the present. Mill says that some taxes are more oppressive than others, and it might be more beneficial to use any current fiscal leeway first to remove the most oppressive taxes and only move on to redeeming the Debt when that has been completed (this was indeed Peel's policy at just about the time Mill was writing).

In 1868 the government decided that it was in the public interest to nationalise the newly-developing telegraph industry and incorporate it into the Post Office (the Post Office was the one civilian industry that the government did traditionally operate. For reasons of its own its investment had always been financed by separate terminable annuities.) The actual purchase

Economists' Views on the National Debt: 6. Karl Marx

For Karl Marx (1818–1883) the evils of public debts are simply one part of the more general evils of the capitalist system as a whole. But in *Capital* Vol I, Ch XXXI he does refer to them explicitly. The evils are fundamentally much the same as other economists have set them out, although in different language: non-capitalist tax-payers are exploited by capitalists and the hangers-on of the capitalist system. 'On this there are not two opinions, even among the bourgeois economists.' He notes wryly that the National Debt is almost the only element of national wealth that common people have a stake in, quoting Cobbett to the effect that all desirable public institutions in England are termed 'Royal'; only the Debt is 'National'.

More importantly, though, he also notes the emergence of public debt as being a very necessary early stage in the development of the capitalist system as a whole. Through its associated stimulation of banking systems, private credit and paper money, it accelerated the development of the crucial institutions of capitalistic production and accumulation.

In Vol III, Ch XXIV, Marx also shows himself well aware of Richard Price's sinking fund ideas. Although commending Price's other activities in support of the working class, he was particularly scornful of the naïve obsession with compound interest.

was messy, finally costing the government £11 million, much more than its original estimate, and much more than most contemporary commentators thought it was worth, and was financed by an issue of Consols.

More successfully, in 1875 the government bought the Khedive of Egypt's shares (44 per cent) in the Suez Canal. While motivated more by strategic than financial concerns, this was certainly a financial success. Financed by an issue of £4 million 3.5 per cent Exchequer Bonds, by 1914 the annual dividends were £1.25 million.

While small compared to the total debt of the time, these purchases should alert us to the dangers of exclusive attention to the indebtedness of government; governments may also have assets to set off against their debts. This has become more significant in the twentieth century as governments have assumed a greater role in their economies. We shall see a more systematic modern attempt to deal with this issue in Chapter 13.

A problem is that many of these public assets are not easily marketable, being investments in infrastructure like roads, schools, hospitals and defence establishments. But in the second half of the twentieth century the British government also built up a large portfolio of industrial assets in its nationalised industries; and for various reasons it has acquired shareholdings in some otherwise private companies (including most recently some very large shareholdings in major British banks after the 2008 crash). Over time many of these assets have been sold off again through privatisation, so that the decline in the government's net financial position is perhaps underestimated by its national debt position alone. On the other hand, the advent of Sovereign Wealth Funds demonstrates that some fortunate governments in the world possess marketable assets well in excess of their marketable liabilities.

NORTHCOTE'S NEW SINKING FUND

By 1875 it was apparent that nothing much in the way of debt repayment had been achieved. An increasingly imperialistic foreign policy and the re-emergence of great-power tensions on the European continent began to cast the shadow of war again. The Crimean War had shown how quickly conflict could undermine the financial position. A wealthy nation should surely do more in times of peace to clear its decks financially and allow room for expansion in any future conflict.

A new Conservative Chancellor, Stafford Northcote, proposed another variant on the sinking fund concept: a Fixed Debt Charge, initially to be set at £27.4 million p.a. but shortly to rise to £28 million. This charge would be responsible for paying all the interest and management expenses on the National Debt, and any surplus would constitute a sinking fund and go towards redemption. As with Gladstone, the initial practical impact fell rather short of the rhetoric: the interest payments alone were running at £27.2 million. An important difference from Pitt's Sinking Fund was that redeemed stock would be cancelled immediately and would not accumulate in the hands of the Commissioners earning interest to be applied to the purchase of more stock.

Although a Conservative minister, in his early career Northcote had been Gladstone's private secretary and had doubtless absorbed some of his master's aversion to debt. Gladstone, still in Parliament, but now in opposition to Northcote, welcomed the general thrust of his protégé's proposals, but was less happy about the dethronement of his favourite terminable annuities. But Northcote correctly pointed out that with his scheme the issue of terminability was simply irrelevant: if people wanted terminable annuities they could have them, and both the interest and the capital elements of their repayments would come out of his fixed debt charge; with perpetuities there would only be the interest payment, leaving a larger surplus in the fixed debt charge to make an equal capital repayment. So his scheme could do all that terminable annuities could, and more. And experience would soon show that terminable annuities were no less vulnerable to raiding than sinking funds.

Northcote's own scheme (like all schemes) would of course be vulnerable too. In his case the compound interest process and therefore success would depend on the government's resolve to maintain the overall £28 million figure over the years as its interest bill began to decrease. Predictably, this would not be so. Successive Chancellors would, and did, argue that having re-done their interest-rate sums they had found that a smaller overall total would now suffice to keep at least some debt repayment going.

Also, on several occasions of financial stringency the Sinking Fund was temporarily suspended (although regrettable, this at least showed an improved level of financial understanding, in avoiding simultaneous new borrowing and sinking fund contributions).

Nevertheless, despite these chisellings the general structure of Northcote's Sinking Fund did actually survive, and governments did begin to make noticeable inroads into the Debt in the last quarter of the century, and in the first years of the twentieth century. They were helped by a largely buoyant economy, low interest rates and healthy tax revenues. As this was one of the few sustained periods when debt was actually being repaid, it might be worth looking at it in some greater detail and considering the possible reasons for its relative success.

One possible explanation, and one certainly held by the Treasury civil servants of the period, was that the very complexity of the arrangements that had now been arrived at was a great safeguard. There were now in fact two sinking funds: Northcote's, colloquially known as the New Sinking Fund, and the original Walpole scheme of accidental surpluses, still in force and now colloquially known as the Old Sinking Fund. Also terminable annuities still existed; although Northcote had considered them to be irrelevant within the structure of his

New Sinking Fund, considerable volumes still existed, and examination of most years' figures shows that the major part of debt redemption in any year through the New Sinking Fund was in fact attributable to them, and only a smaller part of the total was 'free money', available to repurchase any securities the National Debt Commissioners chose.

The Treasury civil servants found that this combination of the New Sinking Fund and terminable annuities was really quite useful. A sinking fund with several million pounds of uncommitted money was very vulnerable to political predation. Even the most upright of Chancellors found some difficulty justifying to themselves raising new taxes for desirable expenditure when the existing taxes already provided money which was not effectively being 'spent'; and procedurally it was not too difficult to divert or suspend a sinking fund. However, the terminable annuities presented a second layer of difficulty for the predator. Repayment of the capital part of the terminable annuities was a legal requirement—or at least it seemed to be. Suspending the Sinking Fund alone would be pointless if its operation would effectively continue through the terminable annuities. Suspending the terminal annuities alone would be pointless if the Sinking Fund remained intact. Only suspension of both simultaneously would be able to divert the funds intended for debt repayment to other purposes, and that would involve correspondingly greater procedural and informational difficulties.

The Treasury suspected—probably correctly—that few people really understood how terminable annuities worked. The further complication that most terminable annuities actually belonged to government departments muddied the water even more. This enabled the civil servants to obfuscate the issues and defeat most proposals to raid the funds by suggesting they would not actually achieve their objectives.

On the other hand it also seemed clear that too large a sinking fund could not be sustained indefinitely. Whereas in theory the whole point is that the fund should grow without limit, and this is what gives it its great power, an ever-increasing uncommitted sum of money would eventually prove irresistible to politicians.

Therefore the civil servants' ideal was a moderate sinking fund of about £6–7 million per year, combined with a sufficient number of terminable annuities to tie up and protect most of this fund's contribution. It would not pay off the National Debt as quickly as the theoretical ideal sinking fund would, but it would make at least some progress and it would be politically sustainable, whereas the theoretical ideal would not be politically sustainable, and would collapse well before it achieved its goal. A situation of this kind did roughly pertain between 1875 and 1914.

It no doubt also helped that with a wealthier economy, sums of this magnitude were now much more affordable than in the first half of the century. Buoyant tax revenues in this period often produced accidental surpluses, so that the Old Sinking Fund also made an appreciable contribution. About £150 million of debt was paid off in the last quarter of the nineteenth century, and another £150 million in the early twentieth century. What would have been an impressive record was only ruined by the intervening Boer War, which put back £150 million in only three years. However, a difficulty in the long run would have been conjuring up more terminable annuities when the existing ones had run their course.

2.5 PER CENT CONSOLS

If the course of debt repayment was a little rocky, interest rate conversion was still firmly on the government's side. Several smaller schemes were eventually crowned by Goschen's conversion of 1888–9. George, Viscount Goschen (1831–1907) was perhaps one of the most economically literate Chancellors of the Exchequer to hold office before the late twentieth century. Born into a London merchant family, he combined practical experience of the markets with an academic intellectual curiosity, rather like Ricardo. He wrote economics books, was a strong supporter of the development of universities, and was both President of the Royal Statistical Society and founding President of the Royal Economic Society. One of his initially minor but lasting achievements was the invention of Road Tax.

He made the opposite political transition to Gladstone: starting as a Liberal he ended a Conservative, and this itself is an interesting story, from which he is sometimes termed the 'accidental' or 'forgotten' Chancellor. Lord Randolph Churchill (Winston's father) was the rising star of the late-Victorian Conservative Party, but he was also an ambitious opportunist and political manipulator. In 1886 he suddenly and rather inexplicably resigned as Chancellor of the Exchequer. His calculation seems to have been that since there was no other suitable candidate for Chancellor within the Conservative Party, the Prime Minister would have to ask him to return, thereby demonstrating his indispensability. But Randolph had overlooked that the Liberal Goschen might be willing to cross the floor, and the Prime Minister seized this opportunity to slap down his annoying subordinate. Randolph's political career never quite recovered from this setback; one can only speculate on the effects on Winston's subsequent political career.

In 1888–9 Goschen carried out a very ambitious and very successful conversion of almost all the 3 per cent debt to 2.75 per cent, with a further reduction to 2.5 per cent due in 1903. With this conversion, Consols reached their final apogee, as 2.5 per cent Consols. This was a very significant reduction in the interest burden, and with the fixed debt charge policy should have resulted in a dramatic acceleration of debt repayment as well. But predictably the government chose to reduce the debt charge accordingly and apply most of the savings elsewhere.

SUMMARISING THE STATE OF THE DEBT
IN THE LATE NINETEENTH CENTURY

After these various exercises, by the 1890s the structure of the National Debt had considerably simplified again, and the annual statement put before Parliament needed only a few lines. The first and by far the largest item was 'Funded Debt', i.e. permanent debt, by now almost entirely Consols; second came 'Capital Value of Terminable Annuities', still a significant amount, showing that Gladstone's initiative had not been entirely in vain; third 'Unfunded Debt', i.e. the floating, short-run debt, almost entirely Treasury Bills and now usually a very, very small proportion of the total, except in crisis periods such as the Boer War. The sub-total of these three items was conventionally identified as the 'National Debt'.

Then comes a fourth line 'Other Capital Liabilities', which added to the previous three, constitutes 'Aggregate Gross Liabilities of the State'. By this time, Other Capital Liabilities comprised only the very small tail-end of an obligation on a Russian-Dutch loan going back to the Napoleonic Wars and the government's obligation to make good the reserves of Savings Banks and Friendly Societies, but new purposes were about to be devised (see below).

Then comes a line of 'Assets', again very small, but including the Suez Canal shares, shares in the Red Sea and India Telegraph Company (but not including the assets of the domestic telegraph and postal industry, whose financing arrangements were kept at arm's length from the central government's finances), and loans made by central government to local authorities. These are deducted from the foregoing, to constitute 'Aggregate Net Liabilities of the State'.

Finally, there is a line of 'Exchequer Balances at the Bank of England and Bank of Ireland' (again small). Although in principle one feels these should also be deducted as assets from the overall Liability figure, in fact they are not, and are just produced for note.

In the entries for Other Capital Liabilities and Assets we see the beginnings of a form of accounting going beyond the conventional notion of the National Debt as being just about Bonds and Bills: a wider notion being the government's entire financial commitments to the future, however expressed, but mitigated by assets which will deliver some income in the future. We will see a more systematic contemporary version of this in Chapter 13. But these headings also open up possibilities of massaging the headline figures of National Debt by hiding some commitments 'off-balance-sheet'. Two episodes around this time are worthy of note.

LOCAL LOANS AND IRISH LAND BONDS

From about 1800, the central government began making small loans to local authorities for public works, and the volumes steadily grew. In 1842 the whole business was entrusted to the National Debt Commissioners, who gained an additional function as Trustees of a Public Works Loans Fund. (PWLF). The Treasury provided the PWLF with funds in cash or bonds, and the latter lent on to the local authorities. However, the accounting of these loans was rather confused, not distinguishing adequately between payments of interest and repayments of principal, and it became difficult to ascertain the true financial position of the central government vis-à-vis the local authorities.

In 1887 Goschen decided to take the activity wholly outside the scope of the central government budget. He converted the existing bonds involved into a new Local Loans Stock and forced this on to the Trustee Savings Bank and Post Office Savings Bank, whose reserves were held and controlled by the National Debt Commissioners. Subsequent issues were marketed to the public. In Goschen's view the Local Loans Stock was not a government security, therefore not a part of the National Debt; nor were the local loans themselves a government asset—the government was merely acting as an intermediary between the investors and the local authorities (as in modern-day peer-to-peer lending). Therefore, the local loan business abruptly disappeared from Assets and an equivalent amount of bonds from the National Debt. But the government accepted responsibility for the payment of interest to the investors in Local Loans Stock, and was clearly guarantor of the scheme—so the Local Loans Stock now appeared in the separate statement of Contingent Liabilities, along with various other loans, mostly foreign, that the government had guaranteed. The accounting of the time made no attempt to put a value on such contingent liabilities.

But after Goschen's separation the National Debt figures clearly represent now only the position of the central government: large local authority indebtedness would not show up, although we would now consider that local authorities certainly constitute part of a wider 'public sector'. The question of definition of the 'public sector' will be taken up again in Chapter 13.

Similar treatment was applied to another troublesome and unusual, but large commitment. In the late nineteenth century, when the British government was struggling to find solutions to the Irish problem, one of the most contentious issues was Land Reform. A scheme was instituted whereby Irish tenant farmers could buy their farms from their landlords, with mortgages on generous terms. These mortgages were financed by the sale of Irish Land Bonds, which were not strictly speaking British government debt but were guaranteed by the government (but as is usual with such arrangements, public perception failed to grasp such subtle distinctions—it was obviously a government scheme). In this case the government guarantee was crucial, allowing an interest rate considerably lower than would otherwise have been the case, given the Irish history of agrarian unrest and nonpayment of rents. The purchasers of these bonds were largely British and Irish banks, the Savings Banks and other British government departments, a similarly incestuous arrangement as with Local Loans Stock, further reducing its transparency. This scheme would create some difficulties after Irish independence in 1921 (see Chapter 11).

NAVAL INSTALLATIONS

The normal rule is that all military expenditure is chargeable to the current year's revenue ('powder and shot'), and therefore any such expenditure running ahead of taxation must produce a revenue deficit and add to the National Debt. However, the practice grew up towards the turn of the century of financing some very large military investment projects, particularly the construction of naval port installations, by separate terminable annuities issued by and chargeable to the relevant spending department. The arguments for doing so seemed to be by analogy with the government's treatment of the telegraph industry (see above): the projects were very long-lived and produced an asset which secured the debt; the responsibility for the debt was the department's own; and the finance was ultimately self-limiting. These annuities did not appear in the National Debt, although they did in Other Capital Liabilities. As rearmament gathered pace at the turn of the century, Other Capital Liabilities accordingly began to grow significantly.

But Herbert Asquith, Chancellor of the Exchequer in the new Liberal government of 1906, strongly objected to this treatment. Asquith's stance was no doubt bolstered by the normal Liberal dislike of military expansionism, but he argued that the practice confused the distinction between capital and current expenditure, encouraged departments to take on long-term commitments too lightly, and tended to conceal from Parliament the true extent of such commitments. Anyway, how was a naval harbour any more of a long-term asset than a battleship?[8] It had never been the practice for battleships to be financed in this way.

To see the significance of these points, suppose a project which might be completed within one year costs £20 million. Financing this with a terminable annuity might see it paid off instead (with interest) by, say, twenty annual instalments of £1.5 million. In the first year the department need only declare expenditure of £1.5 million instead of the whole £20 million, and its budget is more likely to be approved by a parliament not wholly aware of the longer-term implications. In future budgets the annual £1.5 million will appear as a prior commitment, a *fait accompli*, outside the control of Parliament. Making the department 'own up' to the full £20 million at the outset, would beneficially concentrate the minds of both department and Parliament.

Asquith therefore ended this practice and required all such expenditure to be financed out of current revenue, with the implication that large increases in such expenditure would signal the need for either increased taxes or increased explicit borrowing. In fact, despite their continued growth in the years leading up to 1914, tax revenues did largely keep up, and the National Debt continued to fall, as of course did the military contribution to Other Capital Liabilities. However Other Capital Liabilities did continue to grow, through the rather less contentious use of terminable annuities to finance productive investment in the telegraph and other industries, colonial development, and the construction of public buildings.

This episode might therefore be only a small historical curiosity of little practical account, were it not for intriguing echoes both past and future: the practice is reminiscent of the uncoordinated departmental tallies of the early eighteenth centuries, so easily running out of control—hence Asquith's concern—but it is also effectively the same as our current Private Finance

Initiative, and the arguments then made in its favour are much the same as those made for PFI now (PFI will be examined in more detail in Chapter 13). Asquith described it as 'a most unhappy chapter in the history of our national finance'.

THE BOER WAR

One uncomfortable shock was the Boer War of 1899–1902. As with the Crimean War the government initially seriously under-estimated its cost and duration. By its end it had increased the Debt by £159 million—undoing the repayment efforts of thirty years. It was enough to make a Chancellor weep. However, in the first decade of the twentieth century significant repayments resumed, despite the increasing demands of armaments and the Liberal Party's new welfare expenditures.

But, of course, all would pale into irrelevance after 1914.

7

THE FIRST WORLD WAR

JOHN MAYNARD KEYNES AND THE FINANCIAL STRATEGY OF THE WAR

On the morning of Sunday 2 August 1914, at the top end of Whitehall, a tall young man painfully extricated himself from the sidecar of a motor-cycle combination and dusted himself down. John Maynard Keynes, a young and relatively unknown Cambridge don, was about to begin his career as the twentieth century's most influential advisor and commentator on economic policy. He had been summoned urgently by a friend in the Treasury to assist in dealing with the mounting financial crisis caused by the prospect of a major European war. It was a Bank Holiday weekend and the trains were unreliable, so he persuaded his brother-in-law to drive him from Cambridge on his new motor-cycle, stopping only at the top end of Whitehall so he could arrive at the Treasury with greater dignity on foot.

The immediate financial crisis soon eased, but as a result Keynes was offered a job in the Treasury for the duration of the war. It shaped his entire future professional life. By the end of the war, he had risen to become a very significant policy advisor—so significant that he was sent as the Treasury's chief representative to the Paris peace conference in 1919. His disillusion there resulted in his first best-selling book, *The Economic Consequences of the Peace*, which made him a household name. He had enormous influence on the financial conduct of both World Wars.

Like many people in 1914, Keynes thought the war would be relatively short. However, this was not because he thought that gallant British troops would soon be in Berlin. Like most economists he thought that the participants would simply not be able to finance war expenditure for very long, and would be obliged to come to some compromise peace. This was a common view in progressive intellectual circles at the time, perhaps best expressed in an influential book by R. N. Angell called *The Great Illusion*. Modern technology had rendered war increasingly destructive and more and more expensive. In ancient wars, a victor might gain enough loot in treasure and territory from the defeated to make a war profitable. But the wealth of modern countries was not like this anymore: it was tied up in their economic and social networks as going concerns, and defeat would disrupt and destroy the value of these. There could be no gainers and war was therefore irrational. Politicians would either avoid it consciously, or they would be compelled to eschew it through financial constraint.

It is perhaps the most depressing lesson of the Great War that this optimistic conclusion proved wrong. (It was perhaps poorly-founded anyway. The Germans may well have gained from the Franco-Prussian War of 1870–1, which was short, very conclusive, and brought them large gains of territory and a large financial indemnity from France.) Policymakers always managed to prolong the fighting by finding new methods of financing which would ultimately impoverish their nations for decades to come. Paradoxically, the ingenuity of Keynes and other economists would assist that to come about.

The kind of war Keynes and the Treasury wanted to fight was essentially about money. Britain did not have a large army (the Kaiser's reputed sneer of a 'contemptible little army' was quite on the mark: the British sent all their seven home divisions to France in 1914, but the Germans had ninety-eight divisions and the French ninety). Unlike mainland continental countries, Britain's homeland defence relied not on massive armies but on the Royal Navy (on which admittedly she spent as much as those other countries spent on their armies). The main purpose of the British army was to maintain order in the Empire in small-scale colonial conflicts (in fact it was split administratively into two, the Home army and the Indian army, of roughly equal size). And unlike the continental countries the British army was a professional, volunteer force—conscription was, until 1915, an alien concept to the British political system.

So the sensible strategy would be for Britain to use her superior financial resources rather than her inferior military resources: to pay other people to do the fighting—and the dying—for her. It might not have been very noble, but this was after all traditional British foreign policy in Europe: Pitt's government had largely fought Napoleon in this way (but Pitt's subsidies were mainly outright grants, which did not expect repayment; the subsidies of this war would be loans, which as we will see, laid up serious trouble for the future).

On the other hand, Lord Kitchener, the military hero newly appointed as War Minister, was now arguing for an army of seventy divisions. The Treasury was appalled by this prospect. It would be practically impossible to finance the equipping of such a force; the manpower required would denude British industry; nor could such an army be ready until 1916 when the war would probably already be over through financial exhaustion. Better to keep Britain's skilled workers in industry producing munitions and manufacturing exports whose revenue could purchase more munitions from abroad, these munitions then to be provided to France, Russia and Serbia who already had large armies. A short, concerted land campaign by these countries and the demonstration of superior financial resources for the longer term should give the allies a strategic advantage from which to negotiate a rapid and favourable peace—and the more superior the financial resources the greater the strategic advantage and the more favourable the peace. On the allied side, the British government's credit standing was the best in the world—so Britain should borrow, particularly from the US, and lend on the proceeds to France, Russia, Serbia, etc. Such promises of financial support were also used successfully to detach Italy from the opposing side and encourage her to enter the war (disastrously) on the allied side.

Keynes had a further, personal, objection to Kitchener's new army: it would certainly involve conscription. Keynes was not a pacifist (although many of his friends were) but he was an old-fashioned liberal and he objected to the removal of the right to choose whether to fight or not. Keynes was not alone in this: the issue split the cabinet, with several prominent Liberal ministers resigning, and eventually led to the downfall of Asquith as Prime Minister.

But the Treasury lost the financial argument. The vision of an arms-length war on very liberal principles, with minimal loss of British lives and minimal disruption to the accepted economic and social mores, leading rapidly to a negotiated peace, was hopelessly old-fashioned. The European allies did not oblige with land victories (Pitt would have sympathised: his subsidy schemes were almost always undone by one of Napoleon's crushing victories). The genteel nineteenth-century liberalism of Prime Minister Asquith eventually gave way in 1916 to the more ruthless twentieth-century energy of Lloyd George, who appreciated the demands of a more modern 'total war', where the aim would be the complete destruction of the enemy, whatever the cost; and all the resources of the state, human, material and financial, would be mobilised forcibly to that effect. In the later years of the war, such limitless war aims disillusioned many people. In December 1917, Keynes wrote to his friend and ex-lover Duncan Grant, 'I work for a government I despise, for ends I think criminal.'

Against Treasury advice the government pursued both Kitchener's large army and the subsidy of allies: by mid-1916, Britain was paying for the whole of Italy's foreign war spending, most of Russia's, two-thirds of France's, half of Belgium's and Serbia's. 'We have only one ally, France;' Keynes wrote, 'the rest are mercenaries.'

Lloyd George became something of a *bête noire* for Keynes, who wrote a stinging portrait of him for *The Economic Consequences of the Peace* (Asquith advised him to remove it, and it was only published some years later). But the feeling was mutual: Lloyd George personally struck out Keynes' name from a proposed honours list. Lloyd George regarded Keynes as an excitable and pessimistic nuisance, whose prophecies of doom were always unfulfilled: 'If victory shone on our banners our difficulties would disappear. Success means credit: financiers never hesitate to lend to a prosperous concern.'

BUDGETARY CONSEQUENCES OF THE WAR

The British economy had approached the First World War in relatively good condition. As we have seen, in the long period of peace since Waterloo in 1815 the economy had grown, not without setbacks, but overall at an unprecedented rate. Britain's GDP in 1914 is now estimated to have been about £2,400 million per annum. The British population was about 45 million, up from about 15 million in 1815.

Britain's technological superiority had enabled its companies to earn large export surpluses which had been steadily reinvested abroad, so that its citizens had amassed a very large stock of overseas assets: about £4,000 million, which generated a further income of about £2–300 million p.a. (1914 prices were about one-eightieth of present-day prices; during the nineteenth century prices had fluctuated but without any significant long-run trend, so that this price level was almost the same as in 1815; however the price level would almost exactly double during the war so that 1918 prices were about one-fortieth of present-day prices.)

Despite rising expenditure on armaments and the Liberal government's new welfare provisions, the public finances were also quite healthy. Tax revenues kept pace with these new demands, and in most recent years there had been a current surplus (over and above the New Sinking Fund), enabling the government to repay one-eighth of the National Debt between 1903 and 1913.

In 1913–14 total government expenditure was £197.5 million, total revenues £198.2 million (thus almost perfectly in balance, and both less than 10 per cent of GDP). The starting 'reduced' rate of income tax was 9 old pence in the pound (3.75 per cent), payable on incomes between £160 p.a. and £2,000 p.a. (£12,800 and £160,000 at current prices), although a higher 'standard' rate and a new 'Super Tax' raised this to double on incomes of more than £5,000 p.a. (£400,000 at current prices). As much money was raised from alcohol taxation as from income tax.

In the years after 1815, the National Debt had reached an all-time proportional high of about 200 per cent of GDP. As we have also seen, there had been little effective overall repayment, but with the growth of the economy the relative significance of the debt had declined very dramatically. At about £650 million, it now represented only about 25 per cent of GDP. Notice, too, how small it was relative to the £4,000 million of foreign assets now owned by British citizens.

At that time, the government budget was announced in the spring of each year for the forthcoming April–March financial year, so after the outbreak of war in August a supplementary budget was required in November 1914. Income tax and super tax were doubled, the duty on beer tripled, other duties raised similarly. Total government revenue for the financial year would increase as a result to £226.7 million. Unfortunately total government expenditure would increase to £560.5 million, leaving a deficit of £333.8 million, to be met by borrowing.

Much worse was to come the following year. In the spring of 1915 the Chancellor Lloyd George deferred submitting final budget proposals until the war outlook became clearer. He told the House of Commons that the Treasury was working on two alternative assumptions: one was that the war would last a further five months, the other that it would last the whole financial year. The final proposals submitted in September 1915 raised income tax by a further 40 per cent, and similarly raised existing and introduced new indirect taxes. Government revenue would increase to £336.8 million. However expenditure would be £1,559 million, a deficit now of £1,222.2 million.

Table 7.1: First World War Finance[1]

	Government Revenue (£million)	Government Expenditure (£million)	Primary Surplus (+) or Deficit (−) (£million)	Internal National Debt at End-Year (£million)
1913–14	198.2	197.5	+0.7	649.8
1914–15	226.7	560.5	−333.8	1105.1
1915–16	336.8	1559.2	−1222.4	2072.7
1916–17	573.4	2198.1	−1624.7	3643.8
1917–18	707.2	2696.2	−1989.0	4876.6
1918–19	889.0	2579.3	−1690.3	6142.1

Source: E. V. Morgan.

Subsequent budgets during the war followed a similar pattern (see Table 7.1). Even apparently draconian rises in taxation had no hope of matching the phenomenal rises in expenditure. By 1918 income tax was six shillings in the pound and super tax a further four shillings and sixpence (making a combined 52.5 per cent); total revenue had increased to £889 million but the deficit was still £1,690 million. Massive borrowing was therefore required to finance the war effort. From the level of £649.8 million in 1914, the domestic National Debt rose to £6,142.1 million (approximately 120 per cent of the now inflated GDP) by March 1919.

TAXATION VS BORROWING

Most economists now would argue, and many did then, that the government should have relied more on taxation and less on borrowing. However political expediency ruled otherwise: the government's slogan in the early days of the war was 'Business as Usual', and it shied away from presenting the public with the full, appalling, consequences of its actions—the tax rises that did occur were unprecedented enough, and thought to test the bounds of political feasibility. It is difficult to deny that.

Germany and France relied even more on borrowing and less on taxation; but both those countries inflated dramatically after the war (Germany notoriously so), making the debt-holders effectively pay for the war. This had both good and bad (some very bad) effects. Britain did not inflate until after the Second World War, with more modest ill-effects, but only after a cruelly constrained inter-war period.

We have seen that in practice almost all wars involve borrowing, against the usual public finance maxim that each year's expenditure should be covered by the taxation of that year. In justification politicians have drawn an analogy with investment.

It is generally agreed that very long-lived public investments like infrastructure—say a high-speed rail network—will benefit future generations of taxpayers as well as the current generation, so it would be unfair to saddle all the costs of the investment on the current generation alone. Better to do as the private sector would do: borrow and repay over the lifetime of the project, so that all generations will contribute their proportional share. Wars are something similar, it is argued: massive, extraordinary expenditures which fortuitously confront particular generations, although their results, for good or evil, are felt by future generations as well. Therefore it is right to spread their costs.

On the other hand, Arthur Pigou (Professor of Economics at Cambridge during the First World War) argued that the idea of deferring the cost of a war to the future is only a mirage: soldiers cannot fire bullets or wear uniforms that are made in the future.[2] Therefore the real economic costs of war must be borne now, in that today's resources which could have produced nice consumer goods are instead being diverted to produce nasty war supplies. While Pigou's premise is incontrovertible, the implication is in fact only partially true.

In this debate, taxation is generally represented as the policy of making the current generation pay for the war, borrowing the policy which defers the burden to be borne by future generations. This is actually an over-simplification, for two principal reasons. To some extent brute physical laws limit what real costs can be deferred to the future. And even in financial terms the government's tax/borrowing policy cannot determine on its own the time-profile of the burden: individual citizens' reactions to the government's policy also have a role and may actually nullify the government's intentions.

Let us analyse this in stages of increasing complexity. We must first assume the simplest possible case, that a country operates a closed economy, without exports or imports, and that all goods are perishable: they must be consumed in the year they are produced. Before the war the economy's resources are fully employed producing civilian consumer goods; during the war some of these resources must be redeployed to produce war material instead, leading to a fall in consumer living standards. It is this fall in consumer living standards that measures the opportunity cost of the war. At the end of the war the resources will be redeployed again; consumer living standards will return to their pre-war level. However, there is no way that any of this post-war production can be sent back in time to alleviate the sufferings of the wartime population: they went hungry then; nothing in the future is going to change that.

If the war was funded wholly out of taxation, then this means the government has bought its war supplies effectively by confiscating part of the wartime generation's income. When the war comes to an end, no-one has any claims on the government. After the war the wartime generation will be able to resume its previous standard of living, and the new post-war generation will enter into the customary standard of living as if nothing had ever happened. The wartime generation definitely has paid for the war.

But if the war was funded instead out of borrowing, then effectively the government has bought its war supplies by giving IOUs to the wartime generation in recognition of their reduced consumption. After the war this generation will want to cash in its IOUs, but—unless there is economic growth—there will be no net increase in consumer-good production to meet them. The only way the government can honour its IOUs in real terms is by transferring consumer goods from the new post-war generation. This in turn can either be done by taxation or borrowing, and if there is no reason why the government should be any less indulgent now than it was before, it will opt again for borrowing. In this way a bizarre echo-effect of the war will ripple through the generations: the wartime generation may get an opulent retirement—which will in some way compensate them for, but will not eradicate, their wartime experiences—while the post-war generation suffers in peacetime in order to provide that retirement; in turn that generation will attempt to get some recompense out of the next generation.

This is obviously a very inefficient solution, with consumers suffering large swings in standards of living when they would prefer to even them out. The echo effect may die out as economic growth dulls the inter-generational competition, and if the government gradually manages to replace borrowing by taxation, and if inflation is allowed to reduce the value of the IOUs. All these processes will in some way reduce the real value of what one generation can exact from the succeeding. Although these mechanisms do spread some pain around, they do not genuinely spread the cost of the war: the wartime generation has borne the cost of the war; the remaining process is just a distributional struggle for some kind of inefficient recompense.

Now consider another case, in which all goods are now infinitely storable. Here there is some scope for genuine inter-generational shifting of consumption. In the absence of war, some goods would have been produced for laying down for future consumption (savings). These can be diverted to war usage without immediately affecting wartime consumer standard of living, although they will reduce the post-war standard of living, and post-war arrangements will have to settle claims in an efficient sharing-out of what remains. However if the demands of war exceed the current production of savings (and any stocks produced before the war), wartime consumption must fall, and can only be partially recompensed afterwards, as in the previous case.

At a third level of complexity, we may have a mixture of consumer goods and capital goods. Now the citizens can maintain their consumption levels during the war by running down the national stock of capital goods. If war production replaces largely capital investment and the maintenance of capital assets and infrastructure, future generations will pay in terms of not having the productive benefit of these in the post-war period and of having to rebuild them in the future. But this may happen whatever the government's financial policy: if the government decides to tax, will the citizens meet their tax bills by cutting their consumption expenditure or their investment expenditure? And the reverse may also apply: if the government decides to borrow instead, the citizens may prefer to fund their loan subscriptions not by diverting what they would otherwise have saved in private-sector investments but by cutting their consumption expenditure, thereby protecting the capital stock for future generations, but still at the cost of creating an IOU-overhang in the post-war period as in the first case. So the decision is not up to the government alone—excessively profligate (or excessively thrifty) citizens can defeat the government's intentions, and lead to quite complex outcomes, unless the government adopts direct controls over consumption and investment expenditures (as did indeed happen in both World Wars).

Fourthly, in an economy with foreign trade, there are further possibilities open. At the extreme, all additional wartime requirements (material and mercenaries) could be supplied from abroad, with the aim of leaving domestic society untouched. But the imported war supplies must be paid for somehow. The options are:

1. Immediately through increased exports of consumer goods which would otherwise have been consumed at home (or through diminished imports of consumer goods)—either of which will reduce domestic standards of living immediately;

2. Immediately by selling domestically-owned foreign investments—this will not reduce domestic standards of living immediately but will in the future through the loss of the annual income streams that they used to generate;

3. Deferring payment through foreign borrowing—this too will not reduce domestic standards of living immediately but will in the future as increased exports or diminished imports of consumer goods are required to pay the interest and eventually repay the principal of the loans.

The real difficulty with government wartime borrowing lies with one important way in which the analogy with the private sector is misleading. When private-sector firms invest in a long-term project, they create an income-earning asset, which should generate the revenues required to meet the future repayments. When the government conducts a war, this is not the case. At best the wartime expenditures are simply a dead loss; at worst there is also active destruction of productive potential. So government borrowing creates claims without providing any means of meeting them. This sows the seeds of distributional conflict in the future. Taxation, on the other hand, transfers resources without granting such claims.

Secondly, as well as distribution across the generations there is the issue of distribution within the generations. Each generation contains richer and poorer citizens—how should the cost of a war be apportioned across the income ranges? This is by no means an easy decision, and whatever the ethical arguments, each citizen will prefer the burden to be borne elsewhere. It is a very serious distributional conflict. The choice of a particular tax package will determine the result, but a decision to borrow instead is effectively a decision to defer such a determination, unnecessarily prolonging the distributional conflict and significant levels of uncertainty. Citizens may individually prefer to continue to prolong this uncertainty rather than to accept a crystallisation of responsibility which they consider unfair, or more disadvantageous than might conceivably be obtained in the future, although the uncertainty is detrimental to all. In the extreme, as will be seen in inter-war international relations, it can lead to an almost complete paralysis of action.

MECHANISMS OF BORROWING

The unprecedented requirements for finance caused some changes in the way borrowing occurred. Normally policy would have been to borrow very short-term initially through 'Ways and Means Advances'[3] and Treasury Bills, and then mop up this floating debt—either at the end of a short war or periodically through a long war—with issues of Consols which would stabilise the debt into a permanent or very long-term form, hopefully at lower rates of interest. In this war the short-term indebtedness indeed grew alarmingly rapidly, and the need for expenditure was so continuous that the borrowing became continuous too. Previous borrowing practice had usually been a series of discrete events—each issue was a call for subscriptions on a particular day, followed by a long interval before the next issue. But this practice did not meet the new continuous demand, so the practice of borrowing 'on tap', which had been experimented with before the war, became commonplace—a security would remain on sale at the stated terms for as long as considered appropriate.

As well as providing a more continuous supply of finance this might broaden the market for securities to smaller investors as well as the professional bond specialists who frequented the bond auctions. There were other attempts to woo even smaller investors and savers: although the minimum denomination of War Loan itself was £100, smaller denomination vouchers and certificates related to it were sold through post offices and trade unions. Later, War Savings Certificates were introduced, sold in denominations less than £1. These were the precursors of today's National Savings Certificates. Although the propaganda effects of such measures were significant, their net effect on war finance might have been less so. As we have seen, Post Office Savings Bank deposits were all effectively invested in government securities anyway.

In this war the government did not attempt to use its favourite long-term instrument of Consols in the mopping-up of the floating debt. Treasury enquiries in the market suggested that a long-term issue would need an interest rate of 4 per cent. Consols, having been settled now for some years at 2.5 per cent, would therefore have had to be sold considerably under par, with the consequent exaggerated effects on the value of the debt. The enquiries also detected a market preference for a shortish redemption date rather than a perpetuity, perhaps through justifiable fear of wartime inflation, to which perpetuities would be particularly vulnerable.

So in November 1914 came the first of three successive large, redeemable War Loans:

November 1914: 3.5 per cent redeemable 1925–28, issued at 95 (equivalent to 4 per cent), £350 million

June 1915: 4.5 per cent redeemable 1925–45, issued at par, unlimited (£900 million was sold)

Early 1917: 5 per cent redeemable 1929–47, issued at 95, unlimited (£2,075 million was sold)[4]

One can easily see the unprecedented and increasing quantities required, and the consequently increasing interest rates. The increasing expensiveness was in fact greater even than apparent, because the government granted conversion rights to the purchasers of these loans: they were allowed to convert into any succeeding, higher-interest long-term loan without penalty. Unsurprisingly almost all did, so that only the third loan was held in significant quantities by the end of the war.

But after the third loan the government felt that any further long-term loan would be simply too expensive. In its absence the ever-expanding floating debt reached dangerous levels and interest rates exceeding 6 per cent. The government therefore turned to more medium-term borrowing (to which the conversion rights did not apply). A series of Exchequer Bonds and National War Bonds was issued at rates of interest about 5 per cent and for maturities of between five and ten years. By the end of the war about £2,000 million of these were outstanding.

With the entry of the US into the war, maintaining the dollar exchange rate (which had required high short-term money market rates of interest), became less urgent, and short-term interest rates fell, making Treasury Bills attractive again as a source of finance, at rates as low as 3.5 per cent. By the end of the war nearly £1,000 million was outstanding in Bills and £450 million in Ways and Means Advances, without the government having made serious efforts to convert these into longer-term securities. Such a large injection of liquid assets into the banking system tended to increase the money supply and stoke up inflation.

But in addition to the large floating debt there was a more obvious and direct inflationary source of finance. In the first days of the war the government had suspended gold convertibility of Bank of England notes for internal transactions and instituted a new paper currency. For administrative and legal reasons the new paper currency was not simply an expansion of the existing Bank of England notes, but a completely different currency issued by the Treasury, and colloquially known as 'Bradburys' after the Permanent Secretary to the Treasury, whose signature they bore. They were printed in denominations of £1 and 10 shillings, aimed at replacing the gold sovereign and half-sovereign. (The smallest denomination Bank of England note was £5. Since an ordinary working man's wages would rarely exceed £2 per week in 1914, it can be seen that paper currency, although long well accepted in large commercial transactions, only began to impinge on most people's everyday lives at this time.)

Unrestrained by any link with gold, the paper currency could be expanded at whim, increasing the government's purchasing power, but with inevitable depreciation of the currency (the similar situation had pertained in the Napoleonic wars). By the end of the war the price level had doubled.

By November 1918 the government had amassed a Debt of over £6 billion—ten times what it had started with, and now about 120 per cent of GDP. The structure of the Debt was also much less favourable. Whereas the pre-war Debt had been almost entirely in Consols, at very low rates of interest and with no legal requirement to repay, Consols now formed only about 10 per cent of the Debt. The current Debt was at higher rates of interest and had very large repayment requirements in the years not very far ahead. The floating debt, which had caused early eighteenth-century governments such anxiety, was every bit as bad as then. If banks did not wish to renew their massive holdings of Treasury Bills the government would be in serious financial embarrassment very quickly.

Post-war governments would struggle, first to balance the budget, then to reduce or convert the floating debt, then to convert medium-term debts to longer-term forms, then to attempt to reduce interest rates. In addition decisions would need to be taken about the depreciated paper currency and whether gold convertibility should be restored, and if so, should it be restored at the pre-war level.

THE COSTS: INTERNATIONAL BORROWING

Most of the debts above were incurred in sterling to British citizens and organisations who dipped into their savings and prospective future earnings. Patriotism and financial incentives played a part—interest rates rose steadily through the war as the government's needs became more desperate—but probably most important was the lack of any alternative homes for British citizens' money. Government controls (even in the absence of explicit rationing) could restrict the availability of consumer goods, could restrict housebuilding and other real forms of investment, could restrict the issuing of shares and other financial investments, and could prevent the transfer of funds abroad. Better to invest in War Loan than let your money lie mouldering in the bank—and even if you did choose the latter the bank would use your money to buy War Loan anyway.

The government's difficulty in raising these astronomic sums was not quite as great as one might imagine, therefore. However, the first War Loan, of 1914, did encounter some difficulties, and a very large portion of it was in fact secretly taken up by the Bank of England, to avoid the government having to admit that it had been under-subscribed. The secrecy was such that the stock was registered not in the name of the Bank of England, but in the personal names of the Cashier and Deputy Cashier, who had to be specially indemnified for the purpose. Subsequent loans, being unlimited in the aimed-for amount, did not produce such embarrassments.

Most of the expenditure for which government borrowing was destined would also be incurred in Britain and in sterling. Even the armies in France were almost entirely supplied from Britain, not from local sources in France. But much expenditure would also need to be imported, particularly from the US, and American firms would want to be paid. In normal times this would be no problem: both the pound and the dollar were on the gold standard at fixed rates of exchange. Everybody still considered gold to be the ultimate money, but it was expensive to use, so paper and bank transactions were used in practice. American exporters would obviously prefer to be paid in dollars, but so long as the gold standard held the three currencies were effectively identical. The problem was that in the circumstances of the war the gold standard could not be guaranteed for the future. Unlike in 1797, the British government had not suspended gold convertibility for foreign transactions, but the increased wartime risks of gold exportation had similar effects for a transactor wanting to be paid in gold in New York. The value of the now paper pound in the US could fall below its official gold exchange rate, making it less acceptable to American exporters.

So Britain was obliged to keep up its exports of goods to the US, and to borrow large amounts of US dollars in New York through the US banking system (particularly via J. P. Morgan), in order to pay its American bills. Furthermore it had been agreed among the allied nations (the conference that agreed this was one of Keynes' first jobs in the Treasury) that as Britain had the best credit standing in the world, and could therefore borrow at the lowest rates of interest, all the allied overseas purchasing and borrowing would be centralised through Britain, who would then loan on the proceeds to the financially weaker nations such as France, Russia, Italy, Serbia, etc. This, although an efficient use of resources at the time, ultimately created a toxic web of international indebtedness at the end of the war, which bedevilled all subsequent attempts to lay to rest the financial consequences of the war and move on to a new period of peaceful economic relations.

Loans of a modest magnitude would have created no difficulty, but as they built up they amounted to a significant bet by the US investors on the result of the war: if Britain lost, would they be repaid? The effective exchange rate of the pound dipped well below its official gold-standard parity. The official parity was $4.86 to the pound; British policy was to try to keep the effective rate in New York at least at $4.76. This level of depreciation was thought to be tolerable; any further would begin to erode the acceptability of the pound and raise the cost of American purchases. Note that this is very similar to the problem of acceptability of tallies in the early eighteenth century.

In late 1916 the US government became seriously alarmed that the prospect of an allied defeat would bring down the US banking system, thereby forcing the US against its will into the war to avoid such an eventuality. It therefore warned US banks against any further extension of loans to the belligerent powers. This was a desperate crisis moment for Keynes and his Treasury colleagues. Bereft of further loans, American bills had to be settled in cash, running down the reserves of US dollars and gold alarmingly. British citizens' and companies' holdings of American investments were commandeered and sold to raise more dollars or used as collateral to guarantee further dollar loans. Keynes estimated that within a few weeks the reserves would run out and Britain would be obliged to sue for peace. Typically, this left him ambivalent: after all a negotiated peace rather than a long, drawn-out fight to the finish was what he wanted.

Paradoxically the situation was relieved from an unexpected quarter: the commencement by the Germans of unrestricted submarine warfare. Most people believe this was nearly the cause of a British defeat in 1917—in fact it was a disastrous German mistake which saved Britain from default, brought the US into the war, and ensured the Germans were ultimately defeated. The Germans did not in fact have enough superiority in submarine warfare to prevail in the long run. But the immediate disruption to transatlantic shipping meant that there were fewer American bills to pay; and in a short while it brought the US into the war and removed all compunctions about British loans. Keynes was left again pondering the irony that his financial dexterity had helped to keep Britain afloat, to pursue the unlimited war aims he detested.

The overall result was that by the end of the war Britain found itself heavily indebted to the US, nominally offset by large debts due from France, Russia, Italy, Serbia, etc. One can see from the figures that Britain was still nominally a net creditor: it had borrowed, not to fund its own expenditures, but the expenditures of other countries. Unfortunately these countries were now most unlikely to pay up while the US would prove to be a relentless creditor.

Total foreign debts amounted to £1,365 million, most to the US; in addition, the government had forcibly sold £270 million of British-owned foreign securities. Even this does not give the complete magnitude of the loss in Britain's foreign position because many individuals also sold their overseas assets voluntarily, either to maintain their own living standards or to lend the proceeds to the government. Furthermore, the short-term assets of the City of London which had financed pre-war international trade and were the subject of the August 1914 financial crisis were also frittered away as trade dried up. These have been estimated at about £500 million. After the war London never recovered its dominance and much of its business had moved to New York. Thus the overall turnaround of overseas assets is of the order of £2,000 million, about half the pre-war stock and equivalent to nearly a full year's national income.

Table 7.2: British Foreign Debts and Loans at End 1918–19

	Due from: (£million)	Owed to: (£million)
USA	–	1027.3
British Empire	170.9	144.5
France	434.5	–
Russia	568.0	–
Italy	412.5	–
Other Allies	152.8	29.0
Total	1741.1	1364.8

Source: E. V. Morgan.

THE COSTS: PIKETTY

Another way of looking at the losses is provided by the recent book by Thomas Piketty, *Capital in the Twenty-First Century*. Piketty estimates that after the long nineteenth century process of accumulation Britain, like other advanced European nations, had stabilised by 1914 with a capital-output ratio of about seven: that is, its citizens owned capital (of all forms) worth about seven years of national income. By the end of the war this had been reduced to about three years. (Further falls occurred in the Second World War, and we are only now beginning to approach again the levels of capitalisation of 1914.)

This shows that looking at the National Debt alone does not give a full picture of the losses of war. On the one hand the National Debt overestimates, because part of it is owed to other British residents, therefore only a transfer and no overall loss to the economy. On the other hand, the National Debt does not show the loss of assets, both public and private, that might be equally or more significant; nor any increase in private indebtedness.

AFTERMATH AND REPARATIONS

At the end of the war, there were three important and inescapable facts:

1. Almost everybody in Europe was much, much poorer than they were in 1914. To some countries and some people this was immediately and terribly obvious, to others it had not yet really become apparent just how bad it was.
2. Almost everybody owed unrealistically large amounts of money to everybody else. Most individuals didn't even realise this, but there was no way these debts could all be paid to everybody's satisfaction.

Table 7.3: Piketty, National Capital in Europe, 1870–2010

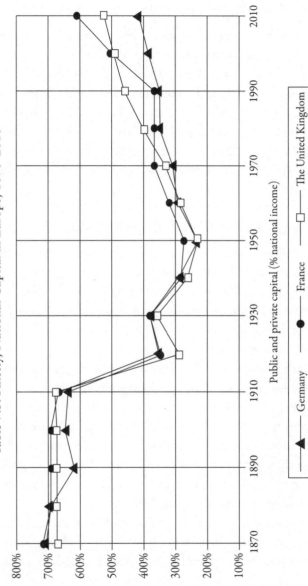

Public and private capital (% national income)

Germany — France — The United Kingdom

Credit: Capital in the Twenty-First Century by Thomas Piketty, translated by Arthur Goldhammer, Cambridge, Mass.: The Belknap Press of Harvard University Press, Copyright © 2014 by the President and Fellows of Harvard College.

3. Everybody blamed everybody else for the impoverishment and had hopelessly unrealistic expectations of compensation.

Therefore, all post-war attempts to restore some kind of pre-war normality of living standards would become a desperate scramble for a larger share of a considerably diminished cake, souring relationships between countries and classes. All demands would inevitably eventually be whittled down. The best tactic would be to pitch one's starting demands as outrageously as possible and then negotiate more intransigently than one's rivals. Not the best recipe for restoring peace and harmony in a post-war world.

THE PARIS PEACE CONFERENCE

As the war came to an end, would there be a financial reckoning? Popular opinion, on all sides, demanded some recompense for the terrible sacrifices. But where could it come from? This was one of the issues facing the Paris Peace Conference, leading to the Treaty of Versailles, to which Keynes was sent as Britain's chief Treasury representative.

Whose fault was the war? To the allies this seemed obvious. The Germans had invaded France and Belgium: it was their fault, so they should pay. But the Germans argued for a wider and longer-term perspective. Subject to an increasing strategic encirclement by France, Russia and Britain, they had been provoked into a desperate attempt to break out before their very survival was threatened. In their view the real fault lay with the pre-war foreign policies of France, Russia and Britain.

And who won the war? How did it end? Again, the allied governments, especially the British and the French, simply thought they had won outright and were entitled to dictate terms. But this again was not the German view—in their eyes they had signed an armistice, not a surrender. An armistice was more like a cease-fire, pending a negotiated (not a dictated) peace settlement, in line with US President Woodrow Wilson's famous Fourteen Points. These had required Germany to 'restore' invaded territory but excluded further financial penalties. German opinion was outraged when the allies eventually presented the Treaty of Versailles as a *diktat*, including heavy financial and other penalties, but by then their military position and social order had completely disintegrated so they could do nothing about it—but the resentment lingered on, and had much to do with the eventual rise of Nazism.

Britain had not been invaded so stood to gain nothing from Woodrow Wilson's formulation, but it had suffered air-raids and some naval bombardment, and lost many merchant ships and sailors, so the British first managed to change the wording to 'all damage done to civilian population and property by German aggression from land, sea and air'. The Treasury estimated total allied losses under this heading would come to about £4,000 million, of which about 15 per cent would be due to Britain. However, they also estimated the maximum Germany could conceivably pay would be only £3,000 million, and that actually £2,000 million would be 'a very satisfactory achievement'.

But between the Armistice and the Paris Peace Conference, public opinion hardened. The French government refused even to commit itself to a figure, on the grounds that any figure would outrage French public opinion as being derisory. Lloyd George, fighting a general election, found that 'squeezing Germany until the pips squeak' was a guaranteed vote-winner. The Australian Prime Minister Hughes demanded that Germany pay the 'total costs of the war', i.e. including the costs of all munitions, service personnel pay, severance allowances (payments to families of absent servicemen), and widows' pensions. Hughes was virulently anti-German, but of course also Australia stood to gain nothing from the more limited formulations, and would gain something from this.

Seizing on this, Lloyd George convinced Woodrow Wilson that severance allowances and pensions were clearly a 'damage done to the civilian population'. Hughes went further, arguing that since all the costs would eventually have to be borne by taxpayers, everything was 'damage done to the civilian population'.

A war cabinet committee chaired by Hughes estimated these total costs (to the allied side) at £24,000 million, which they proposed Germany should pay at the rate of £1,200 million p.a. for 20 years (remember Britain's entire GDP in 1914 was £2,400 million). Keynes and the Treasury roughly agreed with the calculation, although they thought that as a practical proposition it was sheer fantasy. A French estimate was even higher.

Some people seem to have genuinely believed that such fantastic amounts could have been paid by Germany; but most motivations were more cynical. The British negotiators did not seriously believe that Germany could pay a bill including the severance payments and pensions in full, but including them in the demand would increase Britain's proportion of whatever sum Germany could eventually be made to pay—unfortunately France and Belgium would take a much higher share if the calculation were based purely on physical damage.

But there was an additional reason for the victors to make and stand behind these outrageous claims: the toxic web of inter-allied war indebtedness constructed by Keynes and his colleagues. By the end of the war Britain found itself heavily indebted to the US, nominally offset by large debts due from France, Russia, Italy, Serbia, etc. These countries were most unlikely to pay up—Soviet Russia certainly wouldn't, and the others would not unless they could squeeze large sums of money out of Germany. Keynes favoured an all-round cancellation of inter-allied war-debts on the ground that all had been fighting for the same cause, whatever the precise dates of their active participation, and the precise financial terms originally agreed for the assistance were now irrelevant.

This would also kill two birds with one stone, immediately reducing the incentives to make unrealistic claims on Germany.

The US had not suffered greatly directly from German aggression and had no wish to press German reparations unduly. However, American opinion would not necessarily agree that all had been fighting for quite the same cause—a common view was that the war was a typical squabble among irresponsible and archaic European nations which the Americans had ultimately to step in and settle—but it did believe strongly in financial rectitude. A loan was a loan and must be repaid on the agreed terms, so paradoxically the US treated its former allies more harshly than its former enemies. But if the US was intransigent on its British loans, Britain would in turn depend on France paying its, and France would not do that unless it could extract the money from Germany.

So almost all the negotiators except the Americans believed that having raised public expectations to unrealistic levels it would be political suicide at home to be seen to accept any 'reasonable' sum; and the Americans believed it would be political suicide not to insist on their loans and let the Europeans 'get away with it'. In such ways any mutual agreement on reasonable and sustainable levels of compensation which might wipe the slate clean and leave the way clear for a resumption of normal peacetime economic relations became simply impossible. In fact, the Peace Conference ultimately failed to reach agreement on a sum, deferring the issue—without a ceiling—to a subsequent Reparations Commission, leading to years of uncertainty: perhaps the worst of all possible outcomes. (This Commission eventually decided on a figure of £6 billion, but it was still a fantasy.) Various post-war conferences to sort out the reparations tangle continued to flounder with all parties still demanding totally unrealistic and mutually conflicting positions. Eventually the sums were watered down and watered down, and in the end only relatively small sums of money were actually paid, but the resentments and uncertainties contributed indirectly, and occasionally directly, to the dismal economic performance of the 1920s and 1930s.

8

THE INTER-WAR YEARS

When the war came to an end, the Debt had changed both quantitatively and qualitatively. First and most obviously, it was much, much larger—dangerously so to most contemporary opinion.

Its maturity structure had changed dramatically too. Whereas the vast majority of the pre-war Debt had been perpetual Consols (see Appendix I), these now formed only a small minority. None of the debt issued in the war had been of this form. Even the longer-term debt issued had redemption dates, some of which were not too far away. Worse, there was a lot of medium-term debt, with maturities less than ten years, and a very large short-term floating debt, neither of which had figured significantly in the pre-war debt. There was also now an explicitly foreign component: a loan in US dollars.

And considerable inflation had occurred during the war; the price level was now roughly double what it was in 1914 and the foreign exchange value of the pound had slipped below its official gold-standard benchmark. If the return to peacetime normality would also imply a return to the pre-war gold standard (and that

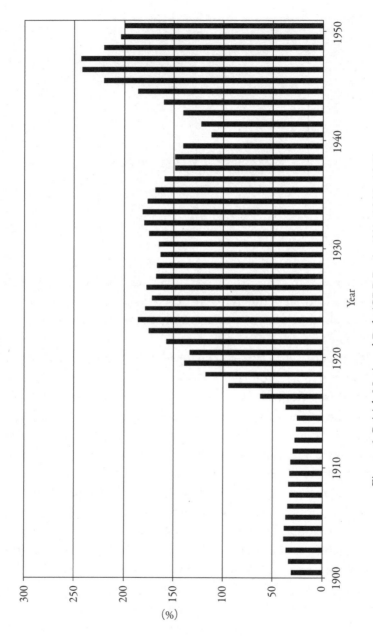

Figure 6: British National Debt/GDP Ratio (%), 1900–1950

was the expectation of the time, for a depreciation of the currency in terms of gold was viewed as akin to a default; and even if British citizens might swallow such a pill, the new US creditors certainly would not), the price level would have to fall again to restore international competitiveness. Thus, debt which had been incurred in a depreciated currency would have to be repaid in a more valuable one, increasing the real value of the debt burden.

The problems facing the government were therefore many. First it had to eradicate the budget deficit to prevent the Debt growing still further. Then it had to reduce the floating debt, which was both a constant threat to the government's credit with its continuous refinancing demands and was a dangerous boost to bank liquidity, exacerbating the inflationary threat. And finally it had to decide what to do with the main body of the National Debt itself. Here the alternatives were the usual: to attempt to repay it; or to attempt to convert it to a more stable, longer-term form; or to attempt to reduce the interest payable on it—or some combination of all three.

'DRASTIC' REPAYMENT?

As was to be expected, there was a lively debate about the desirability and possibilities of rapid repayment. If this was to be the choice, speed was of the essence, before prices fell and the real value of the Debt increased. The problem of course was the sheer enormity of the task. Equally, the enormity was itself a good argument for trying to do something: how could the country cope with any future emergency with an existing debt overhang of this size? The Labour Party favoured a levy on wealth, and quite elaborate proposals were drawn up by Frederick Pethick Lawrence to show that this might be administratively feasible.[1]

Frederick Pethick Lawrence (1871–1961) is largely forgotten today, but he was a significant if eccentric political figure. Born

Frederick Lawrence to a wealthy self-made builder, he was educated at Eton (unhappily) and Trinity College Cambridge (more happily), but social conscience and a strong but individual religious sense combining Christian and Indian influences drew him into left-wing social work and political activity. A conscientious objector in WWI, on marriage he unusually added his wife's name Pethick to his own, and with her became one of the most important organisers of the movement for women's suffrage. Both served spells in prison for this cause but were later expelled from the movement after differences with the Pankhursts. He became a Labour MP and specialised in financial affairs, serving as a Treasury minister in the 1920s, as Leader of the Parliamentary Opposition in the Second World War and as Secretary of State for India in the years leading up to independence. Highly intelligent, but personally eccentric and mild-mannered to a disconcerting degree, he and his wife formed an enduring team well-known for supporting all radical causes in a very English un-radical fashion; but this combination of characteristics meant that he did not achieve the very highest political offices.

Much was made of the analogy that labour had been conscripted during the war, and it was only fair that wealth should be subject to conscription too. But whether such proposals might indeed be ultimately feasible or not, the magnitude of the required transactions would have increased market uncertainties at a time when the government's credit was already very fragile and it was facing almost day-to-day financing crises. Policymakers shrank from the consequences, time passed, and soon the drastic repayment option fell out of the realm of practical politics. The matter was referred to a committee—always a favourite avenue for governments hoping to bury a troublesome issue. By the time the Colwyn Committee's report appeared in 1927, with inevitably an ambivalent recommendation, the time for action was long past.[2]

Nevertheless, the Colwyn Committee's report, and the submissions to it from many notable people, make interesting reading. Keynes gave evidence to the committee: he was initially attracted to the idea of rapid repayment through a capital levy but was convinced by the calculations of Pigou and Josiah Stamp that the net yield of such a levy would be disappointing. High rates of income tax and death duties were already doing a similar job, although more slowly, and much of the yield of a capital levy would be at their expense. One suggestion he made, which was not taken up at the time but eventually became successful in the 1980s, was for index-linked bonds.

Another proponent of very radical measures was Major Clifford Hugh Douglas (1879–1952). Douglas was an engineer who had worked in his early career in various parts of the British Empire, but in the First World War was sent to reorganise the accounting system of the Royal Aircraft Establishment at Farnborough. From his experiences there he became convinced that the capitalist system had a logical flaw: that the incomes generated by production cannot amount to a sum able to purchase the output of that production. This created an inbuilt bias towards slumps and depressions, which were only warded off by the ever-increasing injection of loans by the banking system: loans which in a paper- and bank-money system could be created cost-free by the banks who nevertheless charged exorbitantly for the privilege. The inevitable result was instability and crises, but large profits for the banks. The solution lay in Social Credit, a kind of nationalisation of money and credit: the government would provide, direct to each individual citizen, non-interest-bearing paper credit just sufficient to ensure the national output could be purchased. The amounts of these credits could be increased or decreased as external conditions varied. The exploitative role of banks would be removed.

In such a world-view the National Debt did not really exist: it was just another of the exploitative loans created by the banking system out of nothing, most of it being held directly or indirectly by the banks themselves. As such, the holders had no real claim to interest and should simply be paid off with the government's new non-interest-bearing credit instruments—effectively a monetisation of the debt—and these instruments would subsequently be managed (i.e. augmented or taken away according to circumstance) as part of the total Social Credit supplied by the government in response to macroeconomic conditions.

In the depressed conditions of the 1920s and 1930s, the message of Social Credit struck a chord. Its under-consumptionist theory seemed to provide an explanation of unemployment and unsaleable outputs, and its anti-finance overtones found ready listeners. Many Social Credit political parties sprang up in Britain and elsewhere, with particular success in agrarian parts of the British Empire. For a time a Social Credit party even formed the government of the Canadian province of Alberta.

The problem, however, was that the whole enterprise was based on a fundamental—and frankly embarrassing—error;[3] Douglas's original insight that total income in a capitalist system cannot add up to total production is simply not true. Correct identification of various loose ends is bound by definition to make the two coincide. There will be a mismatch of timing in the realisations of different elements of output and income, which will certainly require some smoothing over by some kind of financial system, but that is a very different matter. While Douglas' diagnosis and prescription have some similarities with Keynesianism, Keynes avoided Douglas' error: in Keynes' theory it is not logically impossible for consumers and firms to purchase the whole of an economy's potential output; but there are obvious behavioural reasons why they might choose not to do so. It is these behavioural reasons that policy must act upon, making for a more subtle and difficult policy process than Douglas suggests. In time the Keynesian approach effectively saw off Social Credit.

It is also difficult to avoid seeing in Social Credit echoes of many earlier disasters associated with the manipulation of unlimited pure paper credit schemes by governments. In principle, so long as the public retains confidence in the government's credit, they might work. But history shows that, without some kind of external underpinning, time and again the public is likely to lose this confidence, leading to a catastrophic collapse. Such was the case with Downing's Orders of Repayment, with John Law's attempt at a wholly paper currency in eighteenth century France, with the *Assignats* of post-revolutionary France, even with the original tally system. More recently we can point to countries like Zimbabwe and Venezuela. It is not obvious how Douglas' scheme could guarantee to avoid such an outcome. (That said, one must concede that most late twentieth and early twenty-first century governments have become rather better at managing purely paper currency systems.)

But Social Credit was not simply an economic theory. Douglas also imbued it with a philosophy, with religious overtones, and with a political theory which was distinctly undemocratic. Although orthodox opinion almost unanimously dismissed it as nonsense—and it certainly made no headway with government committees—it attracted an astonishing range of support from the heterodox, the populist and the disaffected; some entirely high-minded and well-meaning, many distinctly cranky, but also others of a more unsavoury character. Its anti-finance message tended to spill over into xenophobia and anti-semitism, and it attracted supporters from fascist parties. One interesting personality who combined strong views on national debt with Social Credit theory and flirtations with fascism was the poet Ezra Pound—see his *Cantos*.

The Social Credit movement was not itself a single, centralised party;[4] many ambitious would-be leaders set up their own variants, and some of these began to organise themselves along fas-

Economists' Views on the National Debt:
7. John Maynard Keynes

John Maynard Keynes (1883–1946) grew up in the late-Victorian world of a large but very comfortable perpetual National Debt, but most of his career was played out in a very different world of truly massive, intolerable, unstable, almost inexplicable debts. So his attitude to debt was rather ambivalent. Although he had no compunction about resorting to borrowing in emergencies such as wars and economic crises, he was concerned that the legacy of debt should not create more problems than the borrowing had solved. He inveighed bitterly against the dead hand of interest payments and reparation payments. Debt might be a useful servant of public policy, but it should not become the master. He did not believe in the inviolability of debt. If debts became intolerable they should certainly be revised. Unrealistic levels of debt were simply crippling to sensible economic decision-making. This was true both for debtors and creditors, at an individual and at a public level, nationally and internationally.

In the aftermath of the First World War, he was initially attracted to the idea of rapid repayment through a capital levy, but eventually concluded that the result would be disappointing. He perceived the burden of the debt as a distributional issue and therefore a part of overall tax and welfare policy. Radical shifts in wealth and disappointments of expectations were neither expedient nor fair, and he looked more to the steady effects of economic growth, high taxation and moderate inflation to bring about a long-term, relatively less painful 'euthanasia of the rentier'. Although in popular caricature his name is always linked with deficit financing, in fact his ideal macroeconomic policy was one of alternating surpluses and deficits, producing cyclical swings in the national debt but no pronounced trend.

cist lines. Readers will obviously know of Oswald Mosley's Black Shirts; they are probably less likely to have heard of the Social Credit movement's Green Shirts.

After the Second World War, with the eclipse of fascist and quasi-fascist politics and the success of Keynesian economic policies, Social Credit declined, but it continued to exist as a very fringe movement. In the post-2008 malaise, and with the help of the internet, similar views are perhaps beginning to re-emerge.

THE FLOATING DEBT

The immediate consequence of peace was to increase rather than reduce the problem of the floating debt. The government budget did not immediately return to surplus. Large military commitments continued in the uncertainties of the time. Over the course of the war the government had taken on social welfare commitments that could not be reversed. The debt interest burden had grown enormously—by 1925 debt servicing payments accounted for over 40 per cent of the total budget.[5] But an exhausted public expected taxes to fall quickly. Borrowing had to continue, preventing interest rates from falling. The relaxation of controls, and the bloated liquidity of the financial sector unleashed a pent-up demand for consumer goods which produced a sharp surge in inflation. The government could be forced into further short-run borrowing, increasing liquidity further and threatening to produce a classic inflationary cycle.

Ironically, although the government had not formally suspended the gold standard during the war, it had to do so in 1919. During the war the government could rely on internal controls and the natural wartime risks of exporting gold to limit the potential drain due to a trade deficit. When these were removed the weakness of the international position was only too apparent. Restoring the gold standard then became an overriding policy objective, providing another reason why interest rates had to be kept high. The gold standard was indeed restored in 1925, but the effort to maintain it proved too much. In 1931 the government gave up the struggle and allowed the pound to float and interest rates to fall.

Table 8.1: Post-First World War Finance

	Government Revenue (£million)	Government Expenditure (£million)	Primary Surplus (+) or Deficit (−) (£million)	Internal National Debt at end-year (£million)
1919–20	1339.6	1665.8	−326.2	6599.2
1920–21	1426.0	1195.4	+230.6	6453.3
1921–22	1125.0	1079.2	+45.8	6589.0
1922–23	914.0	812.5	+101.5	6614.8
1923–24	837.2	788.8	+48.4	6552.9
1924–25	799.4	795.8	+3.6	6522.8

Source: E. V. Morgan.

But by 1920 the government was able to bring the inflationary boom to an end. The sale of surplus war supplies disguised the budget deficit, and the government announced a commitment to balance the budget and an end to future net borrowing. It further announced a cap on the issue of paper currency and raised the Bank Rate to 7 per cent. Prices fell dramatically. It was probably over-done, and a slump ensued, but after this point the floating debt, particularly the Ways and Means Advances, fell steadily. The interest payable on Treasury Bills also fell, from nearly 7 per cent to 2 per cent before recovering to about 4.5 per cent.

Treasury Bill holders were also wooed with a new Treasury Bond, a medium-term (five years) security at 5 per cent, but with a provision for matching increases in the interest rates if Treasury Bill rates rose. Thus bill-holders could be tempted into a more stable longer-term security without losing the possibility of profiting from any future spike in short-term rates.

In these ways the problem of the floating debt had been largely overcome by the mid 1920s.

With the immediate crisis weathered, and radical repayment ruled out, politicians unsurprisingly returned to the Sinking Fund, which had been suspended during the war. In 1923, Stanley Baldwin introduced a new variant: while the current budget would be responsible for all interest charges, there would be an annual Fixed Capital Repayment, beginning at £40 million and rising to £50 million. The Colwyn Committee criticised this as inadequate, and it was replaced by Winston Churchill in 1928 by a Fixed Debt Charge of £355 million, to cover all interest and repayment, so not unlike the Northcote scheme—although of course enormously bigger. However, Churchill continually undermined its purpose by various sleights of hand, and ironically it was his successor Philip Snowden, the first Labour Chancellor of the Exchequer, who proved perhaps the most fervent fiscal conservative of all. His attempt to maintain the Sinking Fund, balanced budgets and utmost fiscal rectitude through the worst stages of the depression eventually split the Labour government. In subsequent Labour Party mythology, Snowden ranks as one of the great class traitors.

STABILISING THE MEDIUM-TERM DEBT

After the floating debt, the next most pressing problem was the approaching maturity of much of the medium-term debt issued during the later stages of the war. In some cases this was rolled over into new medium-term debt. War Bonds and Exchequer Bonds were replaced by Treasury Bonds of similar maturities.

But increasingly the aim was to replace with longer-term issues if possible.

In 1921, the first of these was the 3.5 per cent Conversion Loan, redeemable after 1961, originally issued to replace £600 million of expiring War Bonds, with subsequent issues for cash and to replace further expiring bonds. This was notable as being the first return to a perpetuity with no fixed redemption date. However the wisdom of its timing was questionable: despite the low nominal coupon of 3.5 per cent—probably chosen to indicate a desired return to peacetime interest rates—the market rate interest rate had not fallen, so the issue had to be floated considerably under par, at an effective interest rate of over 5 per cent, which was now locked in until 1961. A more sensible course might have been to refinance one more time with a medium-term issue until interest rates did fall—which would then be the time to lock in a long-term rate. However, the over-riding political objective of the time was to increase the maturity of debt to remove the permanent feeling of near-crisis over forthcoming redemptions, so policymakers probably wanted to make a statement, and were perhaps a little blind to its long-term costs.

Other conversion loans followed, although these did have fixed redemption dates at twenty to forty years' distance. In 1927 there was another perpetuity issue: 4 per cent Consols, redeemable after 1957. Issued at eighty-five, again this conceded an interest rate close to 5 per cent for at least thirty years.

By far the largest problem was the 5 per cent War Loan issued in 1917. Over £2 billion of this stock existed, and it was repayable between 1929 and 1947. The government's greatest nightmare was having to repay or refinance such an enormous sum in one go, perhaps at an unfortunate time in the markets. But at least after 1929, although not before, there would be a possibility of interest rate conversion. Unfortunately, as we have seen, interest rates initially remained high, first because of the government's continual need to refinance the floating debt, and secondly to support the exchange rate. But the government gradually got on top of the floating debt, and in 1931 finally gave up the attempt to maintain the pre-war gold-standard parity, allowing market interest rates to fall. This in turn allowed the Chancellor Neville Chamberlain to execute an ambitious but successful conversion scheme in 1932, reducing the interest rate to 3.5 per cent, and converting the stock to a perpetuity, redeemable after 1952.[6] Finally the government had been able to achieve its ideal objective of simultaneously increasing maturity and reducing the interest burden. The reduction of the interest burden was very significant—1.5 per cent of £2 billion is £30 million per year. This conversion also marked a dramatic change in the interest-rate climate. For the remainder of the 1930s the government was able to pursue a cheap money policy, with short-term interest rates falling as low as 1 per cent and long-term rates around 3 per cent, so that the interest burden gradually fell further over the period.

REPARATIONS AND INTER-ALLIED LOANS

Attempts to come to terms with the Debt were seriously hampered by the uncertainties surrounding German reparation payments and the inter-allied loans. Why should the country undertake painful measures when there was a possibility that the debts might still be paid off by foreigners? On paper Britain's position looked quite good. It might expect large reparations payments from Germany, and although it owed large loans to the US, these were more than covered by debts due from its former European allies. But in reality, Germany and the allies were unlikely to pay up.

The allied debts were also closely intertwined with German reparations. Fairly soon the British government recognised the futility of German reparations and lost enthusiasm for the pursuit of its own case. But the US was pressing Britain on its loans, and the allies would only pay their British debts if they could extract the money in turn from Germany, so the fruitless attempt to squeeze money out of Germany had to continue. The British government came around to Keynes' view that the best solution was an all-round cancellation of debts, but this was not supported by the US. Attempting to find a way through the tangle, Britain gave out confusing messages. It first announced (the Balfour Note in 1922) that in the absence of an all-round cancellation it would only pursue its European debtors to the extent necessary to cover its own position relative to the US. Later it went further, intimating that it would only consider itself bound to the US to the extent that the European debtors did pay up. This was not a position that the US accepted, but it did unfortunately remove any remaining incentive for the Europeans to pay up. Nevertheless, to set an example of financial good faith, in 1923 the Chancellor Stanley Baldwin negotiated a bilateral long-term settlement of the US loans. These negotiations were fractious on two fronts: first the British negotiators were surprised by American intransigence, and then when Baldwin returned with what he considered the best, although disappointing, deal he could achieve, Prime Minister Andrew Bonar Law threatened to resign on the grounds that the country could not afford the terms. But Bonar Law was persuaded to give way; anyway, he soon resigned because of poor health, leaving Baldwin himself to become Prime Minister. For a while Britain therefore followed the terms of the negotiated settlement.

The American-sponsored Dawes Plan of 1926 and Young Plan of 1930 attempted to find feasible solutions which would deliver at least some money from Germany, but when the latter was almost immediately rendered unworkable with the onset of the great depression, the nations finally gave up the struggle. In 1932 an international conference at Lausanne recognised that reparations were dead. The European nations further recognised that as a result the inter-allied loans were also dead, but this was still not accepted by the US. The British simply stopped paying interest to the US—clearly a default since there had been nothing in the Baldwin settlement about payment being contingent on other events. The US did not retaliate, but nor did it forget. This would cause significant problems at the beginning of the Second World War when Britain again wanted American assistance.

By the end of the 1930s, the government could at least claim that it had stabilised the Debt. As in the nineteenth century, it had not managed to pay off any significant part of it (unless one counts the default on the US loan), but the Debt/GDP ratio was beginning to fall. The government had also tamed the floating debt, lengthened the maturity structure and reduced the interest payable. Government creditworthiness was no longer seriously at risk. The interest burden was still an unfortunately large proportion of the government budget, but the country had adjusted to the higher tax rates that this necessitated. Given another century of peace and economic growth, things might not have turned out too badly at all.

9

THE SECOND WORLD WAR

FINANCIAL STRATEGY, DOMESTIC BORROWING AND TAXATION

The country entered the Second World War in some ways better placed, in some ways worse, than in 1914. This latest conflict did not come as so much of a surprise as the first, and elaborate plans had already been made in advance. But, as is often the case, the most important planning assumption turned out to be wildly optimistic. In 1939, as in 1914, the hope was for a limited, short war. Officials were instructed to plan for a three-year conflict, in the first half of which the British and French armed forces would contain Germany while building up their strength for a decisive offensive. As the war did indeed get off to a relatively quiet start, resources were carefully husbanded for the long-term. But with the fall of France in May 1940, and the imminent danger of invasion and defeat, everything changed: the strategy now became 'money no object'. Everything would be mobilised and if necessary sacrificed to avoid defeat, whatever the consequences. The objective was achieved, but the reckoning would be severe. If, in

Churchill's words, 'This was their finest hour', it was also their most costly.

On the other hand, important lessons had been learnt from the First World War; the current generation of officials had direct experience of that war and were determined not to repeat its mistakes.[1] Perhaps the most fundamental difference, and one reinforced by inter-war experience, was a greater scepticism about the ability of normal market forces to cope with the abnormal demands of wartime. For the first half of the First World War the government's policy had been 'Business as Usual'—as little interference as possible with normal market relationships. Supplies had been bought at market prices, capital and foreign exchange markets had been kept open as far as possible. But in the face of such large shifts in the demand for resources, prices had understandably reacted on a similarly large scale, raising costs and creating inflation, rising interest rates and difficulties in maintaining foreign exchange parities. Over time the government had learnt that in many cases only direct controls could achieve its objectives. So this time, officials had resolved to run a more controlled economy from the outset, superseding the price mechanism and allocating resources more directly through a widespread control of prices and quantities. This worked well in practice during the period of the war.

However, the country would start with a larger debt, already high tax levels and a considerably weaker international financial position, so its ability to rely on the normal market mechanisms was anyway severely limited.

In their borrowing strategy, officials particularly wanted to avoid the expensive increasing interest rates of the first war. The new macroeconomic theories devised by Keynes in his *General Theory* of 1936 were now beginning to seep into the administrative consciousness, and they had included a theory that rates of interest were heavily influenced by expectations of their own future courses in a sort of self-fulfilling feedback. It was therefore decided that all long-term borrowing should occur at no more than 3 per cent, and public commitments would be given to that effect: the public must in no way be allowed to think that the government might weaken in this resolve. This would be easier to achieve, because this time the government would more comprehensively control the banking system and could thereby engineer that there would be fewer alternatives for the public's savings and their terms would be no more generous. It also helped that the public had become used to very low interest rates in the depression years, and economic opinion had grown very dubious about the incentive effects of interest rates on the volume of savings.

The massive single War Loan of 1917 was generally considered to have been a mistake: it was argued that different groups of investors had different time preferences and requirements, so that a series of smaller issues with differing terms would exploit the market more effectively; and the single large redemption requirement had stored up problems for a future date. So instead a series of smaller War Bonds (usually of about five to ten years' duration) and Savings Bonds (usually about twenty years' duration) were marketed with differing redemption dates—but all with interest rates of 2.5 or 3 per cent. These bond issues were a reasonable but not outstanding success.

Significant sums were raised on shorter terms through Treasury Bills and two new instruments, Treasury Deposit Receipts and Tax Reserve Certificates. Treasury Deposit Receipts were a way of mopping up excess liquidity in banks: the Treasury could simply call money in from banks, giving TDRs in return. TDRs were of six months duration, interest-bearing at 1.125 per cent (just a little higher than the typical 1 per cent then payable on Treasury Bills), but not negotiable. They were intended to be a little less liquid than Treasury Bills, and therefore less likely to fuel credit expansion. Tax Reserve Certificates were a way of keeping money out of the banks in the first place. In normal times private individuals would usually set aside money in their bank accounts against future tax demands: TRCs offered instead a tax-free interest rate of 1 per cent outside the banking system. Both measures were quite successful in restraining bank liquidity.

But the government could afford to be rather more relaxed on bank liquidity in this war. With comprehensive rationing and price controls, it was more difficult for excess liquidity to fuel inflation. With few outlets, consumers were effectively forced into saving.

This is shown by the very significant contribution of 'Small Savings': National Savings Certificates, Post Office Savings and Post-war Credits (a form of forced saving through the income tax system devised by Keynes) accounted for nearly £4,000 million over the course of the war, as against nearly £6,000 million from the large longer-term issues. Increase in the floating debt accounted for another £5,000 million.

At the end of the war the domestic National Debt had therefore increased by over £15,000 million. Britain had entered the war with a debt of about £8,000 million; by the time the American loan (see next section) had been negotiated it would rise to £25,000 million, and 240 per cent of GDP. This was worse than the previous peak of the 1820s. In fact, it was a lot worse: the productive and exporting capacity of the economy had been severely damaged in a way that had not occurred in the Napoleonic Wars. What remained of the country's foreign assets after the First World War had now been almost entirely dissipated. There was now also a significant dollar debt (discussed later in this chapter) and overseas sterling debts to empire and Commonwealth countries; and unlike in 1918 there were no offsetting credits with other countries, however unrealistic. Much of the Debt was short-term with redemptions looming.

Although the government had comprehensive controls over the economy, so that a lid could be kept on some of these pressures for some time, the vague commitment under Lend-Lease (see next section) had now crystallised into American pressure to dismantle controls and construct a free trade, free movement of capital, fixed exchange rate international system as soon as possible. British policymakers felt that the British economy could not survive such a shock.

FOREIGN BORROWING: THE US

As in the First World War the problems of obtaining supplies from the US would be a constant headache. Things started off worse. US dissatisfaction with its experience last time around had led it to take an isolationist turn in the 1930s. Two new laws would limit considerably what Britain could expect from the US.

The US Neutrality Acts had reversed a neutral country's usual wish to assert its right to carry on its normal activities with any belligerent power unmolested by that power's enemies. Experience had taught the US that those normal activities would inevitably come under threat, would need defending, and would likely end in sucking the US into hostilities. To avoid this US citizens were instead required to limit their activities with any belligerent power. Armaments could not be sold, loans and credit could not be offered, merchant ships could not carry goods of or visit ports of belligerent powers.

The Johnson Act of 1934 prohibited any financial transaction, public or private, with any country that had defaulted on an obligation to the US. As its date suggests, the Johnson Act was of course inspired by Britain's default on its First World War loans from the US when it became clear that it could not extract the counterpart loans from its other allies, so Britain fell foul of this act too.

The combined effects of these acts practically ruled out any significant economic relations with the US after the outbreak of war. But the Roosevelt government initially relaxed its stance to the so-called 'cash and carry' arrangements: Britain could buy armaments for dollars in cash, and transport them in its own ships. But the country's gold and dollar reserves were now more limited, British factories could not spare many resources for exports to the US, and the submarine threat to the exportation of both gold and goods was greater (although the US helpfully— or unhelpfully—sent a warship to South Africa to collect all the gold stocks there). The only way of mobilising more dollars was commandeering and selling all of Britain's financial assets in the US and Latin America.

However, with the fall of France, and British intimations that they had nearly exhausted all their dollar resources, Roosevelt looked for a way around the legal obstacles, and found it in an obscure nineteenth century act empowering the Secretary for War to lease army property for the public good. In the US's own interest, it would therefore lease, not sell, war materials to Britain; not in exchange for money but in exchange for some vague non-monetary 'consideration'. The US's interest was clearly its own defence, but the American public was not ready to enter the war itself; the 'lease' was a fiction, because it was hardly likely most of the material could be returned; and the consideration was left unspecified. Creative finance indeed. This, to be known as Lend-Lease (and later more officially 'Reciprocal Assistance'—Britain returned the compliment where possible, sharing technology and supplying US forces with material in some parts of the world) became the structure of US support to Britain for the rest of the war. In this way, very large quantities of material—war supplies and essential food and other civilian supplies—were transferred to Britain without creating financial debt.

However not all of Britain's purchases were forgiven in this way. Payments made before this date were not refunded. Some supplies remained outside the terms of Lend-Lease and Britain had to continue to pay for those. Most importantly there was a period between the announcement of the proposal and the enactment of the necessary legislation, during which Britain continued to place large orders, in the belief, but without explicit confirmation, that these would be covered by the eventual legislation. In fact, they were not, and they remained a bone of contention between the US and Britain for the rest of the war.

One of the aims of Lend-Lease was to ensure that the second war did not end, as the first, with a toxic web of indebtedness among the allies (and after the war the Marshall Plan attempted to do the same for the defeated and occupied countries). In this it was only partially successful. The remaining financial debts were large enough in themselves to be insupportable, and the question of the unspecified non-financial consideration (now called Article VII) became itself a significant cause of friction as the war progressed to its conclusion. At the end of the war the Lend-Lease scheme was terminated almost immediately, with no transitional period, leaving Britain with little time to adjust and further large bills for deliveries in the pipeline.

FOREIGN BORROWING: THE STERLING BALANCES

Britain's foreign expenditure was not confined to the US though. Large expenditures had been made in almost every other part of the world open to Britain: for food, raw materials, war materials, and the local provisioning of troops stationed overseas. In some ways this was easier, in others more difficult. The difficult part was that here there was no equivalent of Lend-Lease. These countries did not have the immense wealth of the US and would expect to be paid in some way. Inevitably this would either consume precious current resources or leave a debt to be repaid.

The easier part, though, was that many countries would accept payment in sterling, most obviously the countries of the 'sterling area'. These were mostly the countries of the British Empire and Commonwealth, but also some others like Egypt and Iraq. Since the collapse of the gold standard in 1931, these countries had tended to maintain their currencies in parity with sterling and hold their reserves of foreign currency in sterling in London—in short, they looked to London as their financial centre. They were therefore less likely to require payment in the desperately scarce dollars.

But that was only half the battle. If they could be paid in sterling, what realistically could they do with their receipts? In normal peacetime conditions they could buy British exports in return, or exchange their receipts, say, into dollars and buy American goods instead. But the British had no ability to supply exports in the circumstances of the war, nor any spare dollars to allow an exchange. So payment was made into sterling accounts in London which were simply 'blocked' for the duration of the war. Only after the war, and then at the discretion of the British government, would these countries be allowed to touch their money. By the end of the war there was about £3.5 billion in these 'sterling balances'.

Why did the sterling area countries accept such an unfavourable deal? Partly through patriotic solidarity, but also simply because they had little alternative. There were no other markets open for their produce. They would need to rely on their British market contacts in the post-war world. Better an uncertain claim to be exercised at some time in the future than nothing. Although Britain had little bargaining power with the US, it still did have with these smaller countries, and it did not hesitate to exert it.

But after the war, Britain's basic problems remained. The country was still desperately short of dollars and export capacity and had no realistic possibility of paying off such a large sum in any reasonable number of years. Many British officials would have preferred them to remain blocked for ever, but this conflicted with the commitments to convertibility given in the Bretton Woods agreement (commitments which ironically were required by the US as part of the 'compensation' for Lend-Lease). But if they were made convertible the danger would be that the holders would immediately convert them to dollars, which British foreign exchange reserves could not cope with.

In many ways these sterling balances can be seen as another twentieth-century equivalent of the excess supply of tallies that had so worried early eighteenth century governments. IOUs for out-of-control war debts that the government could neither quite repudiate nor quite honour, cast a shadow over the public credit in much the same way. The sterling balances became the bane of British macroeconomic policy for the next thirty years. Once some degree of convertibility was restored, each successive balance of payments crisis was magnified by the threat of flight of the sterling balances. Only with the collapse of the Bretton Woods system in the early 1970s, the ending of the sterling area, the floating of the pound and the eventual abolition of exchange controls did the problem finally evaporate.

THE AFTERMATH

'The financial problems of the war have been surmounted so easily and so silently that the average man sees no reason to suppose that the financial problems of the peace will be any more difficult.'

John Maynard Keynes

'There can be no greater error than to expect or calculate upon real favours from nation to nation.'

George Washington

By the end of the Second World War, the Debt had increased to about £25 billion, or 240 per cent of GDP—its highest ever ratio. However, despite its magnitude, the domestic debt created surprisingly little difficulty for economic policy in the post-war period. As we have seen, interest rates were very low and remained low for some years. The government's direct controls over the banks and the financial system limited the dangers from the apparently large overhang of liquidity and made it relatively easy to refinance the Debt as it matured. In the longer term economic growth and the appearance of an underlying relentless inflationary trend (although the latter was obviously problematic for other aspects of policy) steadily reduced the relative significance and real value of the Debt without there being any significant actual repayment in money terms.

The real dangers this time came from overseas indebtedness, much smaller in total magnitude, but much more demanding in interest servicing and repayment. There were two important elements of the overseas debt: a new US loan, and the so-called 'sterling balances'.

THE US LOAN

The purpose of Lend-Lease had been to ensure that there would be no repetition of the inter-allied loan problem of the First World War. The second war should ideally have ended with no indebtedness between Britain and the US. As we have seen this was only partially successful. Vast quantities of food and materials had indeed been supplied without creating a debt, but some disputed debts were outstanding from the pre-Lend-Lease period, and from deliveries outside the Lend-Lease framework. But these in themselves could have been manageable. The real problem lay in what Lend-Lease had allowed the British to do to their economy during the war years.

Britain was an open economy. In peace time it depended on large imports of food to feed its population and raw materials to supply its industries. These were paid for through the earnings of its exports and the income from its large foreign investments. It is very important to realise that, contrary to the impression usually given in elementary textbooks, for Britain in 1914 the latter component was as large as the former. But its foreign investments had now, in two world wars, almost completely been sold off, and its export industries had been severely run down in the war: there had been little new investment, plant had not been maintained, shipping to the extent of its entire pre-war merchant fleet had been sunk, skilled workforces were dispersed through the armed services (42 per cent of the workforce was in the armed services), and market contacts had been lost. All the resources of the economy had been devoted to the one, all-consuming object. Paradoxically, during the war this had not been a problem—because of Lend-Lease. The US sent food and raw materials as well as war materials, free of charge. But immediately after the war was over Lend-Lease stopped. Only in peacetime would it become apparent just how badly Britain had impoverished itself in the pursuit of victory.

The realisation was brutally sudden. It had been envisaged that the war against Germany would end in early 1945, but against Japan it would continue for another eighteen months, during which there would be discussions between Britain and the US on a smooth transition to peace. But events accelerated unpredictably. President Roosevelt died in April 1945, to be succeeded by Harry S. Truman. Germany surrendered in May. On 26 July a new Labour government was surprisingly elected to replace the wartime Churchill coalition government; on 6 August an atomic bomb was dropped on Hiroshima; on 15 August Japan surrendered; on 2 September the US terminated Lend-Lease with immediate effect. Supplies currently on the sea would now have to be paid for. New and unfamiliar governments on both sides of the Atlantic were suddenly confronted in a matter of days by a completely new situation.

The British were horrified and aggrieved, but they should not have been. The US Congress had made absolutely clear that, whatever cosy understandings there might have been between Churchill and Roosevelt, Lend-Lease was for the war only and not for post-war re-adjustment and reconstruction.

But to give some idea of the British problem, as new Prime Minister Clement Attlee explained to Parliament in August 1945: 'Our overseas outgoings on the eve of the defeat of Japan were equivalent to expenditure at the rate of about £2000 million a year, including the essential food and other non-essential supplies which we have received hitherto under Lend-Lease but now must pay for. Towards this total in the present year, 1945, our exports are contributing £350 million and certain sources of income, mainly temporary, such as receipts from the United States Forces in this country and reimbursements from the Dominions of war expenditure which we have incurred on their behalf, £450 million.'

Thus, at best, a shortfall of £1,200 million p.a. Exports were running at only 30 per cent of their pre-war level. Although the import bill contained war supplies which could now be run down, they were by no means the only component. Anyway, the peace was only going to be relative, and significant military expenditures all over the world would continue for the foreseeable future.

The Treasury estimated an unavoidable trade deficit of £750 million in 1946, £500 million more in the next two years, until industrial readjustment was able to bring foreign payments into balance. Given the devastation of the rest of the world, the necessary supplies could only be obtained from the American continents, requiring payment in dollars which Britain did not have. At the going exchange rate, the requirement was $5 billion, just to keep the economy afloat for the next three years. On top of that were the unresolved debts outside of Lend-Lease. Government policymakers found it hard to see how Britain could achieve any decent standard of living in the post-war world.

British negotiators, led by Keynes, argued as they had done at the end of the First War, for a complete cancellation of inter-allied debts on the ground that all had been fighting in the same cause. As they put it, it seemed perverse that when the US sent tanks across the Atlantic after 1941, with the additional expense of US crews to man them, it did not expect repayment for either tanks or crews, but before 1941, with Britain providing the crews, it did expect repayment for the tanks. Similarly, if Britain had trashed its own economy in the common cause, then surely the allies should help to put it together again. Interestingly this had also been the French government's original line in 1919— only after it had predictably fallen on deaf ears did the French switch to a harder line on German reparations. But the American position also remained the same as it had been at the end of the First World War: transfers which had originally been structured as grants were not expected to be repaid, but loans were. The original structures presumably had a reason, which should be respected. Britain's own contribution had already been taken into account in the original agreements.

The British felt it was unfair that the Americans seemed to expect them to be bankrupted by the war, whereas the American economy had in fact done very well. Keynes' patience finally snapped at the brutal commercial logic of the American businessmen/politicians: 'You cannot treat a great nation as if it were a bankrupt company!' But Keynes' position was weak: it is not easy to plead both poverty and greatness simultaneously.

It would be difficult to convict the Americans of lack of generosity—they had in fact given the British billions of dollars. Really the British were just asking them to be twice as generous. However, American politicians could not disregard the interests of American taxpayers and the American constitution, any more than British politicians could extract unrequited tax revenues out of the British taxpayer. (One sees very similar patterns in the recent negotiations between Greece and the EU.)

Keynes staked his reputation, and in fact his life, on being able to persuade the Americans to be generous at the end of the war. He led negotiating teams, first for the Bretton Woods Agreement which set up the post-war international trade and financial system, and then in a negotiation for American debt forgiveness and the extension of American support into the post-war world. But he was unsuccessful. Article VII ensured that in most differences of opinion about post-war arrangements the US would get its way. The Bretton Woods Agreement committed Britain to fixed exchange rates and early convertibility, and limited its ability to use discriminatory controls to safeguard its weak post-war international trading position. The Americans would not forgive the remaining debts or grant an interest-free loan to carry them costlessly forward, or make further grants to assist post-war readjustment. The best Keynes could achieve was a loan of $4.4 billion ($3.75 billion of new money and $650 million to cover the disputed pre-Lend-Lease payments; Canada also lent $1.19 billion) at 2 per cent, to cover necessary post-war imports, and to be repaid over fifty years. This time Britain did not default, despite the many vicissitudes of the post-war era. The final payment, after a few contractually allowable deferments, was made in 2006.

Keynes had not been a well man at the beginning of the war, and the continual negotiating wore him out. The loan agreement was signed on 6 December 1945. On 21 April 1946 he died of a heart attack.

In truth, the war aims of the US and Britain, as in the first war, were not identical. Despite the Churchillian 'special relationship' rhetoric, US public opinion was by no means naturally favourable to Britain, with memories going back to 1776, and migrant populations from many European backgrounds, some with pronounced animosity to England. Both countries needed to defeat Germany, but they differed in the kind of post-war world they wanted to create. Churchill wanted to restore the British Empire to its full greatness; the US was understandably less enthusiastic about that prospect, for both idealistic and less idealistic reasons. The British wanted to end the war with sufficient resources still to control their empire; the Americans would prefer that they did not. Americans were willing to be generous to help Britain defeat the Nazis, but they did not want their generosity to be used to help re-establish colonial control over India, Malaya and other such countries, to enable British firms to compete economically with US firms in Latin America, or to exclude US firms from an area of imperial preference. US politicians were willing to help Britain if Britain had genuinely exhausted all its own resources first; but less willing if Britain were trying to hold some of its resources back for other purposes, purposes possibly inimical to their own interests. On the other hand, they knew they could not push their own hand too far—they knew they could not fill the strategic vacuum of an immediate collapse of the British Empire. Like all protagonists in international negotiations, they were balancing several conflicting objectives and constraints, and had little room for genuine or quixotic altruism.

THE STERLING BALANCES

But the American indebtedness was only one of Britain's problems. The sterling balances amounted to £3.5 billion, a temporarily blocked floating debt for which repayment seemed equally impossible. In pre-war conditions each country would have been dealt with separately in a series of bilateral agreements.

Obviously the ideal from Britain's point of view would be for the holders simply to forgive these debts, for the same reasons of solidarity and gratitude that Keynes was trying to argue with the Americans. Indeed, one reason for Keynes' tireless pursuit of generosity from the Americans was that American generosity would serve as an example to the sterling balance holders that could not be resisted. Unfortunately the Americans were more suspicious that the British wanted their money, not to feed themselves, but indirectly to pay off the sterling balances— understandably they did not wish to be exploited in this way.

Alternatively, these balances could just remain blocked, but only at the cost of considerable friction with the holders. The blocking could even be formalised by compulsorily converting them to perpetual debt.

Or they could be released gradually over a period of years. If they were to be released, would they be released unconditionally or would there be restrictions on their use? Common forms of restriction would be to prevent their conversion into any other currency, or to require them to be spent only on British exports. Both would prevent them directly adding to the drain of scarce dollars, although there would still be indirect effects: British export capacity was also scarce, and should not be diverted from its priority target of the US. Both kinds of restriction had been common aspects of many countries' trade policy before the war; however, both would now contravene the commitments of the Bretton Woods system to non-discriminatory trade and currency convertibility.

DEFAULT AND THE NATURE OF THE MONETARY SYSTEM; DEVALUATION

The changed post-war experience demonstrates some very important lessons about the relationship between the possibility of default and the nature of the underlying monetary system.

In the early days of the Debt when money was clearly understood to be gold, with paper notes merely representing the underlying gold, default was always a real possibility: if creditors insisted on being paid in gold and the government's gold stocks ran out, the government would clearly be in default. Avoidance of default meant getting in enough gold through taxation or other means to keep making the repayments. Financially weak governments were weak because their tax-gathering capabilities were weak. But as in reality no feasible level of gold reserves would suffice to pay off all the possible debts, the first line of defence was to maintain an aura of such creditworthiness that the creditors would not in fact demand repayment.

One alternative open to a gold-short government in those days was to depreciate the currency: i.e. to reduce the gold weight equivalent of a pound. The pound was the legal 'unit of account' in which debts were denominated. By depreciating the unit of account a given nominal debt could be paid off with less gold, thereby technically avoiding default. It was legally possible for the Crown to alter the gold equivalent—and it was done on several occasions in the Middle Ages and later. However, the problem was that over time depreciating the currency came to be viewed as just as much of a default as failing to meet one's debt repayments. By the mid-nineteenth century the gold standard was so sacrosanct that this was no longer a plausible way out. But by the mid-nineteenth century default in Britain was very unlikely anyway.

When the gold standard began to break down in 1931, and the only currency was paper, the British government could now never be forced into a position of technical default; they could always print as many Bank of England notes as were needed to pay off any debt. The only difficulty would be purely self-imposed rules about the limits to money supply, like the Bank Charter Act of 1844, which could be suspended in emergencies. However, even self-imposed rules can be restrictive if there is some separation of internal powers; for instance the US famously has a legally binding 'debt ceiling', and on occasions the President may not have a majority in Congress to increase this, leading to the possibility of a 'government shut-down'. Such a situation is less likely to occur in Britain, where the government effectively has to control Parliament. But even here there has been a recent tendency to place some powers in autonomous hands, e.g. the Bank of England's independent control of interest rates; and recent general elections have produced more fragmented and finely balanced parliaments, more difficult for a government to control.

However if a very large expansion of the money supply created inflation, so that the real value of the debt repayment went down, creditors might well consider this as an effective default (the equivalent of depreciation under the gold standard), and the government's reputation for creditworthiness would suffer. But bond contracts are usually specified in purely nominal terms, and the real value of money is not guaranteed. Bond-holders must make their own judgements and take their own precautions against inflation. Of course the gold standard was thought of as maintaining price stability, so that in the gold-standard days this was not such an important issue.

But after 1945, the screw tightened on the British government again. The American debt was denominated in US dollars, which the British government could not print. Avoidance of default then depended on either having enough US dollars in British foreign exchange reserves (which there weren't), or earning US dollars by running a continual trade surplus with the US for the duration of the loan (which was difficult).[2]

Furthermore the British government had signed up to the Bretton Woods system of fixed exchange rates and convertibility. The pound was fixed at $4.03. So although a holder of a sterling balance, or of a domestic British government bond, could still easily be paid off in sterling, the holder might then immediately wish to convert its receipts into dollars—which would only be possible as in the previous paragraph.

So the focus of government solvency shifted rather strangely from its own budget balance (taxation minus government expenditure) to the balance of payments (exports minus imports). For debts denominated in sterling the government could always avoid a debt default, but only at the possible cost of a foreign exchange default. This explains the British obsession with the balance of payments through the 1940s, 1950s, 1960s and 1970s.

In fact, the British were not able to meet all their commitments in the post-war period. They did not default on debt, but devalued, on two occasions: in 1949, from $4.03 to $2.80, and again in 1967 to $2.40. But again, although this was not a technical debt default, the foreign holders of sterling balances had good reason to feel cheated, because their claims would now buy fewer goods in the rest of the world when they were eventually repaid. For this reason some commentators do indeed view a devaluation in a fixed exchange-rate system as a kind of default.

For British resident debt-holders, their situation was a little better because their future expenditures might be expected to be mostly within Britain in sterling. Mostly, but not entirely: foreign holidays would become more expensive, and anyway the sterling price of imported goods would be expected to rise. Harold Wilson's famous 'pound in your pocket' broadcast after the 1967 devaluation was a brave attempt to obfuscate the consequences.

On the other hand, the US government's claim, being denominated in dollars, was unaffected by these devaluations, so they had no grounds for complaint. Devaluation in fact increased the burden of the US loan to the British: more pounds were required to pay it off.

When Bretton Woods collapsed, in the 1970s, the straitjacket relaxed again. Commitments, however clear-cut when entered into, became flexible again.

The next possible twist was the Euro, which Britain avoided, partly because of a disastrous initial flirtation with its fore-runner the ERM. The difficulties of Greece and other similarly affected European countries are sharpened by the adoption of the Euro, which effectively acts like a local gold standard: a currency that an individual country cannot print. Weak Eurozone countries have no easy options: public debts can only be repaid by extracting euros from one's own citizens through taxation, or from foreigners through continuing balance of payments surpluses, which may be near-impossible to achieve. Britain, having stayed out of the Eurozone, with all debt denominated in our own, floating currency, can never be forced into the position of Greece. The worst that can happen to Britain is that foreign (and domestic) creditors may be disappointed with the real returns of their investments, and may adjust their future behaviour accordingly (i.e. refuse to lend in future, or to renew their existing loans when they mature, except on stiffer terms—the consequences may nevertheless be quite uncomfortable).

10

THE POST-SECOND WORLD WAR YEARS

After the traumas and anxieties of the 1940s and early 1950s, the remaining post-war period was kinder to the National Debt. On the face of it one might have expected serious difficulties. The Debt/GDP ratio was close to an all-time high, and there was a significant element due in a foreign currency which Britain did not possess. Each year there would be a large refinancing requirement on account of a steady stream of maturities of the large war issues. The economy was in a terrible condition and the new Labour Government had an ambitious programme of welfare expansion and nationalisation. However, the National Debt itself seems not to have been an issue of high priority in government policy in this period, and there was no recurrence of the agonised post-Second World War debates on desperate measures to repay the Debt.

One very unlikely proponent of radical measures was Hastings William Sackville Russell, 12th Duke of Bedford, who in a series of pamphlets (among them, *The Absurdity of the National Debt*, 1947) argued that the Debt was largely an accounting mirage created for the benefit of the banks, that its importance was

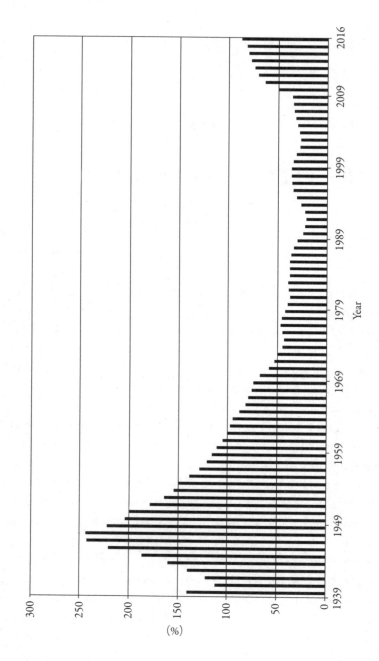

Figure 7: British National Debt/GDP Ratio (%), 1939–2016

almost entirely distributional and that a determined effort to grasp the distributional nettle could settle it without much difficulty at all and cut out the baleful influence of the banks.

In some ways the Duke of Bedford was a post Second World War equivalent of Pethick Lawrence: an Eton-educated aristocrat whom social conscience and a strong Christian ethic had propelled originally into social work and radical left-wing politics. But he had ended up in a very different place from Pethick Lawrence. He had become a convinced adherent of Major Douglas's theory of Social Credit, which informed his views on the Debt and money; and like some others he had moved on from there into quasi-fascist political circles. During the Second World War British intelligence viewed him as a potential traitor and a likely candidate to be a puppet prime minister in a pro-Nazi government if Britain were to lose the war. After the war he led and financed his own nationalist and Social Credit party; he was a clearer exponent than Douglas (who could be remarkably opaque), but Social Credit had passed its peak, and his own position could hardly be considered mainstream, so he gained little traction. Ironically, the government's much less radical-sounding policies achieved almost the same result that Bedford was looking for. By requiring the banks to hold significant reserves in low-interest government bonds at a time of inflation (a policy we would now call 'financial repression'), the government did make the banks effectively pay for much of the war (although no doubt the banks passed most of this on to their customers).

Like Pethick Lawrence, Bedford too was austere and personally eccentric to an alarming degree. But whereas Pethick Lawrence's eccentricities were generally held to be lovable, Bedford's were decidedly not. Family relations in the Bedford family were notoriously poisonous: mutual hatred with his father was in turn replicated with his son, whom he tried to disinherit. Ironically the son overcame all these difficulties to restore the financial fortunes of the family which had almost been destroyed by his father and grandfather and by the death duties necessitated by the National Debt. As Thirteenth Duke he saved from destruction the family home, the architectural gem of Woburn Abbey, by pioneering the idea of opening stately homes to the public as mass tourist attractions, in the relentless promotion of which he became a well-known media public figure.

But so far as mainstream politics was concerned, no significant policies were in fact proposed to repay the National Debt, and the Debt itself was rarely used as an austerity argument against projects of public expenditure. Vestiges of pre-war sinking funds remained, but there was little enthusiasm to reinstate them into a seriously effective system again, and by the 1960s they had been formally abandoned. In the many well-known economics textbooks on performance and policy of the British economy during this period, there are strangely hardly any mentions of the National Debt.

There are several reasons for this apparent insouciance. Firstly, the new Keynesian macroeconomics had dethroned the idea of a balanced budget and freedom from debt as ends in themselves. The public budget was to be determined by its effect on current economic activity: a deficit would be required if there was a need to stimulate activity, a surplus if the need was to damp it down. The effect on the National Debt was incidental and only a second-level priority.[1]

Policymakers viewed the debt concerns of the inter-war period as having been a contributory factor to the Great Depression, inhibiting the use of the more stimulatory policies that the circumstances of the time had demanded. They were determined not to make the same mistake again. Moreover, despite the forebodings of doom in the early inter-war period the country had become used to high levels of debt and the implied high levels of taxation, without a significant threat of financial collapse. This was no longer quite uncharted territory.

The new Keynesian thinking had also assuaged concerns about the effects on capital markets and the rate of interest. Classical economics had viewed public debt as withdrawing national savings from a limited pool which would be better employed as productive investment in the private sector: the competition for the limited resources drove up interest rates, making private sector investment unprofitable, and thereby depressing the economy. But the new Keynesian views had reversed the causality: economic activity and the financial system would always create the savings necessary to sustain any level of investment if supported by appropriate government policy. Furthermore, empirical work in the inter-war period had led economists to question whether real investment expenditure was indeed very sensitive to rates of interest: businessmen seemed much more concerned about expected future levels of demand for their products, which the new Keynesian policies promised to guarantee.

Finally, in Keynes' monetary theory interest rates were determined as much in the money markets and by future expectations, as by supply and demand in the market for real investment. Experience in the war had shown that controls over the banking system and a determined government policy could force the financial system to take up large quantities of public debt while still keeping interest rates low. The banking controls and the determined policy were continued into the post-war period, and the growing pension industry had a voracious demand for government debt, so the government rarely had much difficulty in placing its issues.

However, money interest rates did steadily creep up, partly as the cheap money policy ran out of steam and real rates of interest crept back to their longer-term levels, and partly because of a new phenomenon: a steady inflationary trend. With the success of full employment policies, wage-bargaining power shifted towards labour. The inflationary implications of this occupied macro policymakers for the next four decades. From the narrower perspective of the National Debt this had two opposing effects. As bond-holders began to factor in inflationary expectations the nominal interest rates on new issues climbed still further, increasing the government's debt-servicing charges. However, the same inflation steadily reduced the real value of the entire National Debt.

The period was also one of economic growth. Although the policymakers of the time fretted that the growth was not steady (the era of 'stop-go'), nor as fast as Britain's major economic rivals, the long-run performance was better than any previous historical period. Thus, as in the Victorian age the significance of the Debt relative to GDP steadily fell. Subject to the combined effects of real growth and inflation, the rate of decline of our graph (Figure 7) is quite dramatic. By about 1972 the Debt had fallen to 50 per cent of GDP. But as in the Victorian age there was little actual repayment of debt. There was no Keynesian deficit splurge—in fact in every year up to 1971 the central government ran a comfortable primary surplus and even a small overall surplus. But these surpluses were too small to make much impact on the Debt and were outweighed by two significant new demands for 'productive' investment: the investment requirements of the newly nationalised industries, and local authority borrowing to finance council-house building. There were only a few isolated years in which the Net Debt figure actually went down, and the Second World War Debt of £25 billion had become £33 billion by 1971.[2]

THE EXTERNAL CONSTRAINT

However, although the effects of the domestically-held debt seem to have been relatively benign, this did not mean that governments of the period felt themselves free from constraint.

Quite the opposite—most governments felt highly constrained (and maybe this perception in fact led to policies which ensured that the Debt did reduce in significance). But the constraint was perceived now to arise from the balance of payments and exchange rate—how could the economy now pay its way in the wider world and still maintain a reasonable standard of living and an imperial foreign policy? This problem was greatly compounded by the existence of the overseas debts.

After the early 1950s the world shortage of dollars eased, and the long-term repayment of the US loan proceeded painfully but without too many hitches. However, the sterling balances continued to pose problems. Being more in the nature of floating debts, they were liable to be withdrawn on any hint of a threat to the current exchange rate of the pound. Any weakness in the trade balance (exports minus imports) raised such a threat, leading to withdrawals of much greater magnitude than the trade imbalance and accelerating further pressure on the pound. A significant reduction in the value of the pound would make imports even more expensive in the future. British economic policy was therefore subjected to a series of foreign exchange crises, culminating in a second devaluation in 1967.

Eventually the whole Bretton Woods system of fixed exchange rates collapsed in the early 1970s, ushering in a period of floating exchange rates. But if floating should theoretically have relieved the policymakers of the obligation to support a possibly overvalued pound, in practice it did not do this. The volatile sterling balances could still turn a small correction into a full-scale collapse. In the period of high inflation and escalating oil prices after the first OPEC oil shock in 1974, the effect on import prices, with further detrimental consequences on inflation and the balance of payments, would be too drastic, leading to a dangerous unstable spiral.

Market perceptions about the consequences of government deficits began to change too. A public deficit in the Victorian gold-standard-era era would have been seen as inexorably leading to more borrowing and thus to higher interest rates; if taken too far, the consequence might be a default on the Debt. By contrast the monetarist views gaining ground in the post-Bretton Woods period of no monetary standard saw public deficits as more inclined to expand the money supply, creating inflation domestically and lowering the international value of the pound. Taken too far, the consequence would be a 'default' on the exchange rate and the value of foreign-held debt.

International financiers therefore came even more to see public deficits as a very bad sign for the protection of their investments. In 1976, the Labour government seemed unable to contain an increasing deficit in a period of high inflation, and a serious run on the foreign exchange reserves ensued. The government was obliged to seek a loan from the IMF to avoid a catastrophic collapse in the value of the pound. As with all IMF loans, this came with significant conditions, particularly commitments to restrain public spending. However the financial situation (although not the political situation) stabilised fairly quickly—largely due to the imminent arrival of North Sea oil revenues—and the loan was repaid in a very few years, making little long-term impact on the National Debt. Despite increasing deficits—and therefore debt—during the turbulent 1970s, inflation ensured that the debt ratio continued to drift downwards. The episode was perhaps most notable as a forerunner of the more concerted policies of public borrowing targets to be followed by the Thatcher governments.

MONETARY CONSTRAINT

The Medium Term Financial Strategy of Mrs Thatcher's first government had at its heart a target for the Public Sector Borrowing Requirement (PSBR). But, again, this was not from

Economists' Views on the National Debt: 8. Robert Barro

In 1974 the American economist Robert Barro (1944–) revived interest in Ricardo's approach to public debt.[3] Ricardo had argued that public debt was really just deferred taxation, so the debt was simply 'equivalent' to a tax. But whereas Ricardo's concern was that the public found it difficult to perceive this equivalence, and market imperfections anyway made it impossible to translate this perception into action, the newer macroeconomic theories of Barro's time emphasised 'rational' expectations and perfect markets. In such a world Ricardo's equivalence would be a reality, and there would be no advantage for macroeconomic policy of financing public expenditure through debt rather than taxation. So Barro's interpretation of 'Ricardian Equivalence' was a direct attack on the effectiveness of 'Keynesian' macroeconomic policies. Any stimulus provided by a deficit would be nullified by the public's perception of higher taxes to come: the public would cut back spending to prepare to meet those taxes by just as much as the deficit itself.

But Barro's interpretation does depend on very demanding assumptions. Ever since, debate has raged among economists as to whether those assumptions are tolerably met in the modern economy. The need to formulate a macroeconomic policy response after 2008 on the subject has given the debate a very sharp practical edge. High-profile support for Keynesian policies comes from American economists such as Joe Stiglitz and Paul Krugman; in Britain one of the highest-profile campaigners on the same side has been Keynes' biographer Robert Skidelsky.

any explicit concern for the National Debt itself. The underlying analysis was that since any government deficit must be met by either borrowing or by creating money, with a passive borrowing strategy an increased deficit would imply an increase in money creation. The government's main objective was to control inflation. It saw inflation as fuelled by expansions in the money supply; government deficits would expand the money supply, therefore the route to controlling inflation was through controlling government deficits. This is not the place for a thorough analysis of that policy (after a shaky start it had some success, but not necessarily for the reasons proposed; unfortunately there are some very flexible links in the government's chain of reasoning).

The monetary tightening implied by the policy temporarily drove interest rates sharply upwards. Since similar policies were also being pursued in the US, the interest squeeze was world-wide: mortgage-owners, private-sector businesses, many weaker countries, and some public authorities in the US suffered serious embarrassment, including defaults. However, Britain's public debt, with its fixed interest and relatively long maturities, was affected less significantly than most, since the higher interest rates would only be payable on new or renewed debt.

A PERIOD IN TWO HALVES

Our figure showing the Debt/GDP ratio in the post-Second World War period can conveniently be divided into two halves. First is the sub-period from 1945 to about 1980. This roughly coincides with the 'Keynesian' policy period and it shows an almost smooth decline in the ratio, from 240 per cent in 1945 to 40 per cent in 1973—very reminiscent of, although more rapid than, the similar decline in the Victorian period. As we saw, the reasons behind it are also similar.

Of course at this point there was a major change in economic policy. The Keynesian period has finally run its course and the

Thatcher (and post-Thatcher) period has arrived. For a few years the debt ratio continued to drift, but by 1986 the new government's policies were clearly beginning to work. This was the era of the Lawson boom: GDP rose rapidly and there was even a small amount of net debt repayment, so that by 1991 the ratio had reached an all-time low of 22 per cent. But the Lawson boom ended badly, the Major government rather lost control of the public finances, and by 1997 the ratio was back up to 37 per cent. However, the Major government had worked hard to regain control, and handed over an improving situation to Tony Blair. The first Blair government pledged not to exceed its predecessor's expenditure plans, so again there were several years of net debt repayment; with the additional help of good economic growth the debt ratio again fell, to below 28 per cent by 2002. The second and third Blair governments and subsequent Brown government moved into a more expansionary phase and the ratio increased again, this time to 36 per cent in 2008. At this point the 2008 financial crisis intervenes and the ratio expanded rapidly again, although on the plans of the Cameron Conservative government, even this period of expansion was envisaged to be only about eight years, peaking in 2016. Unfortunately, another shock has intervened in the form of Brexit, and the future course of the Debt is less clear again.

It is tempting to over-interpret this change in the behaviour of the National Debt. The impulse is obviously to divide the period into Keynesian and Thatcherite periods, with the implication that the Keynesian period was more successful in bringing down the debt burden. But this is a little too convenient: the debt performance of the Keynesian period seems very like that of the Victorian period, which was decidedly un-Keynesian in its policies. And the second period covers not only Mrs Thatcher's governments, but all the post-Thatcher governments—Major, Blair, Brown, Cameron—too. Something more fundamental has changed.

The first half of the period fits in conveniently with our general story so far. Wars create massive surges of debt, but periods of peace steadily bring down the debt ratio—almost regardless of the policies governments adopt—if left to run long enough. Small temporary aberrations of expenditure and taxation are dwarfed in the large war and peace story.

But since 1980 movements in the debt ratio have not had to do with war and peace. They are more like a political business cycle. Once the debt ratio has been reduced to a comfortable level, say about 50 per cent, there is no longer any over-riding requirement that it should always be going down. Small movements either way cannot be represented as life-or-death crises, and can be tolerated for some years, although not for ever. Governments may lose control of their finances for a few years but may be able to put them right over another few years. Alternatively, they may work to establish a reputation for fiscal firmness over a few years and then cash in on it over the next few years. This seems to apply to both major political parties equally. Since 1986 there seems to have been one full Conservative cycle and one full Labour cycle, both of about ten to twelve years, with the debt ratio going first down then up; followed by what looks to be the upward first half of a larger such cycle, initiated by the 2008 financial crisis.

Current Conservative propaganda makes much of the previous Labour government's alleged profligacy. It is true that the debt ratio increased between 2002 and 2008, but this is only the second half of one such cycle—and at the end of it the debt ratio was still lower than at the beginning of the cycle, which was inherited from the previous Conservative government in 1997. That Conservative government had itself presided over a larger increase in the ratio, from 22 per cent to 37 per cent.

In 2008, the larger effect of the financial crisis superimposed itself on this pattern, so it is difficult to be certain how it would have continued. The effect of the 2008 crisis is considerably larger than the usual peacetime economic shock, but still much smaller than that of a major war. On its own, the cycle it initiated might have taken eight years to peak and a similar time for its downswing. It is still too early to see what the magnitude of the Brexit shock will be.

The Blair/Brown government was running a deficit of about £40 billion per year between 2002 and 2008. That was about 3 per cent of GDP. This may seem a lot, but the economy was growing well, so that the debt ratio would have remained stable even with a deficit of about £25 billion (see the section on Debt Sustainability in Chapter 12). It was also in line with the government's express policy only to borrow to finance public capital expenditure, which was also about £40 billion p.a. in those years (and in line with the EU's Maastricht criteria, which take 3 per cent as the maximum permissible deficit). The Major government borrowed similar sums over a similar period of years in the 1990s, when these deficits were more like 5 per cent of GDP. In both these cases, the levels of deficit are tolerable for short periods of time but would not be if prolonged.

WARS

Despite a tense international situation, Britain avoided major wars in this period. Probably the most significant for public finances was the Korean War of 1950–3. As well as the costs of the actual fighting this precipitated a sharp burst of general rearmament for fear of a wider conflict. However, against a background of still-reducing military expenditures from WWII, the public finances did not go into deficit, so there is little apparent impact on the debt-ratio figures. (One reason for this was that the Labour government cut back instead on domestic and welfare expenditures to make room for the military expenditure, at the cost of considerable internal party strife. But again the government's concern was more the impact on the balance of payments than on the National Debt.)

The Suez Crisis of 1956 did not last long enough to make a significant impact on debt, although it was of course US leverage over the existing debt that compelled Britain's withdrawal.

Post-Suez governments had to juggle the demands of desirable domestic and welfare expenditure against those of Cold War and colonial military expenditure. It was judged that the last of these was unaffordable, leading to rapid decolonisation with only occasional small-scale military rearguard actions—unlike the French who made major and traumatic efforts in Indo-China and Algeria, and subsequently the Americans in Vietnam.

More recently the Falklands War left little imprint on the Debt, and the wars in Iraq and Afghanistan only a small one. Estimates of the cost of the Falklands War range from about £2 to 3 billion (the value of the National Debt at the time was about £130 billion). Such limited military actions use resources that are probably already committed. The use of existing professional soldiers for short periods does not make much difference to the military wages bill. The true opportunity costs are the diversion from other useful activities such as training, and the use or loss of expensive equipment, some of which would ultimately be replaced through obsolescence anyway.

Iraq and Afghanistan have required much longer and therefore more expensive commitments (Wikipedia reports total British military costs in Iraq, from 2003–2009, of £8.4 billion; in Afghanistan, up to 2013, costs of £37 billion). Before these operations, defence expenditure was on a downward trend after the end of the Cold War. Defence expenditure decreased in the 1990s, but began to increase again from about £28 billion p.a. in 2000 to £45 billion p.a. in 2015. Nevertheless as a percentage of GDP defence expenditure has continued its slow fall, and there is no dramatic spike in the National Debt).

It is, however, worthy of note that the government budget went from comfortable surpluses before 2001 to annual deficits of £40 billion from 2003 onwards, and the National Debt began one of its periods of slow upward drift. Not all of this is attributable to military spending but the Iraq and Afghanistan deployments must have contributed. One might also suspect that these unwanted additions to expenditure added to the pressures to devise inventive off-balance sheet methods of financing other areas of expenditure which the government had hoped to fund from the peace dividend (more on this in Chapter 13).

Other military expenditures have included Northern Ireland, and operations in the former Yugoslavia.

What follows is a list of notable events affecting the National Debt.

NATIONALISATION AND PRIVATISATION

The 1945 Labour government embarked on an ambitious programme of nationalisation: coal, steel, electricity, gas, rail and public road transport. But this was not expropriation—compensation was paid in the form of exchanging the equity shares for government bonds, so the consequence was an increase in the National Debt. In the process the government was also acquiring real industrial assets, at least notionally of identical value, although the public accounting of the period (as we will see in Chapter 13) does not adequately signal this side of the balance sheet. Initially the new bonds were identified with their industries—thus there was Gas stock and Electricity stock—and initially investment within these industries was financed by similarly named bond issues, but clearly there was no possibility that the government could allow a nationalised industry to default, and as the Treasury tightened its financial controls over these industries, there seemed little point in intimating to the market that these were other than normal British government bonds. So the distinctively-named issues gradually disappeared and the nationalised industries' capital requirements were met effectively by borrowing from the Treasury as part of the ordinary National Debt (in much the same way as local authorities were financed through the Public Works Loan Board).

In time most of the nationalised industries were privatised again by the Thatcher and post-Thatcher governments. The revenues from privatisation were treated, bizarrely, as 'negative expenditure' and not used to reduce the Debt. However, the public sector did lose real assets, so its overall financial position was thereby allowed to deteriorate. (Hence Harold Macmillan's jibe that this was like 'selling the family silver'.)

Other elements of the 1945 government's welfare state programme did not affect the Debt as much as might have been feared. The creation of the NHS did not require similar levels of compensation because many of the medical assets taken over were already in local authority or charitable hands. GPs and dentists retained the autonomy of their practices, and hospitals and hospital consultants retained their lucrative private practices. Similarly, in education, independent and direct-grant schools remained autonomous; there was some need for new school-building, but no wholesale takeover of the existing assets of an industry. Conversely, ambitious council-house building programmes saw a significant increase in local authority borrowing.

Welfare payments began systematically, but at levels we would not consider very generous today. They might store up commitments and further aspirations for the future, but there was no immediate large investment requirement and governments comfortably covered the current outgoings with taxation, so again there was little observable impact on the National Debt.

NORTH SEA OIL AND 3G LICENCES

In the 1970s, the advent of North Sea Oil promised a possible revolution in the government's finances, but in reality it was something of a wasted opportunity. Oil revenues helped to disguise the weakness of the government's current budget position, and were helpful in paying off the 1970s IMF loan, but they did not make any significant contribution to repayment of the mainstream debt, much less build up a substantial financial asset position to compensate for the eventual running down of the oil reserves, as occurred in Norway and in Middle Eastern countries.

A similar, but new, kind of opportunity arose in the form of the auctioning of 3G mobile phone spectrum licences in 2000. The British government (unlike many other governments) played its cards well, taking careful advice from economic experts in auction design, and gained £22.5 billion (equivalent to 2.5 per cent of GDP) from the auction. In this case, since it coincided with a brief period of government surplus, the proceeds were treated as a capital inflow and used to reduce the Debt. However, such treatment is exceptional. More usually governments have succumbed to the temptation to treat asset purchases as capital but asset sales as revenue. Such an asymmetry is an obvious bias towards profligacy and leads to a hollowing-out of the state's asset position.

INDEX-LINKED GILTS

An important innovation in 1982 was the introduction of the first Index-Linked Bonds. Until then all bonds had been denominated in strictly nominal terms: their returns guaranteed in money terms, but not necessarily in real terms. In Victorian times, with no long-term inflationary trend, this produced few problems, but the twentieth century, with its wide swings of price level, had created a new source of uncertainty for bond-holders. Victorian holders of Consols had seen them as the epitome of a safe investment, but twentieth century holders had lost three-quarters of their value. With an ordinary bond the only protection a bond-holder could obtain against inflation was to build in the expected inflation rate into the interest rate at first issue, but even this was no protection against unanticipated accelerations in inflation during the life of the bond.

Index-linked bonds bore only a small nominal coupon but promised to up-rate all interest payments and the eventual repayment of principal by any increase in the Retail Price Index. Thus the coupon was effectively a guaranteed real rate of return.

The government hoped that such bonds would be attractive to long-term savers hoping to protect the real value of their savings in times of uncertain inflation; and to pension funds committed to paying out indexed pensions. As risk-averse investors might pay a premium for real-value certainty, these might prove a lower-cost form of borrowing for the government. Such bonds had been suggested before (not least by Keynes in the 1920s to the Colwyn Committee on the National Debt), but the government had baulked at the complexities of administration and taxation. However, a pilot experiment in the 1970s with small-scale index-linked national savings certificates had proved popular, and was now extended into the main bond market, with equal success. Index-linked bonds now account for about a quarter of Britain's National Debt and have been copied by many other countries.

A further reason for issuing index-linked bonds was as a signal of commitment to the government's anti-inflationary policies. If the government were not confident of success their eventual repayment would be more expensive than conventional bonds. Furthermore, once a significant proportion of the National Debt was indexed, this would remove one of the inflationary incentives on government: inflating could not now reduce the real value of the National Debt.

'STRIPS'

With their highly predictable returns, bonds are attractive to institutions like pension funds wishing to match their highly predictable future liabilities. A fund which knows it must make certain payments in ten, twenty, thirty years' time, can construct a matching portfolio of ten-, twenty- and thirty-year bonds. However, achieving perfect matching is hindered by the fact that each bond has interest payments as well as a repayment of principal. In 1997, the government introduced the idea of 'Stripping', whereby each individual payment of a bond might be separated out and have a market of its own, e.g. a ten-year bond has twenty interest payments and one repayment of principal, and so can be divided into twenty-one Strips. The purchaser of such a Strip therefore is entitled to a single payment on a single date, and a portfolio of such Strips can replicate exactly any time profile of liabilities.

THE DEBT MANAGEMENT OFFICE

The Blair government introduced a very important administrative change. In 1997, as part of the government's realignment of financial responsibilities which assigned interest-rate autonomy to the Bank of England but took away from it responsibility for financial regulation, the administration of the Debt was also removed from it and entrusted to a new Debt Management Office, responsible to the Treasury. This brought to an end three centuries of the Bank's management of the government's borrowing. The National Debt Commissioners still exist, but as the DMO's website plaintively notes, little of their original functions remain.[4]

The Treasury under Gordon Brown showed an uncommon interest in the academic basis of economic policy, and in the management of the National Debt. In an unusual book setting out the government's macroeconomic philosophy, the Debt gets three chapters.[5]

THE EURO

Perhaps the most important decision of the Blair government relevant to the National Debt was a negative one: a decision to enter the Euro would have had important implications for the government's control of the Debt and would also have placed it much closer to the centre of events in the post-2008 Euro crisis.

The Maastricht criteria for countries wishing to enter the Euro are worthy of note: they require a Debt/GDP ratio of no more than 60 per cent, and a Deficit/GDP ratio of no more than 3 per cent.[6] At the time, Britain would just about have satisfied those criteria. Subsequent events have shown them to be more honoured in the breach than in the observance by several of the Euro countries, but the fall-out from the Greek crisis has led to a tightening of attitudes.

THE CRISIS OF 2008

The financial crisis of 2008 showed that public indebtedness is by no means the only threat to an economy. In the run-up to 2008 Britain's public finances were actually in quite good shape. There was a small public-sector deficit, but the Debt/GDP ratio was at an almost all-time low and inflation was similarly low. The problem however was that private-sector debt had grown alarmingly, almost unnoticed, and the crisis was effectively a private-sector debt default.

The consequences for the public debt were twofold. First the bail-out of the banks meant that the public sector took over much of the private-sector debt. The way this worked technically was that the government forcibly recapitalised the failing banks. This meant giving them large quantities of government bonds, specially created for the purpose, to boost their reserves in exchange for equity shares in the banks. These bonds are the increase in the National Debt. The National Debt figures though fail to take account of the fact that the government has also thereby acquired assets: the equity shares (see Chapter 13). In ordinary circumstances this could be quite misleading. However, the whole point of the rescue was that the equity shares were almost worthless because the banks' liabilities to their clients exceeded their remaining assets, so unfortunately in this case the National Debt story does not mislead. The whole-of-government accounts explained in Chapter 13 would have told the story rather differently but to the same effect: the bond/equity swap is simply an internal transaction within the now-broader government sector, but the government has taken responsibility for the excess liabilities of the banks. The government may be able to mitigate its losses if the banks can be gradually returned to profitability and the value of the equity shares recovers.

The bank recapitalisation produced a large step increase but it was a one-off event. Secondly, however, the government's budget balance had become unusually reliant on large tax revenues from the high incomes and profits generated in the boom years. These were now seriously reduced and suffered further from the growth of the tax-avoidance industry. The crisis also came at an unfortunate time for the government, as it had just entered an expansionary phase in expenditure. The combined effect of all these was to cause a large recurrent deficit, which would take some considerable time to eliminate. Much policy debate since has centred on the desired time-path for such elimination.

The Brown government initially maintained the deficit in a Keynesian policy of trying to bolster economic activity and employment in the face of the post-crisis contractionary pressures—at the expense of further National Debt growth—but the subsequent Coalition and Conservative governments prioritised earlier elimination of the deficit.

A compensating advantage though has been the very low interest rates induced by the monetary policy measures aimed at reviving the economy, a repetition of the cheap money of the 1930s and 1940s. Britain has also benefited as a relatively safe haven for international funds. Although the National Debt is still increasing, the government has had no difficulty financing its borrowing at very low interest rates and its total debt interest payments have in fact decreased.

VERY LONG-DATED GILTS AND THE END OF CONSOLS

No perpetuities had been issued since WWII. The post-war experience had shown their vulnerability to inflation. Most long-term issues in this period involved maturities of twenty to thirty years. However with the return of low-inflationary conditions and the government's strong creditworthiness, and the very low interest rates after 2008, the government acted to lock in such low interest rates, by introducing very long-dated bonds, with maturities of fifty years.

The historical perpetuities, including Consols, still existed and were traded on the second-hand markets, although they now represented only a very small proportion of the total Debt. Until this time the government had seen no point in redeeming or converting them since their very low historical interest rates could hardly be bettered. However, the extraordinarily low interest rate environment after 2008 made this no longer the case. In 2014 the government redeemed the 3.5 per cent War Loan which had been formed by Neville Chamberlain's 1932 conversion of the First World War debts, and the 4 per cent Consols issued just after that War. The War Loan still amounted to £1.9 billion and had 120,000 holders, the most widely held of all British government stock (although £1.9 billion is now only a very small proportion of the total debt, and in 1932 there were over 3 million holders). Having completed that operation, in 2015 they then proceeded, more out of administrative tidiness, to redeem all that remained, including the 2.5 per cent Consols. As very long-term interest rates were currently about 2.5 per cent, there was in fact no great interest differential to be gained over 2.5 per cent Consols, but once the more numerous 4 per cent and 3.5 per cent bonds had been disposed of, the volume remaining was hardly enough to maintain a liquid market in perpetuities.

Thus were over 250 years of history brought to an end. The only remaining perpetual debt is the original £1.2 million loan from the Bank of England, maintained presumably for purely historical reasons. Notice that although for PR purposes it suited the government to use the language of 'repayment' of old debts, these were effectively only refinancing operations. There can be no genuine repayment while the government is expanding the Debt on other fronts—this is reminiscent of the Pitt fallacy.

All British government bonds now therefore have redemption dates. But despite the lack of perpetuities the average maturity of British government debt is still relatively very long in comparison with other countries. So although current British governments cannot quite enjoy the complacency of Victorian governments, whose Consols could never ever embarrass them with demands for repayment, Britain is still well cushioned against such financial embarrassment.

11

NATIONAL DEBT AND THE 'UNITED' KINGDOM?

Throughout this history, we have tended to refer to the British National Debt, or more correctly to the Debt of the United Kingdom. But the political structure of Britain has changed over the period of this study, and so has the geographic coverage of the Debt. Recent events suggest that the political structure may change again radically in the near future. How have such changes interacted with the Debt in the past?

UNION WITH SCOTLAND

In 1694, there was no United Kingdom of Great Britain and Northern Ireland, so the earliest debts were purely English. The Kingdoms of England (which effectively also included Wales) and of Scotland were distinct entities with their own governments and their own parliaments. Since 1603 there had been a 'personal union', in that the same person was monarch of both, but that was as far as it went. During the seventeenth century there were occasional moves on both sides for closer union, but

209

none succeeded. Towards the turn of the century, two separate issues combined to precipitate matters.

First was the impending death of Queen Anne without issue (despite seventeen pregnancies). To ensure a Protestant succession, England had agreed to offer the English Crown to the German Elector of Hanover, but this was not binding on Scotland, raising the worrying possibility of a separate Scottish monarch again—possibly even the return of the deposed Stuart line, supported by France. This would have been unacceptable to England and to a significant body of Scottish opinion, and concentrated minds on both sides to negotiate the 1707 Acts of Union, which created a single United Kingdom and Parliament.

The other factor was the disastrous Darien scheme of 1698–1700. This, in some ways a Scottish precursor of the South Sea Bubble, was another brainchild of Joseph Paterson, the Scottish promoter of the Bank of England. The idea was to found a colony in Darien, on the Caribbean side of the Isthmus of Panama, open up a short land route across the isthmus to the Pacific Ocean and thereby short-circuit the long and hazardous Cape Horn route to the lucrative Pacific coast trade (the construction of the Panama Canal three centuries later served much the same purpose).

The scheme was originally floated by Paterson in England, Scotland and Holland, gaining potential investors in all three countries, but the English East India Company feared the competition to its own Caribbean trade, and King William's government currently did not wish (at least not unless for its own benefit) to provoke Spain, the power actually in possession of Panama, so forbade any English or Dutch participation. Undaunted, and in something of a patriotic fervour, Scots investors decided to go it alone, contributing about £400,000 to 'The Company of Scotland Trading to Africa and the Indies', estimated to be about 25 per cent of the total wealth of Scotland at the time.

It was a total disaster. The terrain was inhospitable and disease-ridden, and the Spanish were indeed hostile. English colonies in the Caribbean had been instructed to give no help whatsoever. Most of the settlers died, and the survivors gave up after a few months. A second wave of settlers set out, unaware of the fate of the first, and suffered the same. Financially it was a complete loss. The government and almost every household in Scotland had contributed heavily and were practically ruined. It was an object lesson in the riskiness of ambitious overseas ventures for a small nation (not unlike Icelandic banking in the 2008 crisis), and its victims not surprisingly looked to a larger neighbour for a bail-out. This provided fertile ground for conflicts of private and public interest, which the English government doubtless exploited.

The economic provisions of the Acts of Union included the following: for every future £2 million of land tax voted in England, Scotland would also pay £48,000 (so only about 2.3 per cent of the whole). Customs and excise taxes and other indirect taxes would be harmonised, although some with transitional periods, and some indirect taxes were specifically excluded. It was accepted that Scottish customs and excise taxes would have to rise significantly to meet the English levels; the English rates were high to meet the costs of the high English debt, so the consequence would be that Scottish consumers would be contributing to pay off the English debt. As compensation Scotland would be paid an 'Equivalent': a lump sum of £400,000 plus the additional customs and excise revenues arising in Scotland for seven years. This money would be administered by commissioners to support various causes including paying off the Scottish national debt, but also compensating the shareholders of the Company of Scotland (note the suspicious similarity of the £400,000 figure) and winding the company up.

The Scottish public debt, despite the Darien disaster, was small relative to the English, and makes no significant impact on the overall debt figures. Since 1707 there has been no separate Scottish national debt. However, Devolution in the late twentieth century has led to the reconstitution of a separate Scottish Parliament with some independent financial powers, including a limited amount of borrowing: the Scotland Act of 2012 allows a maximum of £2.2 billion borrowing, although under supervision of the Westminster Treasury.

The devolution of financial powers is likely to proceed further over time, but so long as Scotland remains in the United Kingdom Scottish people will remain liable for the overall National Debt as well as their own Scottish Parliament borrowings. If, however, Scotland regains complete independence, the negotiations will have to include a deal partitioning the Debt, a procedure the reverse of 1707.

IRISH UNION

The position of Ireland was slightly different. The King of England claimed also to be King of Ireland but there was really no separate Kingdom of Ireland with a coherent administration and traditions like Scotland. Effective but fragile power in Ireland rested with a minority 'Protestant ascendancy'. There was an Irish parliament, and a small and rather badly managed debt, but powers were severely circumscribed by Westminster. A more effective parliament was granted in 1760, with clearer taxation and borrowing powers; but a serious rebellion in 1798 aided by the French persuaded Pitt of the strategic danger of a potentially independent Ireland.

Consequently the 1800/1801 acts of Union abolished the separate Irish parliament and established the United Kingdom of Great Britain and Ireland. Its economic provisions (Article 7) included that Ireland should be responsible for two-sevenths of expenditure for the first twenty years, and subsequently an equitable share to be determined by the combined parliament. Irish taxes would continue separately to defray the interest and repayments of the Irish public debt unless and until the combined parliament decided that it would be equitable to combine the two national debts. In fact, this happened in 1817, after which year there is only a single British National Debt.

IRISH INDEPENDENCE

The Anglo-Irish Treaty of 1921 provided (Article 5) that the Irish Free State would remain liable for a 'fair and equitable' share of the British National Debt at that point; but after subsequent negotiations in 1925 this was dropped, in exchange for moderate fixed payments and no doubt concessions in other areas. So the Irish Republic did not in the end inherit any British National Debt. However, there was a more subtle debt problem which did cause some difficulties.

In Chapter 6 we noted the introduction of Irish Land Bonds, not strictly speaking British government debt but guaranteed by the government. The 1921 treaty makes no specific mention of these bonds, but in practice the scheme continued, with at least informal agreement between the governments. Administratively Irish farmers continued to make their mortgage payments, 'land annuities', to an Irish government office which relayed them to London, who made the payments to bond-holders. The sums involved were small by British standards, but significant in Irish terms: at its peak the value of bonds outstanding was estimated at 60 per cent of Irish GDP. Payments amounted to £3 million p.a.

But in 1932 with Anglo-Irish relations already tense for other reasons, a new more anti-British Fianna Fail government under Eamonn de Valera withheld the payments. It argued that they should be interpreted as part of the National Debt, which had been forgiven in the 1925 agreement. It further argued that anyway they were morally unjustifiable, being payments to buy back Irish land from English landlords who should never have usurped it in the first place. As such they were highly unpopular with an agricultural population already suffering hardship from the depression, leading to dangerous social unrest.

Rather than be party to a default the British government announced it would assume responsibility for the payments (the bond-holders were mostly either Irish banks, whose head offices were actually in London, or departments of the British government such as the Post Office Savings Bank, so the British government had a strong incentive not to default), retaliating against the Irish government with protective measures, leading to the so-called Anglo-Irish Economic War, which lasted until 1938. This concluded with an agreement which settled several different issues of contention between the governments, including the land annuities. The Irish made a lump-sum payment of £10 million in return for not transferring them in future. Nevertheless, they continued to collect them from Irish farmers, using the revenue for domestic purposes. The British paid off the bond-holders.

WALES AND NORTHERN IRELAND

Wales and Northern Ireland have not quite the same historical claims to autonomy as Scotland and Ireland, and they have never had separate national debts of their own. Welsh and Northern Irish public expenditure has been channelled through the budgets of the Welsh Office and Northern Ireland Office, departments of the Westminster government, financed from overall British taxation and borrowing.

But, as with Scotland, devolution has recently given them some independent financial powers. Under the Northern Ireland Loans Act of 1975, the devolved Northern Ireland Executive now has power to borrow up to £3 billion from the National Loans

Fund. The Wales Act of 2014 gave the Welsh Assembly borrowing powers up to £500 million (subsequently raised to £1 billion); borrowing may be from the National Loans Fund, from commercial lenders, or by issuance of bonds.

THE CHANNEL ISLANDS AND THE ISLE OF MAN

The unusual constitutional positions of the Channel Islands and the Isle of Man (they are 'Crown Dependencies' and not officially part of the United Kingdom) place them outside the scope of British taxation and borrowing. Effectively they run their own finances, including the possibility of borrowing and issuing bonds. There are two Isle of Man Treasury Bonds currently in issue, but they are very small in magnitude. The government of Jersey, with buoyant tax revenues from the financial sector, has a significant positive financial asset position and has only one modest bond issue outstanding. Similarly Guernsey has an overall positive financial asset position and one bond issue outstanding.

LOCAL AUTHORITIES

Until the mid-nineteenth century local government in Britain, like its central counterpart, had fairly minimal responsibilities. These included local law and order, local administration of the Poor Laws, some road maintenance and not much else. Administration was in the hands of local Justices of the Peace, usually appointed centrally from among the wealthier residents. Sources of revenue were very limited—there was a Poor Law Rate—so there was little possibility of repaying any borrowing, hence there could be little borrowing. Any extraordinary expenditures for local amenities were more likely financed from the private generosity or self-interest of wealthy locals.

However, the growth of industrial towns in the course of the industrial revolution brought with it demonstrable problems that required a more systematic local government. Powerful local politicians like Joseph Chamberlain argued that proactive local government was the best safeguard against social revolution. But even short of this, public health required safe water supplies and sewerage, hospitals and sanatoria, better housing and care of the elderly; the development of local industry required all these and roads, public transport, utilities such as gas and electricity, education; municipal pride demanded parks, theatres, museums and art galleries.

Powerful municipal corporations were formed, of which the most prominent example was Chamberlain's Birmingham. Sources of revenue through domestic and business rates were secured. But as many of their initial major activities were in the nature of investments with long lives (e.g. slum clearance, provision of water, sewerage, gas, electricity and transport networks), it was reasonable to anticipate revenue by borrowing. Sources for such borrowing could be found in local banks and other financial institutions, the central government, and in bond issuance.

Central government began making loans to local government for the construction of public works in the late eighteenth century. In 1842 this was formalised by the creation of the Public Works Loans Board (PWLB) in the hands of the National Debt Commissioners. The PWLB effectively automatically incorporates local authority borrowing into the National Debt, allowing local authorities to benefit from the superior creditworthiness of the central government; it charges local authorities an interest rate slightly higher than that which the central government faces on its own debt. However, the PWLB is not a blank cheque for local authority borrowing; it has its own criteria and is usually subject to central government restrictions on the total quantity of its lending. Therefore to maintain flexibility local authorities will also look elsewhere for funding. Such borrowing outside the PWLB does not automatically register in the traditional 'National

Debt', but may be included in statistics covering the wider 'Public Sector'.

The reputation and creditworthiness of the larger and most well-known local authorities was not much below that of the central government, and they could afford to raise money at comparable rates of interest by issuing their own bonds. By the mid-twentieth century there was a very active market in the bonds of many different local authorities and other quasi-public local entities, e.g. the Port of London Authority, The Mersey Docks and Harbours Board, and municipal utilities companies. Such borrowing was a microcosm of central government borrowing: it was secured on the rating revenues of the local authorities, and usually for long terms. Interestingly, it was not guaranteed by the central government, although public perception could hardly envisage the possibility of default. It was often held out of local patriotism by small local savers, and was considered effectively as safe as Consols.

However more recently local authority bonds have fallen out of fashion. The late-twentieth-century bankruptcies of US local authorities, including New York, demonstrated how much more constrained local revenues are than central revenues, that there is no local printing press, and that central government rescue cannot be relied upon. At the same time, central governments operating macroeconomic policies of public borrowing restraint took steps to ensure that these central policies could not be undermined by expansionary borrowing by local authorities under the control of their political opponents. A succession of Local Government Acts limited local authorities' freedom of manoeuvre in various ways: council tax rates were capped, business rates were removed from local authority control, capital expenditure and borrowing had to be approved by central government.

The current framework is laid down by the Local Government Act of 2003. This confirms that local authorities have a right to borrow, but they also have a duty to manage their finances 'prudentially'; and the secretary of state has extensive powers to intervene and overrule, and to set overall or individual limits on local authority borrowing in the national interest. A local authority may not borrow in a foreign currency without Treasury permission. Borrowing is secured on all the revenues of a local authority, and in the case of default creditors may be given powers of administration including the collection of revenues (it would be politically very interesting to see a foreign vulture fund collecting council tax).

Although local authorities are still legally free to use the bond market, few now do: total local authority borrowing is now £84 billion (so fairly small compared to the central government debt), of which 75 per cent is via the PWLB, and most of the remainder is direct with banks or other financial institutions. There is currently some concern among anti-debt campaigners about this bank component: much was taken out before 2008 in complex and opaque derivative-linked loans that have had the effect of locking in high rates of interest for very long terms. Such loans are very unevenly distributed among local authorities: a small number of local authorities have significant exposures.

Such unfortunate experience with financial institutions, and the continued central government squeeze on the PWLB (available lending is now severely limited in quantity as part of the government's target of reducing net borrowing to zero, and the margin over the central government interest rate has been appreciably increased) has led to some renewed interest in local authority bonds. Very large authorities such as Greater London and Transport for London have recently issued bonds to finance large infrastructure projects (e.g. Crossrail), and proposals have been made to form a cooperative bond-issuing venture for local authorities.

SUPRA-NATIONAL BODIES

In the other direction, Britain is a member of various supra-national organisations, e.g. the UN, IMF, World Bank, NATO, and most topically the EU. In principle Britain could be liable for a proportion of the debts of such organisations if they have borrowed. However, in most such cases borrowing powers are severely limited and such organisations usually have to exist on annual budgets financed by current contributions. In the case of the IMF, members make capital contributions, so a decision to leave the IMF would result in a return of assets.

The EU is obviously worth specific consideration. The EU has no formal national debt of its own, so Brexit has needed no negotiations on that score. However, the EU does have future obligations of a non-debt kind, similar to those to be discussed in Chapter 13: particularly the pension liabilities of retired EU staff, and the future costs of long-term collaborative projects. We shall see that such liabilities can be very large, and they have been the central issue of the financial 'divorce bill' negotiations.

If Britain had joined the Euro, the operations of the European Central Bank would probably have created a network of very large debt-like obligations which would need unravelling. Even outside the Euro, the operation of the single market in finance, and EU-wide rescue and guarantee arrangements, will have resulted in similar entanglements.

Another rather different form of supra-national body was the British Empire. While the empire was in full swing, colonial governments levied taxes and paid for some public expenditures in their own territories; the Westminster government might pay for other elements of local expenditure but also might exact contributions for imperial defence and other 'services'. If the local public finances did not add up Westminster could subsidise via grants or loans. Thus the financial relationships between Westminster and local colonial governments were really only the internal book-keeping and political convenience of Westminster in the running of its large multi-national enterprise. The decolonisation in the twentieth century therefore required the renegotiation of any existing debt positions (although it should be noted that some colonial governments were in fact owed money, through the sterling balances, for instance). As in the case of Ireland, the outcome would depend on political realities. India, for instance, agreed to take over responsibility for the colonial Indian government's debts; but other newly-independent countries were probably too poor, and resentful of colonial exploitation in general, to follow suit.

12

THE DEBT

OTHER STANDARDS OF COMPARISON

We have reached the present day. But before attempting to draw some conclusions together from this history, in this chapter we will also consider Britain's debt position from some different standpoints. First, we will consider how it compares to the debts of other countries. Second, we should consider how it stands up against the general theoretical principles of debt sustainability. And third, we should consider whether there is such a thing as an 'optimal' national debt. In the next chapter, we will ask the very important question of whether the National Debt as it is conventionally measured is all we have to worry about.

INTERNATIONAL COMPARISONS

Table 12.1 shows comparable figures for debt and deficits in other European countries, the US and Japan. (The EU uses a slightly different definition of government debt to that of Britain, so Britain's ratio quoted here differs slightly from the one normally used in this book.) Notably there is a wide range

Table 12.1: International Comparisons of Debt and Deficits, 2015

	Debt/GDP Ratio (%)	Deficit/GDP Ratio (%)
Eurozone Countries		
Belgium	105.8	−2.5
Germany	71.2	0.7
Estonia	10.1	0.1
Ireland	78.6	−1.9
Greece	177.4	−7.5
Spain	99.8	−5.1
France	96.2	−3.5
Italy	132.3	−2.6
Cyprus	107.5	−1.1
Latvia	36.3	−1.3
Lithuania	42.7	−0.2
Luxembourg	22.1	1.6
Malta	64.0	−1.4
Netherlands	65.1	−1.9
Austria	85.5	−1.0
Portugal	129.0	−4.4
Slovenia	83.1	−2.7
Slovakia	52.5	−2.7
Finland	63.6	−2.8
Non-Eurozone European Countries		
Bulgaria	26.0	−1.7
Czech Republic	40.3	−0.6
Denmark	40.4	−1.7
Croatia	86.7	−3.3
Hungary	74.7	−1.6
Poland	51.1	−2.6
Romania	37.9	−0.8
Sweden	43.9	0.2
United Kingdom	89.1	−4.3
USA	97.2	−4.2
Japan	233.4	−6.2 (2014)

Source: European Central Bank Statistics Bulletin.

of experience. Most countries' figures have risen significantly since 2008, like Britain's.

Although we have seen that compared to its own historical experience Britain's current debt ratio is relatively low, it is on the relatively high side in this table. But it is by no means the worst. Unsurprisingly, Euro-crisis casualties like Greece, Spain, Portugal, and Cyprus exceed it, but so too do France, Italy, Belgium, the US and Japan. In fact, the only very large country with a lower debt ratio is Germany. Most countries with lower debt ratios are relatively smaller countries, reflecting perhaps a weaker bargaining position in international markets.

The figures for current deficits should also be noted. Clearly a large current deficit is a sign that a debt will get worse. Most countries are at present in some level of deficit; unfortunately Britain's deficit ratio is definitely on the high side.

Outside Europe, the US and Japan are no better. Japan is an interesting case. Although its debt is remarkably larger than any other advanced country, this has so far caused few problems and Japanese interest rates remain low. In the 1980s and 90s, Japan suffered a very extreme property boom and collapse (in some ways a fore-runner of the 2008 crisis), leaving a legacy of fragile banks and a consequent saga of many government attempts to restart the economy through deficit financing. Japan also has an aging population, not very generous welfare provisions but a high degree of social cohesion and respect for the government. The consequence is a large domestic demand for government bonds as retirement savings and bank assets. Little is held by foreign investors and the resulting debt has been very stable, despite much international market disappointment in the performance of the Japanese economy.

DEBT SUSTAINABILITY

Whereas Britain's position may not be that far out of line with other major countries, this would be little comfort if the general level of indebtedness in the world were itself dangerously high. Therefore we need to consider whether there is any absolute standard by which we can judge the level of indebtedness.

Much current concern focuses on whether a debt is 'sustainable' or whether it will spiral out of control. This applies both to national debts and to individual debts. A small loan may be relatively easy to contain, but once a loan exceeds a certain size, even making the interest payments may be a challenge. If one cannot keep up with the interest payments the debt will grow, with possibly catastrophic effects, as many victims of loan sharks can testify.

What is the critical size of a loan, beyond which it is dangerous to go? Some commentators suggest that for nations it is about 100 per cent of GDP. In fact there is no black-and-white answer: it depends on several factors, as the following analysis will show.

Here the analogy with personal finance is not very helpful. We expect personal loans must be repaid some time, but this is ultimately because every individual person is mortal. Even during life, personal incomes will tend to start low in youth, grow to a peak in middle age, and decline in retirement. So sensible lenders will be content to lend several times annual income to young or middle-aged persons with good prospects but will expect to see debt tapering off to zero in later life. Sustainable individual debt must inevitably respect a life-cycle.

But a whole community of individuals is not subject to this life-cycle. As individual citizens decline and die off, they are replaced by new and younger ones. The society's communal debt never faces a point at which it must be paid off. If the population, wealth and age structure remain stable (of course, if any of these do not remain stable, the calculation will be more complicated), any level of communal debt which is considered sustainable at one time will continue to remain sustainable at all other times. So a society can exist for ever with a steady-state level of debt (and if the society is growing the level of debt can also increase with it)—the question is therefore, what is necessary to keep the debt at that steady-state level?

In order to repay a loan, a government has to run a budget surplus, i.e. an excess of tax revenue over current expenditure. In the normal definition of budget surplus, interest payments on the National Debt are included in the expenditure total. But for our purposes here we will find it more helpful to think in terms of the 'primary surplus': the excess of tax revenue over expenditure before taking into account interest payments on the Debt. Clearly, unless the primary surplus is bigger than the interest bill the Debt will continue to grow. But even if the Debt does continue to grow, it will still be 'sustainable' if it does not grow as fast as the rest of the economy. In such a case the Debt/GDP ratio will still fall. What we want to avoid above all is the Debt/GDP ratio continuing to grow. To investigate this more precisely we will need a little more mathematics than we have used so far in this book—but the reader is encouraged to persevere with these few lines, to fully understand the relationships involved.

Let national income in year t be Y_t, national debt D_t, the primary surplus S_t, interest rate r and growth rate of national income g.

Then the current Debt/GDP ratio is D_t/Y_t. What will it be next year, D_{t+1}/Y_{t+1}?

$$D_{t+1} = D_t + rD_t - S_t$$

$$Y_{t+1} = Y_t (1 + g)$$

Therefore, $D_{t+1}/Y_{t+1} = (D_t + rD_t - St) / Y_t (1 + g)$

$$= D_t/Y_t . (1 + r - S_t/D_t) / (1 + g)$$

So D_{t+1}/Y_{t+1} will be no greater than D_t/Y_t if:

$$(1 + r - S_t/D_t) \leq (1 + g)$$

i.e. if $S_t/D_t \geq r - g$

So if the primary surplus as a proportion of the debt is at least as big as the difference between the interest rate and the growth rate, the debt will continue to be sustainable. Clearly if the growth rate is greater than the interest rate we don't even need a surplus at all: the growth of the economy will absorb even the consequences of a small primary deficit. But such a situation is unusual; usually rates of interest are greater than growth rates.

It can be informative to manipulate our equation a little more. Noting that we can break up S_t/D_t into $(S_t/Y_t) \cdot (Y_t/D_t)$, we now have:

$$S_t/Y_t \geq (r - g) \cdot (D_t/Y_t)$$

Interpreted this way, the primary surplus as a proportion of GDP must be at least as big as the difference between the interest rate and the growth rate, multiplied by the Debt/GDP ratio.

Therefore, these are the four crucial variables: primary surplus as a proportion of GDP, debt as a proportion of GDP, rate of interest, and growth rate of GDP. The necessary primary surplus will be higher as the interest rate is higher, and as the Debt/GDP ratio is higher, but lower as the GDP growth rate is higher.

Note that 'sustainability' is not a black-and-white issue: it is a matter of degree of political difficulty. The last equation is perhaps the most informative because the political difficulty of achieving a particular primary surplus is obviously relative to the total community income from which it has to be extracted: what proportion of a community's income does a government need to extract without returning any benefit in the way of public expenditure, in order to keep its debt under control? The higher the debt ratio, the higher the answer to that question. But the degree of difficulty may vary from country to country: a country with high social cohesion and a very efficient tax administration could deliver primary surplus proportions that other less well-placed countries could not.

How do countries shape up to this criterion? In Britain, roughly speaking, D_t/Y_t is about 0.9, r is a low 3 per cent and g perhaps a moderate 2 per cent. So the requirement on the primary surplus is only about 0.9 per cent of GDP—not terribly demanding. But Britain does not have a primary surplus at all at the moment—there is a primary deficit—so the Debt/GDP ratio is continuing to increase. All political parties say they aim to close this deficit over the next few years, although they differ in how fast and in what manner.

Greece, however, has a Debt/GDP ratio of 1.7, and at the peak of its crisis faced high interest rates approaching 10 per cent, with its growth effectively zero, therefore its required primary surplus was about 17 per cent of GDP—much more challenging, and most commentators believed politically impossible. There is a vicious circle here. The more unsustainable a country's financial position appears, the more the interest rates it faces will increase, making its position still worse. But on the other hand a really credible international plan to resolve the crisis would reduce the interest rates, thereby increasing the likelihood of the plan's success.

The 2008 financial crisis bounced many countries almost overnight from a sustainable to a potentially non-sustainable position. Debt/GDP ratios suddenly went up as private bank debt was taken into the public sector, growth rates fell as economies went into slumps, and rates of interest on government debt rose as foreign investors perceived those countries to be now more problematic. All three factors increased the difficulty of sustainability.

'OPTIMAL' DEBT?

The above analysis may tell us whether a particular level of debt is sustainable; it does not tell us anything about whether it is desirable. Is there such a thing as an 'optimal' level of national debt? Many people might be tempted to suggest that zero must be the ideal level. We have an inbuilt feeling that less debt must always be better than more, but this comes from our experiences as individuals: an individual with less debt is obviously better off than one with more debt. However, one cannot transfer this intuition from the individual to the public sphere: in a domestically-held public debt, one person's debt is another person's asset, and society as a whole is not obviously worse off thereby. Even as individuals we do not actually always believe zero debt is ideal: at a particular stage of our life-cycle, we are likely to take out a mortgage to buy a house, in the clear belief that this will be to our benefit. So zero is not an automatic answer—the answer depends on the circumstances.

Similarly, and even more so, with public debts. The trouble is that, as we have seen, there are many possible beneficial reasons to have a public debt, but also many not so beneficial reasons, and similarly many possible negative consequences. An 'optimal' public debt must be some kind of optimal compromise between the various advantages and disadvantages, so the answer is unlikely to be simple. An answer must take into account not only considerations of overall economic efficiency, but also of the distribution of benefits, distribution across several spectra—between rich and poor, young and old, current and future generations. Different economic theorists tend to set up simple models focussing on one or two of the functions and dysfunctions of a public debt, and not surprisingly come up with wildly different answers. Some answers even turn out to be negative, i.e. the state should actually be a net creditor.

Furthermore, there is scope for considerable disagreement about which activities should be funded by public money and which by private: even if it be accepted that the nation should have a particular level of aggregate debt, how much of it should be public debt and how much should be private debt? Thus there is little consensus among economists about an 'optimal' level of national debt.

The question itself is to some extent a utopian one; it is not the actual question we usually have to face. The practical question is: if we start off (for arbitrary reasons—past wars, financial crises) with a particular level of debt, is it a good idea to make sacrifices to reduce it to a lower level? We have seen that governments, for reasons of political expediency, usually prefer to duck that question. But surprisingly that may well be the correct policy on good economic grounds as well.

A large public debt is a cost to the economy because the taxation required to service it distorts economic incentives, thereby reducing total potential output. Reducing the debt now would reduce the taxation required in the long-term, therefore allowing greater output in the future. But reducing the debt will require an increase of taxation in the short run, temporarily increasing the disincentives and reducing output in the short run still further. So the wisdom of such a policy depends on a balance: are the long-term benefits worth the short-term pain? A recent article from the IMF suggests not.[1]

The analysis is complicated, but the underlying reason is simple. It is well accepted by economists that the distortionary effects of taxation increase more than linearly with the level of the tax. But the debt reduction policy replaces a steady time-profile of taxation by higher taxes in the short run and lower taxes in the long run: consequently, the additional distortions created in the short run are greater than the reduction in distortions in the long run. The taxation sacrifice is just not worth it.

We have seen that some politicians and economists over the ages have to some extent shared this intuition (see for instance Sir Robert Peel and John Stuart Mill, Chapter 6).

The correct solution, according to the authors of the IMF report—so long as there is no imminent danger of default, which is an important caveat—is to grit your teeth, continue to pay the interest payments, and wait for economic growth and inflation to cut the problem down to size. Yes, the debt is annoying, costly, and constraining. But attempting to repay it will be more annoying, more costly and more constraining.

Although this is only a very simple model, and therefore suggestive rather than conclusive, it does pose a direct challenge to austerity. In practice, recent austerity policies have focussed more on reducing expenditure than on increasing taxation, and so the impact on distortionary effects may therefore be rather different in detail. But so too the distributional effects will be different: increased taxation would likely be paid more by the rich, while reductions in public services would more likely be borne by the poor. Austerity via public expenditure reduction might therefore have a further question mark against it.

13

IS THERE MORE THAN THE NATIONAL DEBT?

Does the National Debt give a good indication of the total indebtedness of the nation and its citizens? The short answer is 'no', for four main reasons.

1. As we have seen, to a large extent, the National Debt is a set of claims from one group of British citizens to another. To the extent that this is true, it is not a net liability of the British citizenry. Such a net liability only applies to that part of the National Debt that is held by foreigners, and estimates suggest that this only amounts to less than a third of the total debt. So in this sense the National Debt overstates our future real liabilities.

According to the Debt Management Office, in Q3 2017 foreign holdings were £522 billion, UK Monetary Financial Institutions held £624 billion (and of this a massive £468 billion is temporarily held by the Bank of England as part of the Quantitative Easing (QE) programme), Insurance Companies and Pension Funds held £583 billion, and Other Financial Institutions £150 billion. Households held directly only just over £3 billion.

This netting-off of individual claims within the country does not mean, however, that the National Debt poses no problem.

Distorting taxes must be raised to make the interest payments, reducing desirable incentives and thereby total national output. There are also distributional problems: one subset of citizens is indebted to another subset, and it is no comfort to the former subset to realize that their predicament is not totally typical of their fellow citizens. And even if the debt is netted-off nationally, there might still be big imbalances between regions, or between any other kinds of group however defined, for example by gender, age or ethnicity. Some people within the country do have a negative balance and managing their situation may pose an important challenge to the community, even if they are only a minority of the population—much more so if they turn out to be the majority. Others who have a positive balance cannot be complacent either: they may find their expectations are not fulfilled if the affairs of the net debtors cannot be resolved satisfactorily.

The distribution of the Debt is a part of the overall distribution of income and wealth in the country and therefore its resolution should perhaps best be seen as part of a more comprehensive policy on income and wealth distribution. But Britain has rarely had such a policy. If it did, it is not clear that in current circumstances (where the National Debt is not particularly high, nor are the interest rates on it, and its effective distribution through the pension industry may not be particularly unequal) measures aimed at the National Debt would be more effective than taxation measures aimed directly at incomes and wealth. There have, however, been times when the distributional implications of the Debt have been much more pointed: particularly at the various post-war peaks, the unspoken question is always the extent to which the large costs of the war will eventually be borne by the rich or the poor. In the past a rapid repayment of debt could only realistically be met by taxation of the rich, so a policy of deferral resulted in spreading the burden more towards the poor, although necessarily more slowly. In modern conditions, though, an alternative method of speeding up repayment is to reduce public expenditure; to the extent that this is welfare-related expenditure benefiting mainly the poor, the distributional implications are reversed.

2. The National Debt represents only part of the government's responsibilities to the future—that part which can be expressed as a formal, debt-like obligation. There are many other obligations which will, in practice, have to be met in the future, although they are not in the National Debt as conventionally measured. The National Debt is therefore an understatement of the government's future liabilities.

Here we can draw an analogy with our own individual positions. We too may have some formal, debt-like obligations for the future: mortgages, credit card debts, overdrafts to repay. Missing such payments will have immediate and uncomfortable consequences. But we know we also have many less formal liabilities: some time we will have to replace the car, mend the roof, pay for family weddings. Ultimately, we will have to keep feeding ourselves or we will die. But these requirements have some, varying, degrees of flexibility, although the flexibility still has consequences: we can keep the old car for a bit longer at the risk of more breakdowns, or put off mending the roof at the cost of suffering drips when it rains and probably a larger bill for repairs when we ultimately get around to it. We can trim our food intake in quantity and quality; we can skimp on the wedding at the cost of frosty family relationships for ever after.

The government also has many such less formal liabilities for the future. Some are, in fact, quite clear-cut and contractual, although they do not figure in the National Debt. In all sorts of ways the government is required to keep the country on track as some kind of going concern for the foreseeable future. The possibility of large, uncertain liabilities outside the National Debt has become an important and much-voiced concern in recent years. We shall examine this in greater detail in this chapter.

3. Governments do not only have liabilities; they also have assets. A correct overall financial assessment must consider the net balance between assets and liabilities. Looking at the National Debt alone overstates our net indebtedness.

4. The National Debt is the debt of the government, and through our relationship to the government as citizens and tax-payers it becomes part of our individual liabilities. But tax-payers also have their own personal liabilities irrespective of the government—there is private-sector debt as well as public-sector debt, and in some countries and at some times the former may massively exceed the latter.

Major sources of private-sector debt are consumer credit, mortgages and private-sector business investment. But, again, we should remember we also have personal assets, which need also to be taken into the assessment. Some of these assets are of course government bonds, so there may be complex interactions between private and public financial positions.

A country's overall financial health is really measured by its total (i.e. public and private) indebtedness, and the division between private and public can be sometimes quite artificial. Some examples will illustrate why.

It is an interesting feature of the Eurozone Crisis that different European countries approached the 2008 financial crash with very different experiences of public and private debt. Some, like Greece, had excessive public spending and therefore very large public debts. Others, like Spain and Ireland, had more responsible (or more fortunate) governments, and therefore rather small public debts. But Spain and Ireland had very large private-sector housing booms, fuelled by large mortgages, and therefore had very large private-sector debts. When the private-sector banks which had created these debts proved unsustainable and had to be bailed out by the government, the private-sector debt became public overnight, leaving the Spanish and Irish governments in much the same position as the Greek government, although for very different reasons.

Secondly, consider a very extreme example. It is theoretically possible to pay off the entire National Debt at a stroke, by levying, in one year, taxation large enough to do the job. However, the practical problem would be that few citizens would have the cash resources to meet their tax payments. That need not be an insuperable problem if they were able to borrow to meet their tax payments (indeed a government might even compel the banking system to make the necessary loans). The result would certainly be the desired elimination of the public debt. But in reality, it would just have been transferred into the private sector. The citizens' overall indebtedness would remain the same—although their position would almost certainly now be more fragile, as their new private-sector creditors would likely be more demanding than the government bond-holders formerly were.[1]

A similar, but less extreme dynamic, can be seen in the effects of austerity. Governments may aim to reduce their own deficits and debts by reducing welfare payments. But if the recipients of reduced welfare payments cannot reduce their outgoings proportionately, they will inevitably turn to borrowing, ultimately from the most unsuitable and expensive kind of lenders. Again, the result will be at least partially only a transfer of public debt into less efficient private debt.

This is not a phenomenon confined to the poor. If the government similarly aims to reduce its deficit by charging university tuition fees via a student loan system, public debt is replaced by private-sector student debt (although in this case at least so far on terms similar to the government's).

WHOLE OF GOVERNMENT ACCOUNTS

Two recent UK government innovations have considerably helped us to better understand our wider future commitments and prospects. Firstly, the government has been experimenting with 'Whole of Government Accounts', which attempt to remedy some of the defects of traditional national debt accounting. These go some way to meeting the concerns of points 2 and 3. Essentially the idea is to treat the government in the same way as accountants would view a private-sector corporation. Important differences in treatment are:

1. The definition of the boundary of government: the National Debt is basically the debt of the Treasury and the government departments subject to Treasury control, but in private-sector accounting corporations must be consolidated with any subsidiaries that are more than 50 per cent owned or are 'effectively controlled'. So the status of many part-private, part-public agencies must be carefully considered, giving a potentially different definition of the 'Government'.
2. Balance sheets include both Liabilities and Assets.
3. (i) Any 'obligation' to pay money in the future, arising from a past event, must be included in liabilities.
    (ii) A legally binding 'commitment' to pay money in the future for an event which has not yet taken place need not be included quantitatively in the accounts but should be mentioned in 'Notes to the accounts'.
    (iii) Commitments which are not legally binding do not need to figure in the accounts.

The third group of points is particularly important. To elucidate further, let us consider the various stages of 'commitment' in a particular project:

1. The government is aware that at some time in the future, if it is to maintain its existing level of naval capabilities, it will have to replace its aging aircraft carriers. At this point there may be an intention or aspiration, even an expectation, but no

real commitment: the situation is flexible and there are various possibilities, including extending the life of the present aircraft carriers, trying to maintain the naval capabilities without aircraft carriers, or even accepting the scaling down of naval capabilities in the future.

2. The government announces that it will build a new aircraft carrier. This is a political commitment, but not a legal one; if it is reversed there will be political embarrassment but no legal consequences.

3. The government signs a contract with a shipbuilder to build the aircraft carrier. This is now a legal commitment—withdrawing at this stage would be a kind of default and would incur financial penalties—although its precise quantity may still be unclear. Building an aircraft carrier is a long and complex project; specifications tend to change in the course of construction, and this will affect the final bill. But although a commitment, this is not yet a debt, because the aircraft carrier has not yet been delivered, nor the bill presented. It would not appear in the National Debt, and its appearance in the Whole of Government Accounts would be limited to the maximum penalty payments on cancellation.

4. The aircraft carrier is delivered and the bill presented. This is now definitely an obligation, and if the government does not pay it will certainly be in default. It will immediately appear in the Whole of Government Accounts, but it will not figure in the Debt until the prescribed date for actual payment. In our own terminology it would then become part of the floating debt; if the government can pay the bill out of tax revenues then the debt is cancelled and the transaction is complete. If, however, the government does not have sufficient tax revenues it will have to borrow, either short-term or long-term, to pay the shipbuilder's bill, thereby formalising the increase in the National Debt.

But it should not be forgotten that, at each stage of this process, the government is contemplating or actually acquiring a capital asset, although in this case not a commercially very productive one. In theory the aircraft carrier should be valued at its cost, indicating no increase in net liability for the government; but unlike commercial assets, aircraft carriers do not produce a stream of financial returns, so this value will not in the long run be very helpful in paying off the liability.

The latest published version is the Whole of Government Accounts for the year ending March 2016. Because of adjustments in coverage that occurred between 2015 and 2016, the results of 2016 are not quite directly comparable with those of earlier years, so Table 13.1 is compiled, with some amendments, from the reports for both 2015 and 2016.

LIABILITIES

The main liabilities these accounts disclose are, in quantitative order of importance:

1. Public-sector occupational pension entitlements (£1,425 billion)

Public-sector workers, like other workers, have pensions deriving from their employment. In the private sector, such pensions normally have to be funded: i.e. the firm must set aside, in a legally separate vehicle, enough money to cover the expected pension liabilities in the future. This money is normally invested in order to maximise the pensions; much of it is invested in government bonds as they are perceived to be the safest and most predictable sources of long-term returns, and therefore the most suitable asset for long-term, predictable liabilities such as pensions.

The government could do the same for its own workers, but there is little point. The main purpose of requiring funding in the private sector is to protect the pensioners' money against the bankruptcy of the parent company (given the very long-term horizons, quite a plausible possibility, even for well-run companies). But the government is the least likely of all organisations to go bankrupt, and if it did it wouldn't be paying out on its bonds either, so government employees effectively have the same level of protection already; requiring funding would only add unnecessary administrative costs.

Therefore, the government simply pays the pensions of its retired workers out of current taxation, just as it pays the wages of workers not yet retired. This has the unfortunate consequence of disguising the full extent of the government's future pension commitments. It is not committed to paying wages in the future; *in extremis* it could sack all the existing public-sector workers or reduce their pay, subject only to the levels of notice in their contracts; but the past contracts with its retired workers cannot now be altered without default. Proper pension funding would instead have required the trustees of government pension funds to be given large quantities of government bonds, whose interest payments would then pay the pensions.[3] The sums of money actually paid would be the same, but they would now appear in the national accounts as interest payments on a much larger national debt, not as current expenditure.

The Whole of Government Accounts value the future stream of government occupational pensions at £1,424.7 billion at the end of 2015–16. We noted in Chapter 1 that the entire official National Debt in December 2017 was £1,759.5 billion (the corresponding figure for March 2016 was £1,602.6 billion), so this is a very big increase indeed—very nearly as much as the official National Debt itself—but fortunately by far the biggest non-Debt liability. Also, as the table shows, the estimated present

Table 13.1: Assets and Liabilities Summary, 2010–2016

	2010–11 £bn	2011–12 £bn	2012–13 £bn	2013–14 £bn	2014–15 £bn	2015–16 £bn
Property, plant and equipment	714.0	744.5	746.8	812.3	847.8	1,120.2[2]
Gold, cash and other financial assets	254.6	282.1	311.2	350.7	356.1	365.5
Trade receivables	145.1	141.9	138.9	149.6	145.9	154.7
Equity in public-sector banks	59.5	40.8	40.0	43.0	44.2	96.1
Intangible assets	34.8	35.2	34.5	31.9	32.4	–
Other physical assets	26.3	26.1	26.1	27.4	28.9	–
Total Assets	1,234.3	1,270.6	1,297.5	1,414.9	1,455.3	1,742.4
Public-sector pensions	961.0	1,005.8	1,171.9	1,303.1	1,493.3	1,424.7
Government borrowing	908.2	965.5	996.2	1,096.1	1,174.5	1,260.6
Financial liabilities	295.4	374.3	472.8	528.7	542.5	557.4
Trade payables	148.4	158.9	153.5	173.0	172.9	180.2
Provisions	107.0	113.0	131.0	154.6	175.3	305.5
Total Liabilities	2,420.0	2,617.5	2,925.4	3,255.5	3,558.5	3,728.4
Net Liabilities	1,185.7	1,346.9	1,627.9	1,840.6	2,103.2	1,986.0

Source: Table 1.c from Whole-of-Government Accounts 2015 with additions from 2016.

value of this liability has been increasing rapidly in recent years. This is of course partly due to the increasing number and longevity of public-sector pensioners and the increased generosity of pension schemes, but less obviously also due to a more technical adjustment: with the very low current interest rates, all pension schemes' future liabilities are now evaluated at much lower discount rates, leading to much higher numbers. For a private-sector pension fund reliant on the returns from its bond investments, such a revaluation reflects a very real practical difficulty. But as the government does not actually rely on such a fund, the real consequences for the tax-payer are less clear-cut: the actual future payments to pensioners remain unchanged.

On the other hand, the universal state old-age pension is not a contractual commitment:[4] its level is determined year-by-year by political considerations, so its costs figure neither in the National Debt nor in the wider Whole of Government Accounts. Nevertheless, the degree of political commitment to it is very high, and any significant reduction would in practice be very difficult.

2. Government Borrowing, at £1,261 billion

This, which is really the National Debt as we have been discussing it throughout this book, only comes in second in importance. Note that the figure given is considerably less than the conventional National Debt figure we have been using (quoted above), because the Whole of Government approach nets out any holdings of government debt held by departments and agencies within its wider definition of 'Government'. We have seen that many government departments have always held appreciable quantities of government debt, and this tendency has been magnified in recent years by the Quantitative Easing (QE) programme, whereby the Bank of England (considered by the Whole of Government approach to be a part of government) now owns about a quarter of the issued debt.

These QE bonds are in an interesting position, not unlike those bonds that used to be accumulated by the National Debt Commissioners under the Pitt Sinking Fund. If the public fully realised this, they might feel as confused as the early nineteenth-century public as to why the government was paying large sums of interest to itself. If all the QE bonds were now simply cancelled, the government would have rid itself of a large fraction of the debt—without levying taxation—by effectively monetising it. Whether this would be wise, or inflationary, is a moot point.[5]

3. Financial Liabilities, at £557 billion

This item is currently unusually large because it is dominated by the counterpart of Quantitative Easing. The Bank of England bought the bonds involved from the commercial banks, so the commercial banks now have unusually very large current accounts with the Bank of England. If and when the QE programme ends, the commercial banks will buy back their bonds from the Bank of England, using these current accounts—causing this figure to fall and the corresponding figure in point 2 to rise.

Also included here is the ordinary bank-note issue of the Bank of England (about £68 billion), although this does not explicitly figure in the conventional National Debt (but the government bonds held by the Bank of England in exactly equal numbers as security, do).

4. Trade Payables, at £180 billion

This is mostly just the normal short-term throughput of any large business, of bills for purchases to be settled. It is roughly balanced by a similar item of Trade Receivables in Assets. However, one element tucked away here which is worthy of separate note is commitments under the Private Finance

Initiative—this will be discussed separately at greater length in the next section.

5. Provisions, at £305 billion

Within this, the largest components are Nuclear Power Station Decommissioning Costs, estimated at £182 billion, and NHS clinical negligence claims estimated at £58 billion. These have dramatically increased in the last year, not because of any technological reassessment of the real risks, but because of a technical adjustment in the discount rate, which can have very significant effects on the current valuation of very long-term liabilities. The remainder includes HMRC's provisions against disputed tax bills and a variety of compensation schemes for a variety of untoward events, including the Pension Protection Fund. Note, however, that these figures do not give the total amount of compensation in these areas for which the state may be liable in the future. Remember that the accounting principle recognises only the predicted payments arising from events that have already occurred; for example, claims for incidents of NHS clinical negligence occurring next year, although they could possibly be predicted, are not included in these figures (because the government could at this stage still avoid incurring them, if only by shutting the NHS down).

Although the capital value of these items may seem quite high, the period over which they are effectively payable is very long. For instance, the £182 billion of nuclear power station decommissioning costs covers a programme lasting until the year 2137. Health compensation payments may also cover a very long period. Therefore, the annual incidence is rather more modest.

ASSETS (£1,743 BILLION CREDIT)

On the other side, the exercise identifies a significant quantity of government assets. £1120 billion of Property, Plant and

Equipment, being land, roads, buildings, including military equipment (the large apparent increase between 2014–5 and 2015–16 is mainly due to the revaluation of the assets of Network Rail, which had previously been treated differently); £366 billion of Other Financial Assets, including investment properties, the value of intangible military systems, unpaid taxes, the investment in nationalised banks, the student loan book, cash and other financial assets.

The exercise is still experimental, and several issues remain vague or unresolved. The Comptroller and Auditor General is not wholly satisfied with the Accounts and only signs them off with significant Qualifications. These qualifications principally concern the definition of the boundary of the Whole Government (e.g. the accounts still exclude the Royal Bank of Scotland, presumably because the government hopes that its post-2008 shareholding is only temporary, and inclusion would add massive sums to both sides of the balance sheet; but the Comptroller disagrees), and inconsistent accounting principles used in different parts of this enormous enterprise. The valuation of many public assets is very difficult and imprecise because of the very imperfect markets for them. Nevertheless, the areas of uncertainty narrow with each annual exercise.

Overall, the exercise concludes that at the end of the year 2015–16 the government's Net Liabilities under this definition were £1,986 billion in place of the officially recorded Net National Debt of £1,603 billion. Although some very large extra liabilities have been identified, the overall effect is not quite as catastrophic as might have been feared; the extra liabilities are partially offset by the identification and inclusion of assets. Whether that is entirely comforting is a matter of judgement: many of the assets are not easily marketable, or indeed intended to be marketed. Nor are many of them revenue-generating in normal circumstances. On the other hand, the extra liabilities are not tradable market claims either: pension and compensation payments will be made in a steady stream over a very long period of time and their ability to embarrass the government in liquidity terms is limited. Nor are these extra liabilities completely new claims—we have been meeting them quite happily for many years out of current revenue. The real cause for concern is not that they exist, but that they may be on an upward trend.

It should of course be remembered that this exercise only identifies the most clear-cut future liabilities; many of the vaguer liabilities are still excluded. But that is in line with ordinary experience; future evils must largely be left for future generations to sort out, as we in our turn have had to confront problems left over from or unforeseen by previous generations. To some extent we and they must take the rough with the smooth. This exercise only accounts for those cases where our own actions have clearly created, for our own current benefit, definable liabilities for future generations. (Another exercise, the Fiscal Sustainability Report, discussed later in this chapter, does indeed try to quantify some of the liabilities arising only in the future.)

Of course, the government will have to continue to maintain the roads in the future, for example. So one might say that this is a future commitment which should be recognised. But the condition of the roads in the future will be a benefit to future generations, not to the current generation. It is therefore right to leave the costs to the future generations too. It is also right to leave the decision to them too: they will bear the consequences and will be better placed to make that decision. We do not know what their situation will be; technological change may revolutionise modes of transport. Our successors may prefer to let the roads deteriorate and prioritise spending on other matters (as indeed nineteenth-century local authorities did do with the advent of the railways).

THE PRIVATE FINANCE INITIATIVE (PFI)

These are projects such as the construction of hospitals, schools and other infrastructure which might previously have been performed by the public sector with public money, but have been in recent years performed by private-sector firms with private money, in return for long streams of interest payments and long-term contracts for associated services such as maintenance and operation. Crystallised liabilities amount to about £40 billion, although it should be noted that the projects have created corresponding assets valued at £42 billion. But there are larger commitments in relation to future interest payments and payments for future services, which the Accounts only note. The total commitment is likely to be of the order of £200 billion.

PFI is a particularly egregious example of the dangers of over-concentration on the headline figures of indebtedness. It is also a good example of a modern tendency to hide future commitments off the balance sheet. For both reasons it will be worthwhile to spend a little more time on it.

PFI really had its origins in the Thatcher government of the early 1980s. As we have seen, that government wished to reduce public borrowing, not so much from explicit concern with the National Debt but more because of the alleged effect of government borrowing on the money supply, as it was the government's central policy to control inflation by controlling the money supply. Control of the money supply therefore in turn led to a desired control of the Public-Sector Borrowing Requirement (PSBR) expressed in terms of a very public, very high-profile target. This target was obviously designed to put downward pressure on public expenditure, but it put equal pressure on public consumption expenditure and public investment expenditure alike. Some members of the government would have preferred to look more favourably on the latter, as necessary public infrastructure projects would have real productive benefits for the economy, but the public-sector accounting of the time made no clear distinction between the two types of expenditure and the Treasury advised that any public investment must form part of the PSBR. Thus public investment had to be as heavily constrained as public consumption, and, since it is politically much easier to cut or indeed not to start new investment projects than to cut back ongoing and entrenched programmes, the effect was inevitably a disproportionate hit on public investment, with potentially serious long-term effects on the economy.

The Major government inherited the macroeconomic policy framework centred on a borrowing/expenditure target, and sought a way out of this dilemma; a way which was also congenial to its general view that private-sector operation was more efficient than public-sector operation. This view had already found its expression in the privatisation of nationalised industries, but it could also be applied to the effective privatisation of individual investment projects within organisations which would in all other respects remain clearly within the public sector. If these projects could be performed by the private sector, they need not appear in the PSBR, and the government would be less likely to breach its public targets.

But there was a key confusion of interests at the centre of this policy, which is reflected in its name. If private-sector operation were indeed more efficient than public-sector, it was more due to its management skills, not to its financial arrangements. The government's sources of finance were vastly superior to that of any private-sector organisation: it could borrow at lower rates of interest and in larger quantities. What was really needed was not a Private Finance Initiative but a Private Management Initiative. In an ideal world projects might be run on contract by a private-sector management team, with appropriate incentives, but with mainstream finance provided by the Treasury at the lowest possible interest rates.

But private management is difficult to disentangle from private finance, and Treasury advice anyway ruled that this would not meet the requirement to keep a project outside the PSBR. If public investment were involved, and in particular if the public investment were bearing the financial risk of the project, the project would still be in the public sector. To keep the project out of the PSBR, private-sector finance would have to be bearing the risks. Thus Private Finance Initiative it had to be.

But here the true absurdity of the scheme becomes apparent. If private-sector finance must bear risks it will want to be compensated for so doing. This is the principal reason for private-sector finance being so much more expensive than public-sector finance. The government is vastly larger than even the biggest private-sector firm and can spread its risks more widely, as was argued in a very famous article by Arrow and Lind.[6]

To take an example, suppose the government wants to build ten hospitals. Each hospital project contains a certain degree of risk: the eventual construction costs may turn out more than or less than the current best estimates. If each hospital project is contracted out to separate private-sector contractors, each contractor will charge a risk premium to cover this risk. (The contractor in turn must raise its own finance from ultimate investors who also perceive the riskiness of the contractor and will expect their returns to cover it too). But to the government as a whole, the risk of the ten hospitals together is considerably less, through the workings of the law of large numbers. So long as the risks of each hospital are not perfectly correlated, the proportional riskiness of the whole will be less than that of any individual hospital. This is why the government can raise money from the public on vastly better terms than the contractor can. But it is this very substantial advantage that the government is giving up for the sake of political window-dressing. If the government can borrow at 3 per cent and the contractors only at 6 per cent, the taxpayers' future commitments will be double under PFI compared to public-sector investment—although those commitments will not be formally part of the National Debt.

While in opposition, the Labour Party had argued strongly against PFI as an unnecessary and inefficient form of creeping privatisation. But when Labour came to power in 1997, they too found the structure highly convenient for their own objectives. Their macro policy was originally dominated by a pledge not to exceed the Conservatives' former planned expenditure targets (in order to boost their credibility as responsible economic managers). However, other promises committed them to improve social infrastructure such as schools and hospitals, which threatened to exceed those targets. Again, PFI could apparently resolve the dilemma, allowing schools and hospitals to be built and improved in large numbers, but off the balance sheet. The outcome was inefficiently large future commitments, but not formally part of the National Debt. The full size of these commitments is only now beginning to be systematically understood through exercises such as the Whole of Government Accounts.

THE FISCAL SUSTAINABILITY REPORT

The second recent innovation from the UK government is the Office for Budget Responsibility, set up in 2010 to be a quasi-autonomous commentator on the soundness of government fiscal policy. The OBR publishes a series of Fiscal Sustainability Reports, which directly address the question of whether the National Debt is on a sustainable or a non-sustainable path. They apply the basic theoretical methodology we outlined in Chapter 12, focussing on the question of whether the Debt/GDP ratio is likely to fall or rise over the next half-century. But they are able to go into considerably more detail, factoring in the latest projections of population growth and structure, longevity, policy commitments, etc. They also take on board the wider future commitments identified by the Whole of Government Accounts—indeed, they go much further, projecting also commitments that will arise from future events and policies.

Projecting so far ahead is an ambitious venture: the principal assumption is one of 'unchanged' fiscal policy, but this is a slippery concept. For the next few years, up to the mid-2020s, the current government has fairly well-defined plans, but after that point little is actually fixed. Unless there are clear reasons to do otherwise, the OBR assumes that rates of taxation and benefits will remain roughly the same and that the underlying demand for public services will grow as the economy grows.

The overall conclusion of its most recent report (January 2017) is that, in the medium term, the existing austerity policies will succeed in bringing the debt ratio down slightly, from its current approximate 90 per cent to approximately 80 per cent, by the late 2020s. So far, so good. But after that point, long-term unfavourable trends reassert themselves, the public-sector deficit grows steadily year by year, and with it the Debt. By the financial year 2066–67, the debt ratio is predicted to be 234 per cent. Readers will note that such a figure is comparable to the post-1815 and post-1945 debt peaks.

What are the main drivers of this pessimistic outlook? First, the OBR has recently become more pessimistic on the outlook for growth, reducing its long-term productivity growth forecast to 2 per cent p.a. Readers will now be well aware that even small changes in long-term growth can have very significant effects on the long-term debt ratio. But the main drivers are on the expenditure side, arising from the familiar story of a growing and aging population. Total health spending is projected to rise from 6.9 per cent of GDP in 2021–22 to 12.6 per cent of GDP in 2066–67 (this is a truly massive shift, and interestingly it is not simply due to the aging population—it is projected also that the costs of health care will rise faster than costs generally in the economy; new but expensive treatments will continue to be discovered and public opinion will demand their implementation). Over the same period the state pension cost will rise from 5 per cent to 7.1 per cent of GDP, and social care of the elderly from 1.1 per cent to 2 per cent.

These are very large shifts in the demand for resources, and with an assumption of a largely unchanged tax system, it is not surprising that the public finances would be projected as unable to cope: the government's current austerity measures manage to reinstate a primary surplus of 0.8 per cent by 2021–22, but after that the finances steadily deteriorate again to a primary deficit of 7.2 per cent in 2066–67.

What fiscal response would prevent this debt explosion? The OBR recognises that this is not a precisely defined question: there is no generally agreed rule for an optimal long-run debt ratio, and measures to bring the Debt to zero would surely be too draconian. However, it provides projections for achieving various bench-mark debt ratios: 20 per cent, 40 per cent, 60 per cent, etc. It foregrounds particularly the ratio of 40 per cent: that was roughly Britain's level in the years before the 2008 crisis. The OBR provides two kinds of fiscal adjustment that would achieve a 40 per cent debt ratio in 2066–67: (i) a once-and-for-all fiscal tightening of 4.3 per cent of GDP in 2022–23 and onward; or (ii) a gradual fiscal tightening of 1.5 per cent of GDP every decade until 2066–67.

But interestingly the once-and-for-all tightening is not an ideal response. As the expenditure demands are gradually increasing over time, the initial impact is unnecessarily severe, driving the debt ratio below 40 per cent. However, towards the end of the period the 4.3 per cent tightening is no longer enough and the debt ratio begins to rise again. It does meet the target of 40 per cent in 2066–67, but the debt ratio is now again on an upward trend, and the future is actually looking unsustainable again. On the other hand, the gradual fiscal tightening is better matched to the time profile of the increasing costs, and brings the debt ratio down more slowly but steadily, meeting the 40 per cent target in 2066–67 while still on a downward trend, so that seems to be a more genuinely sustainable path. However, one should note the less comfortable implication: after five decades of gradual tightening at 1.5 per cent per decade, the degree of tightening will have reached 7.5 per cent of GDP by 2066–67.

Strangely, the OBR does not provide an estimate of how much additional economic growth would be required instead to achieve the same results. As we have seen from the history it is more usually economic growth rather than fiscal tightening that provides long-term debt resolution. Maybe the OBR's remit precludes it from doing so. But maybe also within its methodology the effects of growth might not be so marked as in the past. In our history, debt problems have largely been requirements to absorb some large but fixed commitment from the past. Future growth can only be helpful in such cases. But in this exercise, many of the expenditure commitments lie in the future, and are assumed to grow with any expansion in the economy. This is a rather different situation and will obviously be expected to damp down the positive effects of growth on the debt. Of course, in practice, another avenue for preventing the debt rising would therefore be to break that assumption. For instance, the state old-age pension is currently protected by the so-called 'triple lock' which ensures that it will grow at least as fast as the economy: withdrawal of that political promise would ultimately lead to a lower pension bill.

So the OBR's view of the future is not a rosy one. But it is not necessarily a cause for panic, and, significantly, the OBR itself emphasises that it does not call for any immediate changes in policy. The timescale is very long: half a century (for comparison, remember that the debt ratio rose from 25 per cent to about 240 per cent in just over thirty years after 1914, and fell back again to less than 50 per cent in the next thirty years). It is also not surprising that any 'unchanged-policy' projection over such a long period for an economy which is not currently running a surplus should trace out an ultimately explosive unsustainable path. As policy will certainly change, in both predictable and unpredictable ways, this is not to be interpreted as a forecast of what will actually happen, more a warning that important decisions will soon have to be taken. Naturally, many other unpredictable things can also happen in fifty years: a half-century ago the IT revolution had hardly begun, and a similar revolution in health-care technology in the next fifty years could completely transform the picture.

The OBR is really spelling out some very significant resource shifts in the economy that will have to be accommodated one way or another. Longer lives and improved health technology are great benefits to us all, but they will imply significant shifts in our expenditure (just as the invention of cars and aeroplanes has meant resource shifts toward transport expenditures in the past). Taxpayers are naturally reluctant to see tax bills increase. The OBR's figures assume that tax revenues hold roughly steady at 36–37 per cent of GDP, a level that some analysts regard as close to the limit of political feasibility in Britain (although some West European countries have ratios exceeding 40 per cent). But if health care and pensions remain in the public sector, the shifting expenditure patterns will require a higher proportion, and taxpayers will have to adjust their expectations. This may be politically difficult, but it is not new. We saw that in 1914, taxation accounted for only 10 per cent of GDP—and was generally regarded as an iniquitous burden—but it significantly increased over the twentieth century. In a famous book, Peacock and

Wiseman argued that public expenditure tends to rise, ratchet-like, only as a result of crises (usually wars), then fails to reverse itself after the crises, and subsequently gains a grudging tolerance at its new higher level from the taxpayers.[7] The aging phenomenon is possibly a similar crisis, and half a century is a long time to allow expectations to adapt.

There are, of course, alternative ways of squaring this circle. One is to accept lower levels of public health care and pension provision; another would be to remove some or all of such expenditures altogether from the public to the private sector. While these would certainly improve the public finances, the real pressures for such expenditures would remain, with corresponding implications for private-sector finances and standards of living. The relative balance between growth, tax increases and expenditure reductions should be a matter of microeconomic calculation, but will also involve political value judgements.

PRIVATE-SECTOR INDEBTEDNESS

The private sector comprises individuals and corporations. In November 2017, total lending to individuals by British financial institutions was £1,566 billion (a very similar order of magnitude to the National Debt), of which £1,360 billion was mortgages, and £206 billion was consumer credit.[8]

Private individuals are much more vulnerable than the government. Individual misfortunes such as illness or unemployment are much more likely to cause serious problems. Of course, the personal sector has assets too—obviously to set against the mortgages should be a similar value of houses. But a balance of liabilities and assets is not the same as having neither assets nor liabilities, for two principal reasons. One is that the assets may be less liquid than the liabilities and therefore not much use to cushion temporary setbacks. And the second is that the dynamics of assets and liabilities may be very different: a comfortable balance may easily become an imbalance if prices and interest rates change. Both these apply particularly to housing.

In the corporate sector, loans to non-financial businesses amounted to £466 billion. Smaller than the personal sector, and these loans have ideally gone to buy productive assets, but the returns from those assets may fluctuate with the fortunes of business while the interest costs remain steady. If the investment decision turns out to have been misguided the asset may be worthless, but the debt still has to be paid—unlike with equity finance where the lender accepts a share of the risk and the payments will vary with the success or failure of the asset.

But all of these are dwarfed by the liabilities of UK Monetary and Financial Institutions, at £8,099 billion. Banks and other financial organisations operate a complex web of borrowing and lending. Transactions are packaged and repackaged and passed on many times among specialists in different kinds of business. The aggregate net position is a small difference between very large apparent assets and very large apparent liabilities, although most of these assets and liabilities are internal transactions within the financial sector itself—somebody's liability is somebody else's asset. Again, these assets and liabilities have varying degrees of liquidity, and obey different dynamics. The financial organisations run on very tight margins, and even small changes in the environment can send some into difficulties; larger changes can provoke wholesale chain collapse. It is this characteristic of finance which makes it so vulnerable.

The financial sector has large international linkages: again, in ideal times a rough balance of very large liabilities and very large assets. But these are very large compared to the size of the British economy, and again small changes in the dynamics could result in a very large net liability to the outside world. This is essentially what happened to Iceland in 2008.

It is beyond the scope of this book to analyse the vulnerabilities of banking systems, but it is clear that the potential for danger is greater by far in the private financial sector than in the public sector.

14

CONCLUSIONS

What, if anything, can we ultimately learn from this history?

First, to recap on the issues foreshadowed in Chapter 1: the Debt/GDP ratio has certainly grown since 2008, but it is still at a level well below its historical peaks. Furthermore, interest rates are exceptionally low at the current time, so that the debt interest burden is in fact close to an all-time low. However:

1. Although the current levels are not historically high, they are moving in the wrong direction, and at a time when they should normally not be.
2. The past historical context has been perhaps relatively kind to Britain and its public debt; we cannot guarantee that it will continue to be so.
3. The official figures for National Debt exclude and conceal other public commitments for the future, which are themselves increasing rapidly.
4. The OBR's Fiscal Sustainability Report has outlined a very challenging long-term future.
5. The National Debt is only the debt of the government (the public sector) but the private sector has debts of its own.

These are of comparable magnitude and have also increased rapidly in recent years. The financial sector has an even larger network of debts. The overall financial situation of the country is the combined effect of all these debts.

With the benefit of our history we can add some further comments.

The Debt continues to rise because the government is still running a current deficit, and this is not due to exceptional wartime requirements, which cease with the end of hostilities. It is, of course, arguable that the financial crisis of 2008 was equivalent in economic terms to a small war, and we are still living through the normal process of debt adjustment following such an event. But we also have a structural deficit of peacetime expenditures such as education, health, welfare and peacetime levels of defence, which are not currently being covered by sufficient taxation; these expenditures are likely to continue to rise, and the government does not yet have a wholly convincing plan to close this deficit.

Although we have had a welfare state for many years, this kind of prolonged deficit is a relatively recent phenomenon. A growing but aging population, environmental issues, and the increasing complexity of society and the economy will keep the expenditure demands high. But the tax base is eroding: wealthy individuals and corporations are increasingly inventive in tax avoidance, and taxation is no more politically popular with lower- and middle-income groups. So a serious problem of adjustment needs to be faced. Either expenditure needs to be trimmed or taxation needs to be increased. Less painful ways out would be a return to higher rates of economic growth, or improvements in the efficiency of delivery of government services, but the latter are much easier to imagine than to implement. History suggests that actually the likeliest saviour is always economic growth.

It is quite remarkable that, whereas the history of our National Debt has been dominated by the problems of absorbing large war expenditures, future projections are dominated by the problems of aging. Although practically very different, the debt implications of the two problems are not dissimilar. Appendix II attempts to show in simple terms how the need to finance longer and more expensive retirements (as projected by the Fiscal Sustainability Report) inevitably leads to larger private and public debts. However, such larger debts are not necessarily unsustainable— indeed they are desirable if proper funding provisions are made.

Our history has shown that actual repayment of debt is rare, and difficult. We have, on the other hand, experienced two long periods of successfully 'growing out of' severe debt peaks. The compound interest effects of economic growth are just as dramatic as those of sinking funds and, given a reasonably stable external environment and at least not unreasonably imprudent budgetary policies, the debt position will almost inevitably improve. But those two conditions are necessary.

There is, however, one period (1875–1914) of quite successful steady repayment. Without the unfortunate intervention of the Boer War, £300 million, or nearly half the National Debt of the time, would have been paid off. The reasons for this success seem to include a strong political (and moralistic) commitment at the time, bolstered by administrative structures of some complexity which could defeat most attempts to backslide. It must be noted also that by that time any air of crisis was long past; the economy was then rather robust compared to the volume of the Debt and the degree of sacrifice required correspondingly less. Just another variant of the usual paradox of debt: it is easiest to borrow, and to repay, when it is least necessary.

The mechanics of the Debt are, at least for the moment, relatively secure. Our Debt is entirely in sterling, which is under our control, and we are committed to no gold standard or fixed exchange rate mechanism. We no longer have the luxury of unrepayable Consols, but the average maturity of our Debt is still very long, so our vulnerability to liquidity crises is low. Low interest rates will not last for ever, and when they eventually rise Britain's public finances will look more vulnerable unless some remedial action has been taken, but the impact on our interest bill will be slow.

National debts have very long-term implications. They are part of the network of implicit contracts between classes and generations within the state, they help to determine the distribution of income and wealth, and any rapid shifts can have dangerous effects on income distribution and on disappointed expectations. Their credibility depends on the state's continued control of tax revenue, and this has become more questionable in recent years. More fundamentally, credibility also depends on the continued integrity of the state—since the early eighteenth century this has not been a significant issue for Britain, but suddenly this too seems less secure.

Control of the National Debt has also required control of the various temptations to leave long-term commitments off the balance sheet. At different times these temptations have taken different forms, and our current time has its own. The expenditures that are financed in this way may be very desirable in themselves, but rational decision-making suffers from the resulting loss of information, clarity and control. Taken too far, they too undermine credibility.

Finally, an existing level of debt makes dealing with a future crisis that much more difficult and expensive. If we are lucky enough to avoid such future crises (as by and large the Victorians were), we may be able to look back on our indebtedness with complacency, even with self-congratulation. But we cannot guarantee this (look instead at the eighteenth and twentieth centuries—we cannot rule out the possibility of another major war in the future). One of the hidden—but significant—costs of indebtedness is greater vulnerability to bad luck in the future. This is as true at the public level as it is at the individual level, and is a good argument for 'mending the roof while the sun shines'. In peacetime we should usually be looking to reduce, not increase the public debt.

As if to exemplify this, Brexit has sprung upon us. While the full financial implications of this are still unclear, it is a shock of potentially the same magnitude as the 2008 crisis. It has already caused the government to relax its plans for eliminating the deficit. With other obvious signs of greater turbulence in world economics and politics, the future prospects of the National Debt have suddenly become more uncertain again.

APPENDIX I

BOND TECHNICALITIES

BOND VOCABULARY

'I will have my bond.'

William Shakespeare, *The Merchant of Venice*

'A small annuity is what I should like you to have—so as to be independent of me.'

Thomas Hardy, *The Mayor of Casterbridge*

'Your money is invested in the English funds.'

Charlotte Bronte, *Jane Eyre*

'Two hundred pound ... vill be inwested in your name in—What do you call them things agin?'

'Wot things?', inquired Sam.

'Them things as is always a goin' up and down in the City.'

'Omnibuses?', says Sam.

'Nonsense', replied Mr Weller, 'Them things as is always fluctooatin' and getting theirselves involved somehow or another with the national debt, and the chequered bills, and all that.'

'Oh! the funds', says Sam.

'Ah!', rejoined Mr Weller, '"the funs; two hundred pounds o' the money is to be inwested for you, Samivel, in the funs; four and a half per cent. reduced counsels, Sammy.'

Charles Dickens, *The Pickwick Papers*

Early forms of long-term borrowing were nothing if not inventive. Major forms were:

ANNUITIES

In return for a capital payment the lender received a fixed annual payment. This could be forever (in which case it is called a *Perpetuity);* or for a specific number of years, short or long; or for one or more lifetimes. In the latter case the lifetime concerned could be that of the recipient or it could be of some other nominated person. In France, where borrowing in this form was common ('rentes', from where we derive the modern term 'rentier' to describe someone who lives on the interest of unproductive assets), a whole industry grew up in identifying and nurturing possible subjects. Young children were obviously best—not too young, because infant mortality was high, but once a child had reached the age of five their prospects were good. Girls were better than boys, because female life expectancy was higher than male, but they had better be kept away from important risks such as pregnancy. Swiss mountain villages were apparently particularly good—fresh mountain air, wholesome food, healthy energetic lifestyle. Genevan bankers were particularly good at exploiting the French and other governments' relative ignorance of mortality probabilities and the superior public health performance of Switzerland. They became adept at forming and marketing syndicates to invest very profitably in life annuities, culminating in a really massive operation, now colloquially known as Les Trente Immortelles de Genève, which seriously strained the French public finances on the eve of the revolution. (Of course fraud was also a profitable possibility—if a subject unfortunately died, an impostor might be produced to attempt to maintain the income stream.)

An important element of this type of contract was that at the end of the term, the payments simply ceased; there was no final repayment of the capital. The advantage to the government was that the debt was ultimately self-limiting, to the lender that they could insure their standard of living for their lifetime, and possibly their descendants' too. But the ultimate duration of a life annuity was a matter of chance: premature death would mean that the lender had struck a poor bargain, but longevity could leave the government with a very long-term commitment.

A more sophisticated version was the *Tontine* (named after its inventor Lorenzo de Tonti of Naples [c. 1602–c. 1684]), whereby a group of lenders would receive a fixed total annuity, to be divided each year equally among all the survivors. This might be thought to be more attractive to potential lenders in two possible ways: as individuals, long-surviving lenders would increase their gains, while those who perished early would hardly regret their losses; and families could reduce the risk of losing family capital through one unfortunate premature death by nominating several family members. For the government the total annuity payable might as a result be smaller than would have been the case with simple annuities.

Tontines were often quite elaborate, with investors being stratified into different groups, with different terms, on demographic characteristics. But although occasionally popular on the continent, tontines were not particularly popular in Britain, being employed on only three occasions, without great success. Their greatest British popularity has been fictional, with writers of detective stories being attracted by the sinister possibilities, giving the tontine a rather raffish reputation—ironically so given its original more sober risk-spreading motivation.

However *Lotteries* were popular in Britain. These could be structured in many ways, but in general they were somewhere between today's modestly risky Premium Bonds and the high-rolling National Lottery. Like today, the government felt that there was an appetite for risk in the population which could be exploited. Sometimes lotteries were another variant of annuities in which failing tickets would receive a standard rate of interest, while successful tickets would receive a higher rate. But although some lottery loans were floated like this in their own right, more often lotteries were used as add-on bonus inducements for the public to subscribe to larger more standard loans.

LOANS, STOCKS, BONDS, GILTS AND FUNDS

These terms are confusingly used almost interchangeably, although there are subtle differences. A *Loan* is simply a payment to the government which will be repaid at a certain (or even an uncertain) date, usually with interest at a fixed agreed rate. The interest may be delivered only with the ultimate repayment of the principal, or it may be paid at intervals (e.g. quarterly, half-yearly or yearly) during the life of the loan. Some loans, as we will see, may by agreement never be repaid, their attraction to lenders then being only the perpetual stream of interest payments.

A loan is often called a *Bond*, and 'Bond' is now used generically to cover almost all organised major loan activity. More strictly, though, the bond is the borrower's promise to acknowledge the debt and its conditions, including procedures and penalties if the debt is defaulted (as in *The Merchant of Venice*), ideally in the form of a written or printed certificate. Such Bonds might also come with a set of *Coupons* which could be detached and presented at the Bank of England for the regular interest payments ('Coupon' is still used in the bond markets to denote the interest payment on a bond, although of course all transactions are now electronic).

Loans may or may not be transferable, i.e. the creditor may be entitled to sell the debt to another individual. The existence of a physical bond and coupons originally facilitated such transfers, and allowed the development of second-hand markets in such loans (the 'Bond Market'). Government bond certificates were frequently printed on elegant, gilt-edged paper; hence the terminology of 'Gilt-edged' or *Gilts* to distinguish government bonds from those issued by private individuals or corporations.

But not all loans had actual bond certificates. Some were acknowledged by being written in a register, in which case they were called *Stock*. In fact this was the case with the principal British government securities, *Consols*. Such stock could also be transferred from one holder to another, but at some inconvenience. Originally the Bank of England only opened its registers to record transfers on certain days, and both transferor and transferee had to attend in person at the Bank; this was very convenient for the London merchants who were the Bank's main customers, but considerably less so for those outside London, and alternative arrangements eventually came in. On the other hand 'bearer bonds' could simply be passed from hand to hand—this was more convenient, and more secret, but also less secure against theft. However, most bonds are not now in fact true bearer bonds in this sense, being simply visible receipts for the true record which is in fact the register, again of course now electronic.

The word '*Fund*' is particularly confusing, having been used in several different ways over the centuries. Originally it meant the tax revenues on which bonds were secured, but gradually came also to mean the bonds themselves—thus 'to be in the funds' meant investing in government securities. However in official terminology 'funded' securities originally also meant only those securities with no date of redemption, such as Consols, as opposed to all shorter-term securities. Hence 'funding' referred originally to borrowing in such permanent securities, or to an operation to replace shorter-term borrowing with permanent securities. But with the gradual eclipse of genuinely permanent securities, 'funding' now refers more vaguely to any operation replacing shorter with longer-term borrowing.

A *Bill* is a bond of very short duration: in Britain, Treasury Bills have traditionally been for 3 months, but current practice allows 1, 3, 6 or 12 months. A Bill Certificate is a promise to repay, say £100, after 3 months. There is usually no explicit separate interest payment: the lender earns interest implicitly by buying the bill originally for less than £100. Thus original purchase of a 3-month bill at £99 is equivalent to an annual interest rate of approximately 4 per cent; purchase at £98 equivalent to approximately 8 per cent.

BOND MECHANICS
Pricing, Interest Rates, Conversion, Borrowing Under Par

BOND PRICING

A bond is normally issued with a fixed interest rate (known as the coupon, see previous section) throughout its life. It therefore offers its holder a fixed annual income stream. A £100 holding of a perpetuity like Pelham's 3 per cent Consols offers £3 per year for ever; a similar holding of 4 per cent Consols (issued in 1927) would offer £4 per year forever. The nominal rate of interest on a bond usually reflects the market rate of interest at the time of its issue, but the market rate will change over time, and as it does so the second-hand market value of the bond will deviate from its nominal value. If the market rate of interest is now 5 per cent, this means that an investor would only be willing to pay £60 for an income stream of £3 p.a., and £80 for an income stream of £4 p.a. If the market rate rose to 10 per cent, the corresponding bond prices would now be £30 and £40.

This illustrates a general rule: the market price of bonds varies inversely with the market rate of interest. In fact, whereas economists like to talk in terms of interest rates, bond market professionals prefer to talk in terms of prices and yields: if they think interest rates are going to go up, they say rather that bond prices will be going down, or that bond 'yields' will be going up. A 3 per cent Consol priced at £30 'yields' 10 per cent.

This effect on market prices opens up possibilities of speculation in what might otherwise be a relatively sober market. If a quick-witted investor foresees that interest rates might shortly rise from 5 per cent to 10 per cent, he will sell his 3 per cent Consols now at £60 and buy them back again at £30 when the interest rate does change, making a handsome profit. A less quick-witted investor who fails to sell in time will suffer a 50 per cent capital loss. Therefore bond professionals are always acutely concerned about the future course of interest rates, and their expectations of future changes are already incorporated into the current prices they are willing to offer.

The case of perpetuities is the easiest to calculate, but other varieties of bonds can be priced according to the same principles, although their calculations are a little more complex. A bond of finite length represents a number of fixed annual interest payments and then a repayment of the £100 principal. The shorter the bond the more the £100 principal repayment dominates the income stream, meaning that its market value cannot deviate far from £100; its value is still inversely related to the market interest rate, but its sensitivity will be less than that of a perpetuity. As a bond of finite length approaches maturity, it becomes effectively an increasingly short-term bond and its market value will converge on its nominal £100, however much it may have deviated through interest rate changes during its life.

Bond pricing can be quite precise because, unlike equities, the income streams of bonds are assumed to be known with certainty. But this is not always the case. If doubts arise about a government's future ability to maintain its payments, the price of its bonds will naturally fall. This opens other avenues of speculation. Quick-witted investors will look carefully for any signs of prospective government weakness, hoping to sell before the signs become more generally apparent. On the other hand, so-called vulture funds (more formally, 'distressed debt specialists') will buy at low prices the bonds of obviously hard-pressed governments, if they believe the market has become more than justifiably pessimistic about the prospects of repayment, or if they trust in their superior ability to extract payment in such circumstances.

But there are also other less dramatic sources of uncertainty. Some bonds do not have a single fixed date of redemption. They may be quoted as redeemable between 2025 and 2035, for instance. In such a case the small print is important. This usually means that the bonds cannot be redeemed before 2025, *must* be redeemed by 2035, and *may* be redeemed, usually at the government's option, any time between 2025 and 2035. (Sometimes, but rarely, bonds may be redeemed at the holder's option.) In such a case an investor is clear what the income streams will be before 2025 and after 2035, but must make a judgement about the government's actions between those two dates. If market interest rates then are higher than the coupon rate, the government will probably let the bond continue until the latest possible redemption date; but if they are below, the government will find it cheaper to redeem as soon as possible and refinance with a new bond issue at the lower rate. So, again, the value of the bond is influenced by the holder's expectations of the future course of interest rates.

Even Consols were subject to this type of uncertainty. Most perpetuities are not in fact true perpetuities: usually the government has no requirement to redeem but it retains an option to do so, and it may well exercise that option if market rates fall below the coupon. Eventually, even with Consols, it did, in 2015.

There are many other ways in which a bond's structure can be made more complicated, thereby also complicating its valuation: a bond may have an option to convert into a different security at a particular time, or contingent on some event; its coupon may not be fixed but may vary according to some predetermined pattern, or to some standard of comparison (index-linked bonds are a particular case of this, where the coupon and the return of principal depend on the rate of inflation). These variations are usually targeted to make a bond attractive to a particular type of investor. But too much uncertainty undermines the very purpose of bonds, aimed at the more risk-averse investor who is looking for a relatively predictable investment.

SHORT AND LONG RATES

We have talked about *the* rate of interest, but experience of the bond market shows that there may be different rates for different periods. For instance in the Second World War the interest rate on long-term bonds was 3 per cent, while the rate on short-term treasury bills was only 1 per cent. How does such a difference come about?

Think about investors considering how to hold sums of money over the next ten years. They could simply buy a ten-year bond, or instead they could buy a series of ten one-year bonds. If the interest rates of all these bonds were known for certain, the total returns of either strategy must be the same, for otherwise all investors would go for the more profitable one, driving its price up, and shun the less profitable one driving its price down until the returns did equalise. This suggests that the ten-year rate of interest must be the average of the ten one-year rates. If the one-year rates are expected to rise over the ten-year period, the ten-year rate will reflect this, being higher than the first year's one-year rate. But if the one-year rates are expected to remain stable, the ten-year rate should be the same as the one-year rate.

However, this is only a starting-point for the analysis, and other factors need to be considered. Obviously the future one-year rates are not known for certain, so the route of successive one-year bonds is a riskier one than the ten-year bond, whose return can be locked in for certain from the outset. The future one-year rates may turn out to be higher or lower than expected: a speculative investor may be prepared to gamble on the former, but a risk-averse investor would prefer to insure against the possibility of the latter. The effect on the ten-year interest rate will depend on the balance between gamblers and insurers in the market.

One very important advantage of the one-year route is its greater liquidity. If, halfway through the ten years, our circumstances change and we need to spend our money rather than continue to save it, or we find a more profitable investment to exploit, we can do so on the one-year route but not on the ten-year route. Investors may be willing to pay quite a high premium for this flexibility, leading to the usual short/long run differential: long rates tend to be higher than short rates because they need to compensate investors for locking up their funds. Strong second-hand markets for bonds will mitigate this tendency, but not completely eliminate it—a second-hand market will allow the investor to get out mid-term if his circumstances change, but not at a guaranteed price.

Again, not all investors want to save for ten years or more; some will only be able to save for less. Therefore, there must logically be relatively more potential takers for short loans than for long loans, again leading to lower short and higher long rates.

The supply side of the market must also be considered. If there is more short-term borrowing than long-term borrowing, short-term rates will tend to be higher than long-term rates. But such a situation is unlikely to last. In a government bond market there is only one supplier. Either the additional short-term borrowing is only a genuinely temporary phenomenon which will soon subside again, or it reflects a more continuous need for additional funds, in which case the government will find it more profitable to convert it to a longer-term form if that is cheaper.

Here the government faces a calculation very similar to that of the investor we have just considered. If the government has a need for funds over a ten-year period, it can either issue one ten-year bond or a series of one-year bonds. If the ten-year rate of interest is greater than the average of the expected one-year rates, then the one-year route is cheaper. But like the investor, the government must also take into account the uncertainty of the future one-year rates and the liquidity implications of the one-year route. A risk-averse government will rightly value the downside risk more than the upside, and will prefer the ten-year route, even at some cost penalty.

(The Northern Rock bank collapsed because of a reckless gamble against this principle. As a large purveyor of mortgages, it lent money out for very long periods. A cautious banker should have borrowed the necessary finance to supply these mortgages over an equally long period ('maturity matching'). But Northern Rock had noted that a series of very short-term borrowings was much cheaper. Well, it was, until the emerging financial crisis in the US in 2006 completely dried up the supply of very short-term money.)

In emergencies such as wars, there is a spike of short-term borrowing which drives short-run rates sharply up. But reasoning as above, the market does not consider that this will be permanent, so long-term rates do not adjust so much. Temporarily the short rate moves above the long rate, but the two rates should converge again on their more usual relationship before too long. How far the long rate itself will move in this convergence process will depend on how permanent the additional borrowing turns out to be.

CONVERSION

Bonds are issued with fixed interest rates, and they are likely to be issued in greatest numbers during wars or other emergencies when interest rates are high. When the emergency has passed, market interest rates may fall again, but the government is still committed to pay the higher rate at which it issued the bond. If the bond is long-lived this may turn out very expensive for the government—whether the government can do anything about it again depends on the small print. If the bond's term is genuinely fixed, or genuinely perpetual, nothing can be done. But governments soon realised that it was wise to write in an option, but not a requirement, to redeem at any time (or usually with a few months' notice). Then if market rates fall below the bond's coupon, the government can issue a new bond at the new market rate to provide the cash necessary to redeem the first bond, thereby making a saving on its interest bill. Making a new borrowing to repay an old borrowing is called 're-financing'.

Alternatively the government may avoid the administrative costs of a new issue by simply using the threat of re-financing to persuade the existing bondholders to accept the new lower interest rate. Usually the vast majority of the bond-holders will do so, since they probably want to stay in government bonds and there are now no better alternatives currently on offer in the market. This is known as 'conversion', and is not a default so long as the government has the legal right to redeem and it also offers the bond-holders the alternative of complete repayment in cash. British governments have used conversion on many occasions. A conversion is judged successful if few bond-holders want to be paid in cash. To achieve this the government must time its intervention well and 'groom' the market carefully in advance.

Bond purchasers are of course aware of the possibility of conversion, and they in turn try to protect their favourable interest streams by insisting on anti-conversion clauses, usually a minimum period of time before redemption becomes possible. Thus we see bonds described as 'redeemable 2035–2055', i.e. cannot be redeemed before 2035, must be redeemed by 2055, may be redeemed between those two dates; or 'redeemable after 2045', i.e. a perpetuity, but one that cannot be redeemed before 2045 but may be redeemed thereafter.

The purpose of re-financing and conversion is to reduce the government's interest bill, but a badly-judged exercise may leave the government worse off in other respects. Suppose the intention is to replace a 4 per cent bond with a 3 per cent bond, but the market is not quite ready to accept a 3 per cent interest rate. Perhaps the re-financing will only be accepted if bond-holders are offered £120 of the 3 per cent stock for every £100 of 4 per cent. The government will still have achieved some interest saving—each £4 of interest will be replaced by £3.60—but at the cost of increasing the total value of the National Debt, which will make repayment of the Debt more difficult, if repayment becomes the favoured policy in future.

Very occasionally a government may make use of this mechanism to make repayment easier in future. An upward interest-rate conversion involves offering to replace a 4 per cent bond by, say, an 8 per cent bond. Bond-holders would be able to maintain their interest payments by accepting only £50 of the 8 per cent stock for every £100 of 4 per cent, thereby halving the total value of the National Debt. But canny bond-holders will probably want a better bargain than that—they can see that their income streams would now be easier to redeem. (Otherwise the government could pursue this policy to the extreme: refinance to an astronomically high interest rate—and consequently very small total value of the National Debt—and then immediately redeem, with very little pain. Problem solved.)

BORROWING UNDER PAR

If a bond is a true perpetuity, and never to be repaid, its nominal capital value is irrelevant: what is important is its annual income stream. A £100 bond at 6 per cent is effectively identical to a £200 bond at 3 per cent—both offer the investor a perpetual income stream of £6 p.a. If the current market rate of interest is 6 per cent, the investor would be willing to offer £100 for either bond, i.e. he would be willing to take the first bond from the government at par, but the second only under par, at a 50 per cent discount.

But if, as usual, the government has an option on redemption, the investor might prefer the latter bond, because if the market rate of interest subsequently falls, say to 5 per cent, the government will redeem the 6 per cent bond, replacing it with a 5 per cent bond, so that the investor's perpetual income stream will turn out less than the anticipated £6. However, at 5 per cent the government will not find it economical to redeem the 3 per cent bond (borrowing £200 at 5 per cent would cost it £10 p.a. in order to save the current interest payments of £6), so the investor's perpetual income stream remains unchanged. Conversion will only become economical if interest rates fall below 3 per cent. So by lending under par, the investor is able to lock in a higher effective rate of interest—another tactic for avoiding conversion.

To some extent the government can take advantage of this preference: investors as a result will offer slightly more than 50 per cent for the 3 per cent bond, so that lower-interest bonds do indeed seem to offer the best effective interest rates to the government. But there is a sting in the tail: for each £100 actually raised, the nominal value of the National Debt will rise by nearly £200. If at some later point government policy should favour paying off the National Debt, the cost of doing so will be twice as high.

Nevertheless, faced with market realities, governments do from time to time issue bonds at prices below par, and sometimes also offer ultimate redemption at more than par. By so doing they are offering further incentives to potential lenders, complicating the time profile of the gains to lenders in ways which might be thought to be more attractive to the lenders, but less expensive to government.

APPENDIX II

RETIREMENT, AGING AND THE NATIONAL DEBT

The problem of trying to provide for our retirement is in some ways the inverse of the problem of paying for a war. In the latter we are faced with expenditures beyond our means in the present and would like to try to defer the reckoning into the future; in the former we are faced with expenditures beyond our means in the future which we would like to provide for in the present. In both cases we have to distinguish between the legal and financial claims we might construct on the one hand, and the brute physical transferability of real resources on the other. If the government involves itself in any way in the business of providing for its citizens' retirements, it will inevitably and naturally build up a national debt or similar debt-like obligations. If longevity increases, this debt will naturally increase with it.

A similar analysis also applies to health care: as one's need for health care steadily rises with age, the financial provision for the NHS is not unlike a pension scheme in that one pays in more in early life and takes out more in later life.

Let us proceed as we did in the analysis of paying for a war in Chapter 7: building up the analysis in stages of increasing complexity. Let us assume that each person works for four periods, then is retired for one period, and then dies. The country has a population of 5, with a balanced population structure: one person in each age-bracket. In a working period each person can produce 100 units of a consumable good. GDP is therefore 400. Each working person could consume up to 100 in each working year, but in that case they would starve in their retirement. To maintain a constant standard of living throughout their life they should only consume 80 a year, and for simplicity we will assume people very much prefer a constant standard of living to a varying one. How can this come about?

The easiest situation is when the consumable good is infinitely storable: this is just like squirrels and nuts. Each year each worker consumes 80 nuts and sets aside 20; by the end of their working life they have accumulated 80 nuts, on which they can live in their retirement. There is no need for any social arrangements (other than security of private property). At any one time the country has a total of 200 nuts in individual stores (20 for the youngest worker; 40 for the next youngest; 60 for the next; and 80 for the worker just about to retire). Although individuals (and therefore the country) clearly have savings, there are no private or public debts; each individual's saving is covered by their own accumulated assets.

Although there is no need for a social arrangement, a social arrangement is perfectly possible. Suppose instead of each squirrel maintaining its own hoard, squirrels deposit their nuts in a central hoard, receiving receipts in return, which can be cashed in on retirement. The central hoard is now like a pension fund. It has liabilities (200 receipts) but also has the corresponding assets (200 nuts) to cover their redemption. But this arrangement has now also created the institution of debt: the individuals' savings are now held with the fund rather than at home. This has created an equal and opposite debt for the fund; and the fund now has the assets to cover this debt.

This pension fund need not be a government fund—its operations as so far described would be perfectly viable in the private sector. So the debt thereby created could be either private debt or public debt. But a government fund could do some things that a private-sector fund could not. A private-sector fund relies on voluntary contributions and therefore must give legally binding, or at least credible, guarantees for their redemption. A government could choose to operate in the same way—in which case the receipts would be like government bonds, and the government would have a national debt of 200 (and therefore a debt ratio of 50 per cent), which citizens might worry about, but unnecessarily, because the government has the assets to cover it. However, it could instead collect the contributions as compulsory taxation and give just a political commitment to 'look after citizens in their retirement'—in which case it would not have a formal national debt, but citizens would probably worry instead about the government's vague future commitments (see Chapter 13). They would also probably overestimate these commitments at 320—pensions of 80 for all 4 workers currently alive and therefore an apparent debt ratio of 80 per cent—whereas the actual commitment at any point in time is indeed only the correct 200, because the younger workers have not yet put in enough time to generate their full pension entitlements. Comparing the overestimate of 320 with the 200 nuts in the government store would make the citizens worry even more. Nevertheless, in the stable situation we have assumed, all worries are unnecessary, and all arrangements in fact turn out identical; but if circumstances begin to change they might not.

Say, for instance, longevity increases, so that workers now begin to live two periods in retirement. If this is initially unforeseen, under the private-sector arrangement or the public sector mimicking the private sector, the first workers to live longer will have an uncomfortable retirement (although not strictly speaking an unfair one—they consume, over two periods, as much as they saved in the previous four). As workers begin to take on board the new information, they will begin to save more, attempting to restore some smoothing to their remaining consumption patterns. But no one is directly affected by the misfortunes of their predecessors. Eventually a new steady state is reached, with workers evening out their consumption at 66.7 per period, hence saving 33.3 in each working period. Each worker therefore accumulates 133.3 by retirement, and the government store steadily contains 333.3 nuts with an equal number of receipts/bonds outstanding. The National Debt has therefore risen, quite naturally and voluntarily, as a result of the increased longevity—the debt ratio is now 83.3 per cent.

However, in the second public-sector version the government may initially continue to provide pensions at the original annual rate to the first long-lived retirees, thereby running down the store. When realisation kicks in, pensions will be reduced and contributions of the later generations will be increased to fund their own retirements, and to make good the deficit in the store. Thus in this version the early generations are insured against this unexpected change in the environment, passing the costs of it on to the next generations. The same new steady state will eventually be reached. The vague future commitments become even more worrying to citizens, jumping first to an apparent 640, genuinely unsustainable at the original rates of contribution, but falling back after revision of pensions and contributions, to an apparent 533.3 (or 133.3 per cent of GDP) in the new steady state, which although high is nevertheless sustainable. Again, the government's future commitments have increased, quite naturally, because of the increased longevity.

So far, in either arrangement, the fund has always been a 'fully-funded' one: there should always be enough nuts in the store to cover all the existing liabilities, whatever might happen to the flow of contributions in the future. It all works smoothly, but from an economic point of view it is not quite as efficient as it might be, because of this quantity of nuts always in the store. Some people have worked to produce these, but they are never consumed. This seems an unnecessary waste of resources. Suppose either in one year, or over a period of years, they were consumed. The store would now be empty, but all future payments out of the store could still proceed just as before, because the future in-payments would continue to cover them. The fund has now been converted to a 'pay-as-you-go' basis—the pensions of the retirees are effectively paid directly from the contributions of those still in work. In economic terminology this is a 'Pareto improvement' on the former arrangement: some people have been made better off (through the consumption of the stored nuts) and no people have been made worse off, hence an obviously good thing to do.

However, a private-sector fund would have difficulty operating in this way. The fund's credibility now must rest entirely on its ability to continue extracting contributions in the future. For a private-sector organisation this is difficult to guarantee—which is why pension-fund regulation insists on private-sector funds being fully-funded—but not so difficult for the government, with its apparently infinite life and its power to tax compulsorily.

But the public-sector version will now encounter difficulties if longevity increases: the current contributions will immediately be insufficient to maintain pensions at the original annual rate. Contributions will have to rise; the speed with which they rise determines the extent to which the earlier generations are insured. In this case the next succeeding generations do not lose out either: all generations actually manage to consume a little more (over two periods) than they have saved until a new steady state is established. The fund's 'losses' are effectively deferred into the remote future. The government's vague future commitments have increased, but they are now covered by the government's increased future tax plans.

The public fund in fact has another alternative open to it. It could instead have borrowed nuts from the working population in order to maintain the payments to the earlier generations. The suppliers of these nuts will effectively be investing in top-up pensions for themselves, and the fund will now be in debt to the lenders—therefore more bonds. This is really only a policy of delaying the inevitable because the top-up pensions can only be repaid by raising contributions or reducing the mainstream pension at some time in the future. The government now has both formal and informal commitments to the future, adding up to at least the same total as before. But if there is a permanent demand for these top-up pensions, the borrowing can be rolled over indefinitely to future generations. So here we have the beginnings of a permanent public debt, but equally the beginnings of greater uncertainty about what the government's future commitments really are.

Now let us consider the other simple case: where the consumer good is perishable, and cannot be carried over to a future year. Here there is no way we can individually guarantee our own retirements. We cannot stockpile the consumer good, and therefore must rely on the production of others if we are to eat in our retirement. Why should they do this for us? One possibility is altruism; another is the 'implicit contract' whereby we look after our parents and in turn expect our children to look after us. To some extent informal social pressures can support this kind of transfer, but it cannot be legally enforced if some people are not willing to play ball. Here we really do need the social organisation of the pension fund with its legally binding receipts.

Each year the 4 workers sell 20 units of the consumer good to the fund in return for receipts. The one retiree purchases them all immediately with his accumulated 80 receipts. Because of the perishability, no goods can be retained in store. But again, in balance it could all work smoothly. As before, the fund will have liabilities of 200 receipts outstanding, but in this case there can be no real assets to balance the liabilities. So as before, the fund's credibility rests entirely on its ability to continue extracting contributions in the future. In this world the fund is, in real terms, necessarily pay-as-you-go, whatever paper commitments might be given.

But the institution of money can restore the illusion of a fully-funded private-sector fund. Money is another commodity, which is no use for consumption purposes, but it is infinitely storable, and it is exchangeable for consumption goods. In reality the pension fund's dealings with its clients will not be in real goods but in money. The workers will be paid their wages in money; with £80 they will buy consumer goods for current consumption, and the remaining £20 they will give in cash to the pension fund in return for receipts. When they in turn retire the pension will be paid out similarly in cash, with which the pensioner can then buy consumer goods from shops. The pension fund therefore again ultimately accumulates liabilities of 200 receipts, but in this case also accumulates assets of £200 in cash to cover them. In money terms the scheme is fully funded, but in real terms it is not: if for some reason in the future the production of consumer goods is disrupted or their price level rises, although the money income of pensioners remains guaranteed the real consumption that this income can buy cannot be.

In the same way as before, the £200 in cash is effectively sterilised; it stays in the pension fund's safe and is never spent. If money is a real commodity like gold this is again a waste of resources as people spent time and effort in digging it out of the ground and refining it. But if money is paper money there is effectively no loss.

Now if longevity increases, again the private-sector fund can offer no insurance to the surprised early generations,[1] while the public-sector fund can, by enforcing higher contributions on the working population, or by borrowing money from them. Furthermore, the government can also, if it chooses, offer the same kind of insurance against price rises and other adverse surprises.

So providing for retirement in society inevitably creates future commitments for the nation and the government. They may be formal commitments like bonds or contractual pension schemes, or vague, like generalised pension aspirations. To the government, bonds represent fixed future claims, whereas their generalised pension aspirations may represent claims to the same value but are revisable in the light of events. Bond obligations are much more transparent, and clearly limited; but they rule out insurance possibilities which might be very valuable to citizens. In fact, the claims of bond-holders can only ultimately be satisfied out of future taxation, just the same as the vague generalised pension aspirations. Increased longevity will naturally increase the government's future commitments, either formal or informal.

To individuals, the fixity of bond returns makes them relatively immune from government attempts to redistribute income to insure other pensioners. Conversely, they cannot benefit from any such redistribution themselves. On the other hand, vaguer generalised pension claims on the government are subject to these possible government interventions, for good or ill.

All government pension commitments could therefore be met by issuing all potential pensioners with the appropriate quantity of government bonds. This would have the merit of making the government's future pension commitments absolutely clear. But it would remove the government's freedom to operate insurance among pensioners.

NOTES

1. INTRODUCTION: SHOULD WE WORRY?

1. Precise definitions can be important: this is 'Public Sector Net Debt, excluding public sector banks', from the Office for National Statistics (ONS), January 2018, https://www.ons.gov.uk/economy/government-publicsectorandtaxes/publicsectorfinance/timeseries/hf6w/pusf. Other concepts will be met with in the course of this book.
2. A new (2017) pound coin is 2.8 mm thick; the average distance to the moon is 384,400 km.
3. The land area of the United Kingdom of Great Britain and Northern Ireland is 243,610 km^2. The diameter of a new pound coin is 23.43 mm; so £1.7595 trillion would cover only 966 km^2 (even without taking into account the effect of close packing). But perhaps this would at least be enough to pave the streets of London?
4. ONS, June 2017, population estimate at 30 June 2016, https://www.ons.gov.uk/peoplepopulationandcommunity/populationandmigration/populationestimates
5. ONS, November 2017, estimate for 2017, https://www.ons.gov.uk/peoplepopulationandcommunity/birthsdeathsandmarriages/families/bulletins/familiesandhouseholds/2017
6. ONS, November 2017, estimate for Third Quarter 2017 GDP, projected forward one quarter at a quarterly growth rate of 0.4 per cent, https://www.ons.gov.uk/economy/grossdomesticproductgdp

7. Since 'debt' is measured at a particular point in a year (end, middle or beginning), while GDP is a rate-of-flow measure covering a whole year, there is inevitably a small degree of ambiguity in the Debt/GDP calculation. But this will normally be only of the order of 2 or 3 per cent, and will not make any significant difference to any of the numerical conclusions presented throughout this book. Similar numerical ambiguities can occur between statistics using slightly different definitions, or different sectoral or national coverage. But in general the movements in the national debt magnitudes which we will follow in this book are so pronounced that any small data inaccuracies cannot affect the broad picture. Readers are advised to concentrate on the broad magnitudes, and not worry too much about excessive precision.

8. ONS, January 2018, Central Government Total Revenue, 2017.

9. ONS, October 2017, Central Government Interest Paid, 2016,

10. According to The Money Charity, January 2018, Money Statistics, Figures for end November 2017, http://themoneycharity.org.uk/money-statistics/

11. I cannot claim originality for this chart; you can encounter several versions of it on the web and elsewhere. For the data behind these particular charts I am grateful to Stephen Broadberry and Nicholas Dimsdale, who directed me to their very long-run dataset 'Three Centuries of Data', originally prepared for a Bank of England article, and now incorporated in an even larger dataset 'A Millennium of Macroeconomic Data', available on the Bank of England website. The source data for national debt come originally from B. R. Mitchell, *British Historical Statistics*, Cambridge, 1988, now also incorporated in the Bank of England data. Updates for recent years are from ONS.

2. PRE-HISTORY

1. Strictly speaking it was only the English and Welsh National Debt at the time—in Chapter 11 we will follow the various subsequent changes in the composition of the 'United' Kingdom and their effects on the debt.

2. S. K. Mitchell, *Taxation in Medieval England*, New Haven, 1957, p. 158.

3. The full story can be found in Caroline Shenton, *The Day Parliament Burned Down*, Oxford, 2012.

4. See D. M. Palliser, The Age of Elizabeth: England under the Later Tudors, 1547–1603, London, 1983, p.108.

5. C. D. Chandaman, *The English Public Revenue, 1660–1688*, Oxford, 1975.

6. See for instance S. Pincus, *1688: The First Modern Revolution*, New Haven, 2009. Interpretations differ as to this significant event: for some it was the quintessential reassertion of Englishness against unhealthy foreign influences, but to others it was a Dutch takeover; and with the Dutch King came Dutch methods, including, significantly, finance, where they had been pioneers in banking, securities and public debt.

3. THE BEGINNINGS OF THE NATIONAL DEBT

1. See C. D. Chandaman, *The English Public Revenue, 1660–1688*, Oxford, 1975.

2. Tallies always eventually required some written order for repayment actually to take place; Downing's innovation was therefore really simply to pre-commit the production of such orders, and required little adjustment to the traditional administrative procedures. But if the Order was in the hands of the creditor from the outset, and the Register was in the hands of the government, the tally was really redundant; if the system had survived it would indeed have become effectively a paper, not a wooden, currency.

3. Some writers, indeed, count the Bankers' Debt as the beginning of the 'permanent' National Debt, preceding the usual date of 1694 and the foundation of the Bank of England. But the Bank of England's debt was officially recognised from the start as intended to be permanent; the Bankers' Debt was unintended, and it would be truer to say that until 1699 its status was 'unclear' rather than 'permanent'.

4. Parliament did not actually forbid unauthorised royal borrowing after 1688, but a combination of several measures effectively closed it off. Firstly, the large uncontrolled permanent income was replaced by an itemised 'Civil List', so there was very much less fungible revenue that could serve as security for royal borrowing; secondly, Parliament gained the right to audit the government's expenditure as well as its income, so borrowing therefore became pointless as a way of secretly financing dubi-

ous expenditure; and thirdly, after 1694 the Crown could not compete with the parliamentary guarantee that the public rapidly came to expect in lending to the government.

5. See, for instance, John Carswell, *The South Sea Bubble*, Stanford, CA, 1960 and Malcolm Balen, *A Very English Deceit*, London, 2002.

6. At 38 Threadneedle Street, the opposite end from its rival the Bank of England, but close to East India House in Leadenhall Street. It is the subject of a well-known memoir essay by Charles Lamb (Lamb's day job was as a clerk in East India House but he had started his career with a few months in the South Sea Company) and the essay evokes the sadness of its past glories and current pointlessness, and the harmless eccentricities of its staff. This South Sea House was demolished and rebuilt on the same footprint in elegant banking-baroque style by the British Linen Bank in 1902, although the original side entrance still exists complete with South Sea Company ironmongery and a charming but eroded bas-relief representing South-Sea trade and navigation. Apparently, and appropriately, even this is not quite what it seems: the bas-relief was allegedly commissioned by the company but never paid for, and only installed, as a gesture to the past, by the British Linen Bank's architect. The British Linen Bank was in time absorbed into other banks, ultimately Halifax Bank of Scotland. But HBOS in turn was a serious casualty of the 2008 financial crisis and the building was at the time of writing a Jamie's Italian restaurant, but apparently not for much longer—the South Sea curse lives on! The East India Company was absorbed by the government after the Indian Rebellion of 1857, and the site of East India House is now occupied by the ultra-modern Lloyds Building.

4. WAR AND PEACE IN THE EIGHTEENTH CENTURY

1. The Consolidated Fund is essentially the central government's main bank account, which is held at the Bank of England. All taxation and other revenue goes in, all expenditure comes out, and the National Debt was therefore effectively the overdraft on this account. A further refinement was instituted in 1968 with the creation of the National Loans Fund, through which all the borrowing, lending and repaying of the Consolidated Fund is now carried out. So now the Consolidated Fund

balances every day, any imbalance is taken up by the National Loans Fund, and the traditional National Debt is now the net liability of the National Loans Fund. But as these are the bank accounts only of the central government, and since 1975 the government has preferred to publish a broader 'Public Sector Net Debt' statistic, statisticians now also have to add any debt of public bodies (e.g. local authorities) held outside this system.

2. The public were well aware of the dreadful consequences of profligacy and bankruptcy; this was after all the era of Hogarth and *The Rake's Progress*.

3. This can only be a thumbnail sketch of the French situation. For lengthier treatments of a really intriguing story, see J. F. Bosher, *French Finances, 1770–1795: From Business to Bureaucracy*, Cambridge, 1970; Antoin E. Murphy, *John Law: Economic Theorist and Policy-Maker*, Oxford, 1997; William Doyle, *Venality: The Sale of Offices in Eighteenth Century France*, Oxford, 1996; Guy Rowlands, *The Financial Decline of a Great Power: War, Influence and Money in Louis XIV's France*, Oxford, 2012.

5. PITT'S SINKING FUND AND THE FRENCH REVOLUTIONARY AND NAPOLEONIC WARS

1. The Commissioners comprised the Speaker of the House of Commons, the Chancellor of the Exchequer, the Master of the Rolls, the Accountant-General of the Court of Chancery, and the Governor and Deputy Governor of the Bank of England, most of whom were more genuinely independent of the government than might be thought today (the Commissioners still exist to this day, with some amendments). But as was commented at the time, a future government could simply starve them of funds by repealing or reducing the £1 million taxes, or with some greater difficulty, even abolish the whole structure. This did not happen: Pitt's stature was such that the system was rigorously adhered to even throughout the stresses of the forthcoming wars. The flaws which eventually led to its undoing were less obvious.

2. This is not to deny that there are indeed other ways in which lower interest rates can increase the difficulty of repayment. Lord North's preference for issuing low-interest bonds under par is one; and some con-

version exercises only achieved their results by offering an increase of capital as an inducement: e.g. by offering, say, £120 of 3 per cent stock to replace every £100 of 4 per cent.

6. THE NINETEENTH CENTURY: A CENTURY OF PEACE

1. See for instance N. Draper, *The Price of Emancipation: Slave Ownership, Compensation and British Society at the End of Slavery*, Cambridge, 2010.

2. More neutral, but of course not perfectly neutral: abolitionists might see this as a process whereby slave-owners previously parasitic on the physical efforts of their slaves had managed to transfer by stealth their parasitism to the future taxpayer.

3. This is actually a conceptual error, but one common in these debates. Taxes used to repay a wholly domestically-held national debt do not simply disappear; they move from one set of pockets to another, and the owners of the second set of pockets might be as likely to invest in industry as the owners of the first. Of course, the move may not be costless, and there may be a time-lag. Also the polemicists of the time would probably have disagreed with the second half of that argument: they tended to contrast the 'industrious classes' who paid the taxes with the idle drones who held the National Debt and would probably spend their proceeds on luxurious consumption rather than productive investment. John Stuart Mill held the reverse: the debt-holders were by definition savers, not profligate consumers.

4. Gladstone's aversion to debt combined with his high moral principles to resist British military expansionism and foreign adventures. But one of the few such adventures he did sanction was the annexation of Egypt on the Egyptian government's default on its foreign debt. Niall Ferguson, *The Cash Nexus*, London, 2001, p. 266 has pointed out that Gladstone was himself a holder of Egyptian debt.

5. The lesson had been learned that operating a sinking fund while net borrowing was occurring was a bad idea; Lewis' Sinking Fund would therefore only begin at the end of the war. But that made it even more vulnerable.

6. This is still true today: a surprising amount of government debt is held by the government itself or government agencies in various ways. It is

one of the factors that make interpreting national debt statistics quite complicated. In very recent years, a further twist to this has been given by the policy of Quantitative Easing: currently a very high proportion (about a quarter) of the existing stock of British government bonds has been temporarily bought back from the commercial banks by the Bank of England.

7. These two institutions had been set up by government to provide risk-free savings vehicles for small savers and for those with trustee responsibilities. They were obliged to invest their reserves in government bonds, which were held for them by the National Debt Commissioners. So in practice they were being obliged to help finance the National Debt.

8. To be a useful 'asset' in an accounting sense, a project certainly must be long-lived, but it should also be capable of providing income-generating services during its lifetime, and of being marketable itself in case of financial emergency. The government's expenditures in the telegraph industry therefore qualify, but most military expenditures, however long-lived, fail either or both of these latter two tests.

7. THE FIRST WORLD WAR

1. Budgetary figures for the First World War are from E. Victor Morgan, *Studies in British Financial Policy 1914–25*, London, 1952.

2. See for instance A. C. Pigou *The Economy & Finance of the War*, London, 1916, or *The Political Economy of War*, London, 1940.

3. This quaint parliamentary term harks back to the days of borrowing to anticipate tax revenues. Once Parliament has approved the financial plans ('Ways and Means') for the year, the government may immediately borrow short-term from the Bank of England up to the limit of those plans, subject to repayment before the end of the financial year. In normal circumstances this is used merely to smooth out day-to-day fluctuations in expenditures and tax revenues. In earlier days the Bank would have directly provided the loan in new bank notes in exchange for government bonds or bills; in an era of universal banking the government can effectively short-circuit this process by just sending out cheques to its creditors, which the Bank of England is obliged to honour, allowing the government to run an overdraft with it. The government's former cred-

itors now have larger current accounts, so the broad money supply has increased. So although this is a convenient device to iron out very short-run fluctuations in revenue, if used continually the money supply will grow continually, leading ultimately to inflation.

4. There was also an alternative issue at 4 per cent which was exempt from taxation, but this did not prove popular, selling only £52 million.

8. THE INTER-WAR YEARS

1. See for instance F. W. Pethick Lawrence *The National Debt*, London, 1924.

2. Great Britain, *Report of the Committee on National Debt and Taxation*, HMSO London, 1927.

3. To be fair to Douglas, the error was not perhaps so obvious in his time as it is now. Anyone reading the correspondence of Keynes and his colleagues at about the same time will be impressed by how they too were struggling with definitions of income, output, saving and investment, and how to keep these consistent with each other. The detailed science of national income accounting—which makes things very much clearer—only really established itself after the Keynesian revolution in the 1940s.

4. See for instance Frances Hutchinson and Brian Burkitt, *The Political Economy of Social Credit and Guild Socialism*, London, 1997.

5. See Mitchell, *British Historical Statistics*; also Bank of England Millennium dataset.

6. With the recent resurgence of interest in debt and default, many internet bloggers strangely seem to count this unilateral reduction of the rate of interest as a British government default. This is incorrect—it was a perfectly legitimate and standard conversion operation. After 1929 the British government had a contractual right to redeem the stock for cash and refinance at whatever terms it could achieve. As it did indeed offer a cash alternative, the 3.5 per cent offer was just the usual convenience to those who would prefer to remain in government stock (as the vast majority did). On the other hand in 1932 the British government clearly did default on its US loan (see below later notes).

9. THE SECOND WORLD WAR

1. A good reference for Second World War finance is R. S. Sayers, *Financial Policy, 1939–45*, HMSO, London, 1956.
2. Note that this is typically the situation faced by Third-World countries. Unable to persuade foreign lenders to offer loans to be repaid in a weak local currency, they are obliged to borrow in hard currencies like the dollar, exacerbating their difficulties when exchange rates turn against them or their export revenues falter for some reason.

10. THE POST-SECOND WORLD WAR WORLD

1. But Keynesian theorists did not entirely ignore the debt problem. James Meade, 'Is the National Debt a Burden?', *Oxford Economic Papers*, 1958, outlines a more mainstream series of concerns.
2. The most protracted such period was 1968–70, when Roy Jenkins as Chancellor of Exchequer ran a determined policy of public expenditure restraint. But, again, the effect on the debt was incidental: the real target of this policy was not the debt itself but the protection of the exchange rate and the balance of payments in the wake of the 1967 devaluation. Economically the policy was quite successful, but many commentators point to its unpopularity as a major contributor to the Labour government's defeat in the general election of 1970.
3. R. J. Barro, 'Are Government Bonds Net Wealth?', *Journal of Political Economy*, 1974
4. Their official title remains 'Commissioners for the Reduction of the National Debt'. Apparently the last officially recorded full meeting of the Commissioners was in 1860. Since then, necessary decisions have been taken by civil servants or by the Chancellor of the Exchequer and the Governor and Deputy Governors of the Bank of England.
5. H. M. Treasury, *Reforming Britain's Economic and Financial Policy*, Basingstoke, 2002
6. Although the EU prefers a Gross Debt measure rather than the Net Debt measure preferred by the British government and normally used throughout this book. The difference lies in financial assets and money balances that are actually held by the government.

12. THE DEBT: OTHER STANDARDS OF COMPARISON

1. J. D. Ostry, A. R. Ghosh & R. Espinoza, 'When Should Public Debt Be Reduced?', IMF Discussion Note, June 2015.

13. IS THERE MORE THAN THE NATIONAL DEBT?

1. Readers familiar with economic theory will recognise this as simply the crystallisation of the 'Ricardian Equivalence' of the debt (see the Box on Robert Barro in Chapter 10). Writers like Ricardo would probably feel that at least there might be some gain in transparency here—the citizens would now really know where they stood financially, instead of being lulled into complacency through ignorance of the National Debt. But this example also shows one reason why Ricardian Equivalence does not quite work: the government can borrow on our behalf at lower interest rates than we can ourselves. If we have to be in debt, we might prefer the government to do our borrowing for us. Consider a country with a serious housing shortage, say, after a protracted war. The obvious private-sector solution is for individuals to borrow and build houses for themselves (or borrow and buy houses from private-sector house-builders). Wealthy and high credit-status individuals may do just that. But that course might be impossible or very expensive for poorer and low credit-status individuals. They might be better off if the government borrows to fund a public-sector housing programme, the resulting houses being rented (or even mortgaged) to tenants at a lower overall cost.

2. Includes an accounting adjustment (£228 billion) in the treatment of the assets of Network Rail.

3. An interesting complication from this system arose during the privatisation of the Royal Mail: the government could easily find potential purchasers of the Royal Mail's current operations, but who would be likely to take over responsibility for the very large pension payments, current and future? In fact, the Royal Mail, being historically a rather semi-detached part of the government did have its own funded pension scheme, but poor recent performance and the turmoil of the financial crisis had left it rather under-funded. While in the public sector this was no great problem, since the government would pick up any resid-

ual bill for the pensions anyway. But on privatisation the new owner would be obliged to make good on the pension fund, which would require the injection of an unrealistically large sum of money. The government was therefore obliged to formally adopt the pension responsibilities of Royal Mail before privatisation. You might think this would cost the government a lot of money; in fact, the immediate consequence was apparently the reverse. Arguing that it did not operate funded pensions, the government sold off all the remaining assets of the pension fund, giving it an additional windfall on top of the privatisation receipts. The additional liabilities incurred, however, went unrecognised.

4. Although it might be argued that it was meant to be: entitlement nominally comes from National Insurance contributions, and the original intention was for an actuarially sound National Insurance Fund covering pensions, unemployment, healthcare and other welfare benefits, and therefore available as of right to those (and only to those) who had made the appropriate contributions. Many people do still cling to the 'Insurance Principle' as a rationale for the welfare system. But in practice there are too many potential recipients who cannot be expected to make contributions, and the National Insurance Fund has never built up to an adequate level, so that the payments are heavily subsidised out of general taxation. National Insurance Contributions still exist, but they are really just another form of income tax.

5. The whole purpose of QE was to counteract a dangerous potential fall in the money supply, as frightened banks after 2008 called in too many loans in a mutually destructive attempt to protect their own reserves. After several years it has not so far proved inflationary. Formalising it as a long-run situation would not necessarily be inflationary if prudential regulation prevents banks from returning to their pre-2008 excesses.

6. K. J. Arrow & R. C. Lind, 'Uncertainty and the Evaluation of Public Investment Projects', *American Economic Review*, 1970.

7. A. T. Peacock and J. Wiseman, *The Growth of Public Expenditure in the United Kingdom* (1961).

8. Bank of England, Bankstats (Monetary and Financial Statistics), November 2017.

APPENDIX II: RETIREMENT, AGING AND THE NATIONAL DEBT

1. This is perhaps too black-and-white. In practice many private-sector pension schemes have offered standard rates of benefit over a pensioner's life-time, however long; and some have operated index-linked pensions too. But their ability to command the resources to guarantee these is much more constrained than the government's, and the increased pressures of recent years have seen an almost universal withdrawal of such schemes.

SELECT BIBLIOGRAPHY

There is a voluminous literature on all aspects of public debts. The following is a short guide to accessible further reading on the British national debt and its contexts:

Bosher, J. F., *French Finances 1770–1795: From Business to Bureaucracy*, Cambridge: Cambridge University Press, 1970.

Brewer, J., *The Sinews of Power: War, Money and the English State, 1688–1783*, London: Routledge, 1989.

Carswell, J., *The South Sea Bubble*, Stanford, CA: Stanford University Press, 1960 (much republished).

Chandaman, C. D., *The English Public Revenue, 1660–1688*, Oxford: Clarendon Press, 1975.

Chernow, R., *The House of Morgan*, London: Simon & Schuster, 1990.

Daunton, M. J., *Trusting Leviathan: The Politics of Taxation in Britain, 1799–1914*, Cambridge: Cambridge University Press, 2001.

———, *Just Taxes: The Politics of Taxation in Britain, 1914–1979*, Cambridge: Cambridge University Press, 2002.

Dickson, P. G. M., *The Financial Revolution in England: A Study in the Development of Public Credit, 1688–1756*, London: Macmillan, 1967 (much republished).

Ferguson, N., *The Pity of War, 1914–1918*, London: Penguin, 1998.

———, *The House of Rothschild* (2 volumes), New York: Penguin, 1998 (also published in one volume as *The World's Banker*, London: Weidenfeld & Nicolson, 1998).

————, *The Cash Nexus: Money and Power in the Modern World, 1700–2000*, London: Penguin, 2001

Hargreaves, E. L., *The National Debt*, London: Edward Arnold, 1930 (republished 1966 by Frank Cass & Co.).

Hope-Jones, A., *Income Tax in the Napoleonic Wars,* Cambridge: Cambridge University Press, 1939.

Hutchinson, F. and B. Burkitt., *The Political Economy of Social Credit and Guild Socialism*, London: Routledge, 1997.

Knight, R. J. B., *Britain Against Napoleon: The Organisation of Victory, 1793–1815*, London: Penguin, 2014.

Morgan, E. V., *Studies in British Financial Policy, 1914–25*, London: Macmillan, 1952.

Pethick-Lawrence, F. W., *The National Debt*, London: The Labour Publishing Company, 1924.

Piketty T. (translated by A Goldhammer), *Capital in the Twenty-First Century*, Cambridge, MA: The Belknap Press of Harvard University Press, 2014.

Pincus, S. C. A., *1688: The First Modern Revolution*, New Haven, CT: Yale University Press, 2009.

Price, R. R., *An Appeal to the Public, On the Subject of the National Debt*, London: printed for T. Cadell, 1772.

Sayers, R. S., *Financial Policy, 1939–45,* London: HMSO, 1956.

Shenton, C., *The Day Parliament Burned Down*, Oxford: Oxford University Press, 2012.

Wormell, J. (ed.), *National Debt in Britain, 1850–1930* (9 Volumes), London: Routledge, 1999.

————, *The Management of the National Debt of the United Kingdom, 1900–1932*, London: Routledge, 2000.

Official Publications

Report of the Committee on National Debt and Taxation (Colwyn Committee), London: HMSO (Cmd.2800), 1927.

Great Britain, HM Treasury (G. Brown, E. Balls, G. O'Donnell), Reforming Britain's Economic and Financial Policy: Towards Greater Economic Stability, Basingstoke: Palgrave, 2002.

Great Britain, HM Treasury *Whole of Government Accounts 2015–2016*, Gov.uk.

UK Office for Budgetary Responsibility *Fiscal Sustainability Report*, January 2017.

Sources of Data

Mitchell, B. R., *British Historical Statistics*, Cambridge: Cambridge University Press, 1988.

Bank of England, *A Millennium of Macroeconomic Data*, Bank of England Website.

UK Office of National Statistics

UK Debt Management Office

European Central Bank Statistics Bulletin

References for the views of notable economists (in boxes)

Hume, D., *Essay on Public Credit*, first published in *Essays, Moral, Political and Literary*, 1752.

Smith, A., *An Inquiry into the Nature and Causes of the Wealth of Nations*, first published 1776.

Maitland, J., Earl of Lauderdale, *An Inquiry into the Nature and Origin of Public Wealth, and into the Means and Causes of its Increase*, first published 1804.

Ricardo, D., *On the Principles of Political Economy and Taxation*, first published 1817.

———, 'Funding system', first published in *Encyclopaedia Britannica*, 1820.

Mill, J. S., *Principles of Political Economy*, first published 1848.

Marx, K., *Capital* (3 Volumes), first volume published 1867, first English translation 1887.

Keynes, J. M., *The Economic Consequences of the Peace*, first published 1919.

———, *Essays in Persuasion*, first published 1931.

———, *The General Theory of Employment, Interest and Money*, first published 1936.

Barro, R., 'Are Government Bonds Net Wealth?', *Journal of Political Economy*, 1974.

INDEX